LISTENING TO SUBTITLES

Anna Matamala & Pilar Orero (eds)

LISTENING TO SUBTITLES

Subtitles for the Deaf and Hard of Hearing

PETER LANG

Bern · Berlin · Bruxelles · Frankfurt am Main · New York · Oxford · Wien

Bibliografische Information Der Deutschen Nationalbibliothek
Die Deutsche Nationalbibliothek verzeichnet diese Publikation in der Deutschen
Nationalbibliografie; detaillierte bibliografische Daten sind im Internet über
‹http://dnb.d-nb.de› abrufbar.

British Library Cataloguing-in-Publication Data:
A catalogue record for this book is available from The British Library, Great Britain

Library of Congress Cataloging-in-Publication Data

Listening to subtitles : subtitles for the deaf and hard of hearing / Anna Matamala & Pilar
Orero (eds).
p. cm.
Includes bibliographical references.
ISBN 978-3-0343-0353-8 (alk. paper)
1. Telecommunications devices for the deaf. 2. Closed captioning. I. Matamala, Anna,
1973- II. Orero, Pilar.
HV2502.5.L57 2010
384.55'3–dc22

                                                            2010006218

Cover design: Thomas Jaberg, Peter Lang AG

ISBN 978-3-0343-0353-8

© Peter Lang AG, International Academic Publishers, Bern 2010
Hochfeldstrasse 32, CH-3012 Bern, Switzerland
info@peterlang.com, www.peterlang.com, www.peterlang.net

Printed in Switzerland

To Ana Pereira,
who started it all up

Acknowledgements

This book was published thanks to the financial aid of the Spanish *Ministerio de Ciencia e Innovación* (<http://web.micinn.es>) with the project ref. no. HUM2006-03653FILO. The original Spanish title was *La subtitulación para sordos y la audiodescripción: Primeras aproximaciones científicas y su aplicación* (English translation: *Subtitles for the deaf and hard of hearing and audio description: First scientific approaches and their application*). The project is also part of the EC ongoing project within the ICT Policy Support Programme of CIP-ICT-PSP-2007-1 with the reference DTV4ALL 224994. It is also part of the Catalan Government Consolidated Research Group scheme with the reference 2009SGR700.

Contents

Anna Matamala, Pilar Orero, Ana Pereira

Introduction

This book is one of the outcomes of the project *Research and development of the criteria regarding the creation of subtitles for the deaf and hard of hearing for digital television*.[1] The project was a research collaboration between lecturers who come from an interdisciplinary background and who are active at the following Spanish universities: Universidade de Vigo, Universitat Autònoma de Barcelona, Universidad de Deusto, Universidad Carlos III, and Universidad Rey Juan Carlos. The book also publishes some results from the R + D project,[2] which was financed by the Spanish Ministry of Education and which is considered to be a first step in the new international pilot project financed by the European Commission entitled *Digital Television for All*.[3]

The aim of all three projects is the improvement of the quality of audiovisual accessible material whose users have hearing problems of an either age-related or illness-related nature. These collaborations are a first step towards a European comprehensive scientific study, which may serve as point of departure for drafting new guidelines for subtitling for the deaf in digital television. These new guidelines, which may be or become part of local legislation, should be seen as an attempt to standardise subtitles in different platforms, a claim which Spanish deaf and hard of hearing users have been requesting for years.

---

1   The project was originally drawn up under the Spanish title *Investigación y desarrollo de criterios para la elaboración de subtítulos para sordos en la televisión digital* and was financed by the Spanish Ministry of Work and Social Affairs. [reference: SUBSORDIG 76/06]
2   The project was originally drawn up under the Spanish title *La subtitulación para sordos y la audiodescripción: Primeras aproximaciones científicas y su aplicación* (English translation: *Subtitles for the deaf and hard of hearing and audio description: First scientific approaches and their application*). [reference: HUM2006- 03653FILO]
3   Digital Television for All (DTV4All) [reference: 224994], which is part of the EC Competitiveness and Innovation Framework Programme. ICT Policy Support Programme (ICT PSP), ICT for accessibility, ICT PSP/2007/1 PILOT TYPE B.

The SUBSORDIG project

The percentage of subtitled products in Spain is increasing in quantity. Nevertheless, researchers in the SUBSORDIG project have come to the conclusion that quantity should not be achieved at the expense of quality and this view has always been the basis of our work in the field. Bearing in mind this philosophy, the SUBSORDIG project was drawn up with three specific objectives. The first objective, and probably the most logical point of departure for our research, was drawing up a comprehensive bibliography (see Pereira & Arnáiz Uzquiza in this volume). The second objective was establishing a set of technical, orthotypographical and linguistic criteria for quality subtitling for the deaf and hard-of-hearing (SDH) in digital television (DTV). The third and final objective was the reception of quality subtitles with users. The project had the following stages: analysis and recompilation of the literature available, the new possibilities offered by digital television, various studies of SDH practices on DVDs and on TV networks in Spain and in other European countries, preliminary reception studies and papers on UNE 153010 (AENOR, 2003).[4]

After setting the goals of the project, the challenge was choosing one of the following two paths:

1. The ideal situation would be to create two types of SHD which would be accessible to the two main reception groups with hearing disabilities: prelocutive deaf people whose language of communication is Spanish Sign Language (SSL) would be offered simpler subtitles with basic vocabulary and a slower reading speed. Readers whose first language is oral would be offered more complete subtitles with a higher reading speed, richer vocabulary and more cultural references.
2. Market policies favour only one type of subtitling, hence a solution that would satisfy the two main reception groups would have to be found when designing the research.

Finally, a decision was taken to work with only one type of subtitles which would be accessible to all deaf audience members. In so doing, the results

---

4   AENOR (2003): Norma UNE 153010: *Subtitulado para personas sordas y personas con discapacidad auditiva. Subtitulado a través del teletexto.* Madrid: AENOR.

of our research can be applied to current practices in SDH, which will apparently not change in the near future.

Technical criteria included elements such as the following: the ways in which the relationships between characters and their words are indicated, the number of lines of subtitles and their positioning, character format, time of exposition on the screen, and subtitle synchronisation. As far as orthotypographical criteria were concerned, it was decided how best to convey sounds produced by characters, sound effects, music and songs in SDH. Finally, as far as linguistic criteria were concerned, the most innovative contribution was that SSL features which conform to the Spanish syntactical and lexical structures and norms were included in the subtitles.

Once the subtitling criteria had been established, the third aim was to test the criteria by means of reception tests. Appropriate audiovisual products were selected and subtitled according to the following criteria: one chapter of the cartoon series *Shin Chan*, selected for the young(er) audience members participating in the tests; the beginning of the first chapter of the Spanish series *Los Serrano*, selected for the adult audience members participating in the tests, and an excerpt from the movie *Stuart Little 2*, selected for tests dealing with positioning, font type and font size. Additionally, these products were chosen because they were popular programmes, widely accepted by most if not all of the audience members when preparing the tests.

Subsequently, the reception studies were designed in order to test the functionality of the selected criteria at all levels: font style and font size, colour, gaps between letters, relationships between characters and words, number of lines and positioning, time of subtitle exposure on the screen, synchrony, volume adjustment of voice, tones, pauses, hesitations, stuttering, voice sounds, sound effects and background noises, music and songs, vocabulary, syntactical structures, etc.

Subtitled clips and questionnaires were sent to each university and shown to a group of 15 to 20 prelocutive deaf informants (children and adults), 15 to 20 postlocutive deaf informants (children and adults) and 15 to 20 hearing informants (children and adults). The hearing informants were all part of the control group. Although the relationship with the deaf audience was difficult and time-consuming, it was extremely enriching and the informants provided invaluable information for our research. Working with children was especially challenging and, in some instances, it was not possible to create groups with the desired number of postlocutive

deaf informants. The reason was that in Galicia, for example, the informants attended schools located in a vast geographical area and in some instances the children had not been diagnosed as deaf but as hearing children with comprehension problems.

The book

In the following articles in this book SDH research in its many stages is
described. The objectives, aims, different stages of research and methodologies, along with the results are developed. The book also includes a
number of articles which provide contextual information for the development of the research. In so doing, the articles offer new perspectives and
insights as well as hints for possible, new avenues or research approaches.

The book starts with a prologue to digital television written by Peter
Olaf Looms. In his article, Looms asks whether DTV will be a service for
everyone or just for some, pointing to some of the challenges posed by
analogue shut-off. After this general introduction the book turns to more
detailed studies on user-related and language-related elements. Inmaculada
Báez Montero and Ana Fernández Soneira revise the many features that
characterise the broad spectrum of SDH users, ranging from deep deafness to a partial loss of hearing. The linguistic peculiarities of deaf people,
regardless of their degree of loss of hearing are also discussed in an attempt
to establish a taxonomy of specifically targeted subtitle recipient groups
that may benefit from the many technological advantages offered by digital broadcasting systems.

The relationship between the user and the text, and understanding the
metalinguistic knowledge of deaf people with a language with no written
form is a key issue when creating subtitles for the deaf and hard of hearing,
and this is the topic that Carmen Cabeza-Pereiro addresses in her article,
in which the concept 'grammatisation', which is used in linguistic
historiography, is revised.

From the studies which take into account the users and their relationships with language, we move to articles related to the SUBSORDIG project
referred to above. Francisco Utray, Belén Ruiz and José Antonio Moreiro
discuss the results of a series of tests developed to establish the maximum

acceptable font size for subtitles in standard definition television (SDTV). In their contribution they define the specifications for a subtitle magnifying application, which will allow users to increase character size optionally when broadcast reception is user-mixed. Eduard Bartoll and Anjana Martínez Tejerina present the results of the tests devised to discover the most suitable font, font size and font position for SDH, focusing on the positions of SDH. Testing the reception of complex data with users is what both Ana Pereira and Lourdes Lorenzo set up to do in their investigations. While previous articles have dealt with separate formal subtitling features, Ana Pereira presents two closely related articles and does so from a holistic approach. The first article deals with the many tests taken on board to check the functionality and validity of a set of technical, orthotypographical and linguistic criteria designed to elaborate quality subtitles for deaf and hard of hearing adults in Spain. The second article describes the many Spanish Sign Language (SSL) features and the instances where they coincide with the features found in the Spanish language and where they diverge. The question of adapted subtitles whose syntax is that of SSL is also studied. The objective is to check if subtitles which follow SSL syntax enjoy a better reception by deaf audiences whose mother tongue is SSL. Lourdes Lorenzo also provides contributions in the form of two related articles. The first article presents a case study based on an episode of the cartoon series *Shin Chan*, subtitled for deaf and hard of hearing children. Lorenzo reports on the results of its viewing with regard to communicative efficiency. The intention behind the study was to verify the functionality of the existing criteria in the Spanish subtitling standard UNE 153010. Lorenzo's second article presents some proposals in those areas where UNE 153010 does not provide solutions (mainly linguistic issues) with a view to a possible validation for DTV. In their search to find more synthetic subtitles Clara Civera and Pilar Orero analyse the use of icons (in SDH) to represent sound context and, more importantly, to represent the speakers and the speakers' moods. In their analysis, they use Face Alive Icons (FAIs), a technology developed at the Industrial Technology Research Institute in Taiwan.

This book presents all the work carried out jointly during one year of research but it goes beyond simply describing a finished project. As with any form of experimental research, many hypotheses were confirmed, and others paved the path for new avenues and further experimentation. This is the case for the following four contributions.

In her article Verónica Arnáiz Uzquiza describes the possible influence of local subtitle conventions on subtitling preferences, and proposes the adoption of scientific tools such as eye-tracking technologies. Pablo Romero-Fresco uses his contribution to present the European project *D'Artagnan*, which has been inspired by the SUBSORDIG project. The epigonic nature of his research offers both the possibility of taking on board similar tests in different European countries and also the room to manoeuvre, adding new testing possibilities which were possibly overlooked in the Spanish research as a result of time constraints.

Pierre Dumouchel and other researchers from the *Centre de recherche informatique de Montréal* (CRIM) were asked to contribute to the volume in order to offer an overview of their experience in the challenging task of offering subtitles in real time. Their experience in shadow speaking for real-time closed-captioning of TV broadcasts in French is described in their contribution. This new approach offers an innovative field of research in SDH, that of using speech recognition for live closed-captioning, describing the solutions implemented to the problems found.

By way of concluding the book, we asked Ricardo Vizcaíno-Laorga, Álvaro Pérez-Ugena and Deborah Rolph to present their experiences with the use of subtitles for the deaf and hard of hearing in a virtual avatar environment created for the project *ULISES* (The logical and integrated use of the European System of Sign Language). Their chapter presents the project-related experiences and the outcomes of their research.

Many people have been working on the SUBSORDIG project and we would like to thank them here: Irene Pazó Lorenzo, Almudena Pérez de Oliveira and Santiago Rodríguez Bouzas (Universidade de Vigo), Verónica Arnáiz Uzquiza (Universitat Autònoma de Barcelona), Rubén Rojas (Universidad Rey Juan Carlos) and José Luis Teigell (Universidad Carlos III de Madrid); also Natxo Canto and Gonzalo Eguíluz (Universidad de Deusto), María Martínez Ortiz (Universidad de Valladolid), Mónica Souto (CESyA).

We would also like to thank some people and the associations who helped us with the tests: Carmen Jáudenes and Begoña Gómez Nieto (FIAPAS), the Asociación de Sordos (Vigo), Asociación de Sordos (Ourense), Instituto la Farisa (Ourense), José Luis Arlanzón from ARANSBUR and MQD (Burgos), Asociación de Sordos de Alcorcón CODIAL, Centro Altatorre de Sordos (Madrid), ACAPPS (Barcelona), AICE (Barcelona) and Asociación de Personas Sordas (Bilbao and Bizkaia).

We would like to end this introduction by thanking all the authors who have contributed to the volume. In addition, we would also like to acknowledge and thank the anonymous editors who checked the manuscript and suggested changes to optimise the reception of the articles. In many cases changes were related to the problems that often arise when authors' mother tongue is different from English and when examples and references are given from other languages. We would also like to thank Jimmy Ureel, from Artesis University College (Antwerp)/the University of Amsterdam (Amsterdam). His proofreading skills and witticisms made editing this book an enriching and enjoyable activity. Any remaining mistakes in this book are, of course, our own. Our gratitude goes also to Martina Fierz, who accepted the original idea of the book, and has waited patiently throughout the preparation of the manuscript for publication. We would also like to acknowledge Henrik Gottlieb's help in finding the inspiration for a title. The book would not have come into existence without the generous and anonymous help that we received from many people with sensory difficulties who took the many tests, gave feedback and shared our belief in a better future. This better future may arrive sooner than expected if technology, governments, associations and quality research manage to interact without limiting their interaction to their own interests and to strive for excellence and quality for those who deserve only the best.

Girona, 4 May 2009

PETER OLAF LOOMS

Prologue: Digital television for some or for all?[1]

For most people around the world, watching television is a simple matter. In the 'good old days' of analogue television, buying a new TV was not a problem either. Some of the channels needed to be preset. Viewers needed to read the manual or ask for help, after which they could turn on the television set and find something to watch. In the course of the next five years, most countries will switch on digital television and switch off analogue transmissions. Hong Kong launched the world's first commercial digital cable service more than a decade ago. It started digital terrestrial television (DTT) on 31 December 2007. Analogue shut-off is planned to take place in the course of 2012. The question is whether digital television (DTV) is as easy to set up and use as analogue television. DTT has some unique challenges, as it is commonly used as the means of distributing free-to-air programming (i. e., television channels paid for by advertising, a broadcast licence or out of the public purse). Public service and state broadcasting aim to be socially inclusive and have the obligation to make television accessible to all. The following article is my view on the challenges and their solutions.

1. What are the main problems?

1.1. Getting started

Watching digital terrestrial television (DTT) requires that the viewers purchase either an integrated digital television receiver or a digital set-top box and that they connect the receiver or box to the existing television set. This may require having to change the aerial or buying a new one altogether.

---

1   A shorter version of this article can be consulted at <http://www.rthk.org.hk/mediadigest/ 20080715_76_121914.html> (Retrieved 20 May 2008).

On the face of it, this should not be a big problem. However, recent studies indicate that the elderly and those with visual, hearing or intellectual impairments are more likely to have problems getting started than the young or those without sensory impairments.

Good product manuals and help facilities in the receiver, preset to the appropriate language, are important. Compliance regimes – independent confirmation that a given product meets minimum requirements – can make a difference, provided that there are incentives for manufacturers to submit (and pay for) their products to be tested.

In markets where consumers have the right to return a product that does not meet their requirements, the lack of product testing may be financially onerous for both retailers (lower profits as a result of purchase refunds) and for broadcasters and service providers (spiralling costs as a result of increased traffic at broadcaster and service provider call centres).

1.2. Digital television for some or for all?

Once digital television has been set up, the next set of challenges is the extent to which it is truly a service for all. Do people truly have problems using a digital television set? In Hong Kong, about four per cent of the population reports having some kind of physical, sensory or mental impairment.[2] By international standards this number seems to be quite low. In the USA, "approximately 1 in 5 Americans has some form of disability, and 1 in 10 has a severe disability ... Disabilities can occur at any age, but they are most prevalent among those over the age of 65".[3]

Overall,

> people with disabilities constitute about 15 % of the European population ... Accessible ICT products and services [including digital television] have now become a priority in

---

2   "Persons with disabilities and chronic diseases", Special Topics Report (STR) Number 28, Census and Statistics Department, Hong Kong SAR, 2001.

3   "Disability Status: 2000" U.S. Census 2000, C2KBR17, U.S. Census Bureau. March 2003 and "Disabilities and Age: October 1994–January 1995." Census Brief, CENBR/ 97-5. U.S. Census Bureau. December 1997, p. 2 (Retrieved 20 May 2008, from <http://www.atp.nist.gov/factsheets/1-b-3.htm>).

Europe, due to the demographic shift: 18 % of the European population was aged over 60 in 1990, while this is expected to rise to 30 % by 2030.[4]

The transition from analogue to digital terrestrial transmission in Europe by 2012 represents a unique opportunity to provide better access to television and other services for people with disabilities. In Europe, hearing impairments seem to be somewhat higher than the one per cent number quoted for Hong Kong. Mellors explains that variations from one country to another are often due to different criteria being used to ascertain what actually constitutes impairment.[5]

Assessing the size and nature of the demand for access services is not straightforward either. An Ofcom review in the UK has shown that the demand for access services such as subtitling is extremely significant. 12.3% of the population said that it had used subtitles to watch television and approximately six million people (10%) did not have a hearing impairment.[6]

It seems that subtitling in particular is used not only by those with hearing impairments but also by those who find it difficult to understand young people speaking quickly or using slang; in countries with two or more official languages where it is useful to facilitate the understanding of all of these languages by offering opt-in subtitles; and in countries with significant immigrant groups for whom subtitling in their mother tongues may promote integration and social cohesion.

Audio description and signing for those with hearing impairments are increasingly common.[7] "Those who had used audio description regarded it as very helpful in understanding programmes better, and ... a

4　Communication From The Commission To The Council, The European Parliament And The European Economic And Social Committee And The Committee Of The Regions eAccessibility [SEC(2005)1095] Brussels, 13.9.2005 COM(2005)425 final (Retrieved 20 May 2008, from <http://eur-lex.europa.eu/LexUriServ/site/en/com/2005/com2005_0425en01.pdf>).

5　Mellors, W.J. (2006) WGHI – Working Group on Hearing Impairment Statistics on age and disability and in relation to Telecommunications: A significant market (Retrieved 20 May 2008, from <http://www.tiresias.org/wghi/stats.htm>).

6　OFCOM (UK) Television access services. Summary (2006) (Retrieved 20 May 2008, from <http://www.ofcom.org.uk/consult/condocs/accessservs/summary/>).

7　See <http://en.wikipedia.org/wiki/Audio description> (Retrieved 20 May 2008).

significant proportion that had not used audio description was keen to try it".[8]

We can conclude that the elderly and those with various impairments may well have difficulties getting started with DTT, but also that the DTT platform has considerable potential to make television accessible to all.

2. Is accessibility a medical or a social problem?

Offering access services usually lies between the following two extreme scenarios: on the one hand, a focus on disability and equating disabilities with diseases that require medical attention and, on the other hand, a focus on "the social model of disability where a distinction is made between the terms 'impairment' and 'disability'".[9]

In the first scenario, the (public) health system uses medical science to take corrective action as far as disabilities are concerned. Solutions often require public funding and assuring action is ultimately up to those directly affected. In this scenario, those with impairments buy specialised DTT set-top boxes themselves or get them from the public health system. Solutions often ignore the self-esteem of those involved, tend to be ad-hoc, and run the risk of being expensive from a macro-economic perspective.

In the second scenario, however, society at large assumes a collective responsibility for being inclusive. DTT solutions in this scenario focus on hammering out consensus among all the stakeholders in the value chain, including the viewers and organisations representing those with impairments and the elderly. Where consensus is reached, DTT is synonymous with inclusiveness, respect for the rights and well-being of all.

---

8   DCMS consultation on the Television Without Frontiers (TVWF) Directive Response from RNIB and RNID (Retrieved 20 May 2008, from <http://www.culture.gov.uk/ NR/rdonlyres/709879D2-6860-4D62-A3D3-5EC259C24A2E/0/RNIBRNID. doc>).

9   See <http://en.wikipedia.org/wiki/Social_model_of_disability> (Retrieved 20 May 2008).

3. What DTT access services can we offer now?

DTT already has a range of options. There are many mature access services solutions that broadcasters and transmission companies can offer. However, tough choices will have to be made. They depend, in the first instance, on the regulatory climate governing access services and, subsequently, on the application of three criteria:

1. Is the service to be offered acceptable and does it have a demonstrable benefit to its intended audience?
2. Is there a technology that can be integrated into existing work flows and is this scalable?
3. Is there a sustainable business model for the service in question?

For a service to be viable, all three criteria have to be met. A prerequisite is that each stakeholder in the value chain understands the interests and resources of everyone else in the value chain. Unless the solutions chosen constitute a win-win for all parties concerned, coercion will lead only to services that cannot be sustained.

4. What can be done in the medium term?

The problem facing DTT in particular is that in the course of the coming five years, new production and distribution technologies will emerge that will either enhance or disrupt our existing access services.

A good analogy is deciding whether a solution is an ugly duckling (i.e., something that will grow into a beautiful swan (read: solution)) or an orphaned tiger cub brought up by a dog (i.e., cute to begin with but a risk to its poor adopted mother within months) as represented in the pictures below.

Ugly duckling vs. orphaned tiger cub.

All services have a finite life. The challenge is to find the optimum switch-over point where first generation access service 'sunset' solutions should give way to second generation 'sunrise' solutions. There are many dilemmas when deciding on the societal 'return on investment' – which services are to be offered? Public service broadcasters in particular often work within modest, fixed budgets and they need to cope with finite resources and almost infinite demand. There are no easy answers in this respect.

Deciding whether en emerging solution is an ugly duckling or an orphaned tiger cub can be quite difficult. Among the things to be considered are the following: the transition to high definition pictures and multichannel audio, the use of MPEG-4, the emergence of hybrid terrestrial and IPTV solutions and the option of ultimately moving from digital broadcast to other IP-based options. Text-to-speech is rapidly becoming a reality as affordable chip sets in car navigation systems find their way into digital television. Spoken EPGs and voice-activated controls need to be carefully assessed too.

Agreeing on new solutions for DTT takes a great deal of time and hard work, which ultimately pays for itself. This is why in Europe we are seeing special-interest groups, broadcasters and hardware manufacturers embark on collaborative endeavours to discuss options and come up with scalable solutions that will ensure that digital television is accessible to all. In other words, there should be something to report on well before analogue shut-off in Hong Kong in 2012.

Inmaculada C. Báez Montero, Ana Mᴬ Fernández Soneira[1]

Spanish deaf people as recipients of closed captioning

Closed captioning – commonly known as subtitling for the Deaf [2] or hearing impaired people – constitutes a fairly complex issue. If the movement from a direct system to a substitute system (i. e., spoken language/written language) is problematic in itself, the difficulty increases when you take into account that the switch of linguistic mode is a rather difficult process for a vast majority of the members of the Deaf community (whose main communicative language is acquired through the visual-gestural channel). Solving specific translation problems is even more complex because there seems to be no general agreement on which language constitutes the recipients' main language or mother tongue. The lack of an established practice when writing this particular kind of subtitling does not justify a further delay in offering a final result that meets the quality standards required by such a task. Thus, the following article intends to revise the manifold features that characterise subtitle recipients (i. e., Deaf readers of closed-captions/subtitles) who present deep deafness or suffer from a partial loss of hearing (i. e., hypoacusis). The linguistic peculiarities of Deaf people, regardless of their degree of any loss of hearing, will also be discussed in an attempt to establish a taxonomy of specifically targeted subtitle recipient groups that may benefit from the many technological advantages offered by digital broadcasting systems.

1   This research has been supported through the project *Basis for the linguistic analysis of the Spanish Sign Language* [subsidised by the MEC, reference: HUM2006-10870/ FILO]. We would like to acknowledge Rosa Pérez Rodríguez, Jorge Luis Bueno Alonso, Helen Catherine Avison Harwood and Patricia Álvarez Sánchez for their comments, suggestions and translation of an early version of the paper, which helped for the completion of this work.
2   Throughout this article the convention of using the adjective *Deaf* with a capital D will be used to refer to hearing impaired people who are members of a community which shares a common sign language and a common sense of identity.

1. Introduction

Subtitling for the Deaf is, quoting Pereira (2005),

> [...] una modalidad de trasvase entre modos (de oral a escrito) y, en ocasiones, entre lenguas; consiste en presentar en pantalla un texto escrito que ofrece un recuento semántico de lo que se emite en el programa en cuestión, pero no sólo de lo que se dice, cómo se dice (énfasis, tono de voz, acentos e idiomas extranjeros, ruidos de la voz) y quién lo dice sino también de lo que se oye (música y ruidos ambientales) y de los elementos discursivos que aparecen en la imagen (cartas, leyendas, carteles, etc.). (p. 2)[3]

In the scientific field the terms *deafness* and *Deaf* or *hard of hearing* are used to refer to those people who have a partial loss of hearing (also referred to scientifically as *hypoacusis*) but also to those people suffering from congenital deafness. In general terms, we will use the term *Deaf* to refer to people who have some impediment of an acoustic nature which may cause problems for them in the reception or comprehension of oral language. The variety of recipients that we include in this term and the recipients' diverse needs force us to consider different kinds of captioning. However, we normally use the expression *specific subtitling for the Deaf* as if it were possible to reduce all the varieties to a single type of captioning which meets the needs of the Deaf community.

As we will see later, a significant group of people inside the Deaf community use sign language as their mother language. These people tend to have serious difficulties communicating in our society, in which almost everything, ranging from entertainment to information, has an oral basis. For them, captioning for the Deaf will consist of the translation of oral language into their mother tongue, that is, sign language.

On the contrary, many Deaf people do not have sign language as their mother tongue and their reading levels are largely determined by the na-

---

3 [...] a modality of transfer between modes (from the oral to the written mode) and, sometimes, between one language and another. It consists of showing the script on screen, which offers a semantic account of what is being broadcast in the programme: not only what is being said, how it is being said (emphasis, tone of voice, accents and foreign languages, voice noises), who is saying it, but also the sounds that may be heard (music and environmental noises) and other discursive elements that appear on screen (letters, captions, signs, etc.) (our translation).

ture of their loss of hearing. The various types of deafness show important differences that we cannot ignore if we want to try to address the expectations of the Deaf community, which demands and requires the use of captions, not only as a source of information but also as a medium for overcoming the communication barriers which the members of the Deaf community have been encountering for centuries and which need to be abolished as soon as possible.[4]

Nowadays, the communication difficulties in a society with an oral basis are being reduced. The historical segregation of the Deaf is starting to become a thing of the past thanks to technological advances. However, the debt is undoubtedly one that is yet to be settled.

2. Special features of the communicative process model on visual languages by Shannon and Weaver (1949)

We are interested in studying communication, not because of the individual nature of the speech acts but because of our interest in discovering the systematic phenomena and identifying the principles underlying these phenomena. As pointed out by Escandell (2005, pp. 9–10): "Si analizamos muestras concretas de comunicación es para tratar de encontrar en ellas regularidades que remitan a principios comunes".[5]

We will now revise the communicative act of Deaf people reading subtitles, taking into account the elements of the communicative process laid down by Shannon and Weaver (1949) and the revision of the communicative act carried out by Escandell (2005).[6] In so doing, we can clearly observe the special features of communication through visual languages (together with the common regularities of any communicative process)

---

4 Although we are focusing our analysis on the current situation of deafness and the Deaf, we cannot forget that auditory problems have been interpreted in the same way throughout history as highlighted by Gascón Ricao and Storch de Gracia y Asensio (2004) in their historical overview of the issue.

5 "If we analyse specific samples of communication, it is in an attempt to try to find regularities in them which may lead us to common principles". (our translation)

6 Because of space considerations we will dispense with other elements discussed by Escandell (2005) (e.g., redundancy, context).

and therefore the transfer of information to the Deaf recipient through captions.

1. The speaker and the recipient may be Deaf or hearing (both hearing, both Deaf, a Deaf speaker and a hearing recipient, or a hearing speaker and a Deaf recipient).

2. Codes are conventional matching systems by which any given signal is paired with a message and vice versa. Just like Escandell (2005) has pointed out, codes may be *simple*, that is, a reduced set of fixed and invariable signals, or complex, that is, structured sets formed from isolated units combined with each other through a fixed rule system. These codes are recursive and compositional. Gestural languages are not based on versions or translation of words from oral languages to gestures. They are systems with inherent degrees of consistency and, as such, systems which have not emerged from the restructuring of other linguistic systems. They also possess recursion and compositionality like any other language.

3. The message may be sent out through oral or sign languages. It may also be transmitted through a direct system or a substitution system. Sign languages may perform exactly the same functions as natural languages with an oral basis. They are not limited codes simply designed for specific purposes, as is the case with, for example, legal, chemical or mathematical language.

4. As far as the channel is concerned, it must be pointed out that sign languages (SLs) are communicative codes of a gestural nature. This means that while oral languages use the auditory channel and send out audible messages for their expression and reception, sign languages use the visual channel and use gestural messages which are received visually.

3. Brief revision of the features of visual languages

Serna (1994, p. 45) points out the following main differences between oral languages (OLs) and sign languages (SLs):

SL	OL
manual	vocal
visual	auditory
spatial	temporary
simultaneous	linear

As we have already said, sign languages are communicative codes of a gestural nature which encode information through gestural signs and decode information through sight. Such languages are developed in time and space but the spatial dimension is the most dominant.

We will point out some of the main similarities with the oral languages:

1. Separation of the organs of transmission and reception (eye-hand/ mouth-ear);
2. Secondary nature of the linguistic articulation with regard to other functions;
3. Lack of homogeneity between receiving and transmitting capacity;
4. Accommodation of articulation to receiving capacities.

We will broadly highlight the special features of oral productions and compare them with visual productions. The features can be divided into two groups: those features that depend on the intrinsic properties of each medium (e.g., linearity vs. simultaneity, use of iconic resources) and those features that depend on the extrinsic properties of each medium (e.g., development of a written tradition, grammatical tradition, institutionalisation).

Gestural unities of communication, called signs, constitute linguistic signs in the same way as morphemes and words do in oral languages. The difference between the two lies in the different nature of the signifier: SLs have a specific grammatical structure mainly determined by their visual nature, meaning that, for the exchange of information between the speaker and the recipient, the use of space with grammatical purposes is required. Space in front of the signer (particularly between the limits of the head and the length of the arms in any direction), movement of the hands, facial expression, etc. are parts of the basic units of gestural communication. Their combinations allow the signer to form countless linguistic statements with full meaning.

Other features of SLs are, among others, the simultaneity that shows the formative parameters of the signs, the use of three-dimensional space, the high rate of iconicity in sign languages, etc.

4. Writing is a substitution system for oral languages

As it has been already pointed out by Buyssens (1943), systems may be formed by direct *sémies* or substitutive *sémies*. The difference lies in the fact that signifiers of direct *sémies* are signifiers of meanings, and not of other signifiers.

Writing is defined as a substitutive code; according to Buyssen's terminology writing is a substitutive *sémie*, that is, a code in which graphic signifiers address meanings that are linguistic signs themselves.

Signifiers of a substitutive *sémie* of sign languages are writing systems or those called transcription systems, sign language notation, etc. Among the most used in the last decades, we may point out the following:

1. *SignWriting*, created by Valerie Sutton, based on the written representation of sign languages with graphic representations of the human body completed with a series of symbols that represent the sign;
2. *Signfont* (source of signs), created by the Salk Institute for Biological. Studies in San Diego in California, which, as has been pointed out by Pinedo (1989) tries to "create a written transcription, easy to read and write, both by hand and using a computer" (p. 199);
3. There are also systems such as the alphabetic one created by Herrero Blanco (2003) or *Hamnosys*, which refer to other visual signifiers and not directly to other meanings.

We may also differentiate various steps in the captioning process. For example, symbols in Braille alphabet reproduce the letters of the Latin alphabet embossed, which, at the same time, refer to phonemes in languages.

There are also manual systems which are substitutive. This is the case for fingerspelling, which is used as an assistant for sign languages to reproduce words from oral languages which do not have a sign, or a sign which is unknown to a participant in the communicative act (particularly in conversations with hearing people). Thus, fingerspelling is a substitutive *sémie* of a second grade that reproduces writing and not voiced units from oral languages.

Bimodal systems such as Signed Spanish or Signed English may be considered substitutive to the degree that they reproduce aspects of the signifier from the corresponding oral language (in this case Spanish or English respectively), such as the order of constituents or even particles

which do not exist in Spanish Sign Language (SSL) (e. g., articles, preposi-
tions). These restricted systems are used when educating Deaf children, as
a bridge between pure sign languages and oral language.

5. Deaf recipients[7]

As we already pointed out more than ten years ago (Báez Montero &
Cabeza-Pereiro, 1997), the lack of a census of Deaf people forces us to resort
to statistical studies to quantify the possible number of Deaf recipients. The data presented below comes from the website of the Spanish
National Statistics Institute (*Instituto Nacional de Estadística* (INE)).

Although the number of Deaf people in Spain, according to the last
INE survey, is just under one million people (967,445),[8] the number of
users of SSL is estimated to exceed the 400,000 mark. This number contains not only Deaf people but also those who, as a result of different
reasons (generally family-related, emotional or professional reasons), have
learned SSL.

In the INE statistical counts hearing impaired people are grouped by
age, type of deafness, or the disability that deafness generates.

1. Regarding age they form three groups: people who are younger than 6,
    people between the ages of 6 and 64, and people who are older than 65.
2. Regarding the type of deafness, several groups are drafted depending
    on age. In the group of people who are older than 6 three groups are
    distinguished: people with prelocutive deafness, people with postlocu-
    tive deafness, and people with bad hearing. In the group of people
    who are younger than 6 two groups are distinguished: people who are
    totally Deaf, and people who are hard of hearing.

7   Official INE data: percentage of users of SSL with respect to the total amount of deaf
    recipients.
8   Encuesta de Discapacidades, Deficiencias y Estado de Salud (Survey on disabilities,
    deficiencies and state of health 1999. Madrid: Instituto Nacional de Estadística,)
    2001 (Retrieved 19 January 2009, from <http://www.ine.es/prodyser/pubweb/discapa/
    discapamenu.htm>).

3. Regarding the classification of hearing-related handicaps, three types of handicap are distinguished: impairment for receiving any sound, impairment for louder sounds, and impairment for listening to speech.
4. They also establish a classification on the communicative disabilities for: communicating through speech, communicating through alternative languages, communicating through non-signed gestures, and communicating through conventional writing and reading.

The data below are the quantitative data that the report shows:

People aged 6 to 64		
hearing impairments	278,654	(total amount)
prelocutive deafness	24,070	
postlocutive deafness	20,738	
hard of hearing	229,549	
balance disorders	5,904	

People aged 65 and older		
Hearing impairments	542,219	(total amount)
Prelocutive deafness	2,168	
Postlocutive deafness	39,705	
Hard of hearing	496,909	
Balance disorders	8,028	

Regions[9]	total number of hearing impaired people	% of deaf people
Andalusia	185,582	2.26
Aragon	32,636	2.46
Asturias	29,352	2.93
Balearic Islands	15,628	1.56
Basque Country	42,924	1.99
Canary Islands	19,684	1.96
Cantabria	12,328	2.11
Castile-La Mancha	43,373	2.12

9   Children under the age 6 are not included.

Regions	total number of hearing impaired people	% of deaf people
Castile-Leon	102,325	4.00
Catalonia	161,231	2.18
Ceuta	673	0.85
Extremadura	26,694	2.43
Galicia	67,964	2.44
La Rioja	4,383	1.38
Madrid	100,878	1.60
Melilla	1,216	1.70
Murcia	27,181	6.31
Navarre	11,460	1.85
Valencia	92,369	1.84

Type of deafness	Children under 6
Hard of hearing	5,042
Profound deafness	871

Taking into account the type of disability, it is stated that hearing problems affect 9.5% of the Spanish population.

6. Specifications for Deaf recipients

In our grouping, we will take into account classifications of hearing impairments from both a strictly medical point of view and a linguistic perspective. Thus, we will also bear in mind the degree of communicative development of the Deaf with the purpose of designing different groups of Deaf caption readers.

From a medical point of view, we may classify the types of deafness according to the following four criteria:

1) the degree of loss of hearing;
2) the location of the injury which causes the deficiency;
3) the moment of appearance of the loss of hearing;
4) the etiology of deafness.

From a communicative point of view, we distinguish the degree of linguistic development. In order to make this distinction, we will take into account any element that may influence this determining aspect of the Deaf community (e.g., mother tongue, education).

a) Types of deafness from a medical point of view

1) The degree of hearing loss is measured in quantitative grades, both in intensity (using decibels) and in frequency (using hertz). Following the standards of the *Bureau International d'Audiophonologie* (BIAP), four groups or types of deafness are established: mild loss of hearing (21– 40 dB HL), moderate loss of hearing (41–70 dB HL), severe loss of hearing (71–90 dB HL) and profound loss of hearing (>90 dB HL). This last type of deafness means an important obstacle for the Deaf when acquiring and developing linguistic skills common to oral languages (e.g., writing). However, the key factor is not the degree of loss of hearing but the hearing functionality that this deafness allows, even when hearing aids are used.

2) Using the location of the injury which causes the deficiency we are able to distinguish two types of loss of hearing: transmission (or conductive) deafness and perception (or neurosensorial) deafness. Transmission or conductive deafness affects the mechanical part of the ear, preventing the sound from properly stimulating Corti organ cells; they correspond to pathologies in the outer and middle ear. Perception or neurosensorial deafness locates the injury in the Corti organ or in the hearing superior centres or canals. Both transmission and perception deafness may occur together. This is called mixed deafness. Obviously, the differences, when overcoming the common difficulties of transmission or perception deafness, are big and require different treatments.

3) Using the moment at which the loss of hearing appears enables us to recognise the type of deafness, taking into account the stage of language acquisition and the chronological age. Thus, we will be able to distinguish the following types of deafness:

    a) prelocutive or prelingual deafness which occurs before the appearance of language (0–2 years);

b) prelocutive deafness which appears between the ages of 2 and 4;

c) postlocutive or postlingual deafness, which is found after all the fundamental linguistic acquisitions are consolidated.

Postlocutive Deaf people, unlike prelocutive Deaf people, know at least the rudiments of oral languages even if they have lost phonation skills. It is also easier for postlocutive Deaf people to read because they already know the oral language.

4) The etiology of deafness seems to be insignificant for the classification of the linguistic aspect of the Deaf. However, it may be necessary to evaluate aspects that fundamentally affect the access and development of language and communication. We may distinguish the following aspects:

a) genetic origin: congenital or degenerative deafness;

b) antenatal origin: embryopathy (rubella) or fetopathy;

c) neonatal origin: prematurity, perinatal suffering, etc.;

d) acquired during childhood: infectious causes (e.g., meningitis), toxic causes and traumatic causes.

b) Types of deafness from the linguistic point of view

Medical classifications start from the degree of loss of hearing, which needs to be fixed in Deaf people. However, in order to have a wider perspective, another form of differentiation is necessary, bearing in mind not so much Deaf people's impairments but their degree of communicative and linguistic development.

1) The fact of being born and of living in one's own linguistic community is significant for the cognitive and communicative development of human beings. Thus, it is also important to take into account the linguistic communities in which Deaf people were born.

We must not forget that Deaf children are frequently raised within hearing families, which makes the conditions for communicative interchanges highly unfavourable. When the Deaf children grow up in oral environments, surrounded by hearing people, they will be subjected to situations of isolation. They will not receive proper stimuli to reach a communicative development at the same time individuals do when they develop in their natural language environments. Nevertheless, if parents, siblings, grandparents and other relatives in the home environment share hearing problems, communication pathways emerge, which are vital to aiding gradual and full communicative development. In such cases, Deaf people will learn the languages of their close environments, without delays in time, which, on occasions, may be irreconcilable. Thus, the Deaf people's languages would be the natural languages of the Deaf community and sign language would be Deaf people's mother tongue.

2) Education is one of the decisive factors in the linguistic development of the Deaf community and this should be taken into account if we hope to understand the special features of this community in an attempt to prepare suitable captions for its members.

We should also bear in mind the fact that in the education for the Deaf the duality between oralists and manualists is still in force. The former are supporters of an education focused on the acquisition of oral language and the latter believe that Deaf students should have a communication tool specific to the development of their community.

Education in special schools is no longer commonplace. On the one hand, special schools brought about the socialisation through their natural language (sign language) as a vehicle for communication outside the classroom. On the other hand, specially designed methods for overcoming the linguistic impediments were encouraged and applied inside the classroom. Results have not been good mainly because of the rootlessness of the small Deaf children who were separated from their families for long periods of time to live in boarding schools which were, in most cases, not even in the same province that their families were living in.

Given that in recent years the inclusion of Deaf children in the same classroom as their hearing counterparts has been encouraged, we should deduce that the purpose of the socialisation of the Deaf is focused on the need to prepare them to live in an oralist world.

Defenders of a mixed or bilingual option think that the education of Deaf children should meet the demands of inclusion in an oralist society but also allow Deaf children to communicate in the modality that they feel most natural in. This option is becoming more widely accepted.

The associative Deaf movement characterised by the defence of SL as the identity language of the Deaf has significant influence in Spain.[10]

c) Other

Reading speed is not a parameter which can be used to measure the comprehension of captions by the Deaf. It is known that visual discrimination is stimulated much more among the Deaf from birth than in hearing people. Nevertheless, this fact, which could mean a greater capacity for reading, does not take place because reading is much more than visually discriminating written symbols. Reading means, apart from decoding the symbolic values of written symbols, deciphering the combination relations of the elements that constitute words, and the relations and values of the grammatical relations in a language. In this respect, Deaf people are not experts but rather have a certain knowledge of this language in various degrees, which may be quantified but with difficulty.

Going back to the main aspects, we may highlight the following four features:

1) When the loss of hearing is bilateral and of severe or profound intensity, or prelocutive and perilocutive, it interferes with and hinders the development of the oral language, which leads to individuals whose natural language is sign language.

2) Communication for the Deaf, as with hearing people, is directly related with their level of language development, not with the language itself (oral or signed) but with their own skills and relation possibilities (social and home), their educational experiences, their possibilities of receiving information from their homes, educational and social environments, which should be as broad and accessible as possible.

---

10 We do not have official information on the number of Deaf enrolled in associations. Nevertheless, it is extremely risky to establish a percentage relation between the number of Deaf enrolled in associations and the use of SL. However, we cannot deny the relation between the number of Deaf registered and the number of signers. The associative Deaf movement in Spain is characterised by the identification of the group as a linguistic community and its defence of the language of the Deaf community as a language of identity and culture.

3) The ability to read subtitles in Deaf individuals is not related to their reading speeds but to their capacities to understand the language. They are quick at decoding the written symbols but slower at establishing the relation between the signifiers and the meanings of the things that they read.

4) Two types of subtitles: in their natural language (there is no captioning but a side window in SL) and in adapted written language. In both cases, we should take into account the linguistic features of sign languages.

7. The acquisition of reading in oral language

Reading provides access to information. Deaf people have traditionally had great difficulties when writing and reading, even when reading has been part of and is currently part of programmes which try to develop oral language skills through reading. The levels acquired by the Deaf, most of them prelocutive, have not been satisfactory.

At present, the Deaf with cochlear implants are achieving good results, both in the development of oral languages and their reading skills. The problem is yet to be solved because not all the people with implants obtain the same results. In addition, not all Deaf people may have implants. Moreover, there is still a large percentage of the Deaf population, both young and old, who have not received a good education and need other solutions. As Villalba Pérez, Ferrer Manchón and Asensi Barrás (2005) point out, reading skills stem from a good development of the linguistic capacity:

> En el desarrollo del pensamiento lógico, los chicos sordos pasan por las mismas etapas que los oyentes pero lo hacen con un retraso variable según la competencia lingüística alcanzada. Los resultados de los estudios experimentales reflejan menor habilidad en la representación mental de la realidad, en la formalización del pensamiento, en la formulación de hipótesis, en la planificación de estrategias, en la abstracción y en la memoria verbal. Señalan, asimismo, importantes dificultades académicas y un pobre nivel lector (p. 21)[11]

11   In the development of logical thought, Deaf children go through the same stages as hearing children but they do so with a varying degree of delay, depending on the linguistic competence reached. The results of the experimental studies show less ability in the mental representation of reality, in the formalisation of thought, in the

Research on the reading levels of the Deaf reveals that the population that generally finishes compulsory school reaches a reading-writing level comparable only to the reading-writing level of a hearing counterpart aged 10.[12]

Authors	Period	Age	Results
Quigley & Paul (1984)	1920–1980		
Pintner & Patterson	1916	Deaf about to finish school	Reading delays of 7/8 years
Myklebust	1960	564 Deaf students 201 hearing	Reading delays of 7/8 years Reading level reached related to their lip reading capacity and their level in oral language
Furth (1966)	1960s	North American Deaf population	8% reaches a reading level of a 10-year-old child
Gallaudet College (Demographic Studies Office)	1970s	17,000 Deaf Between 16 and 20 years	Average reading levels at the end of schooling: 10-year-old child
Di Francesca	1972		10% of the 18-year-old Deaf reach a level of a 14-year-old student
Conrad	1979	468 Deaf 15 to 16 years (end of schooling) England and Wales	Reading level of hearing impaired: 9 years. Hypoacusis: 10.6 years; 35% exceed the functional reading level. Profound Deaf: 8.9 years Only 5% had a reading level comparable to those with the same chronological age.
Asensio	1989	106 Deaf students from 7 to 14 years 157 hearing students from 7 to 11 years and a low socioeconomic level	Similar levels to other countries. 14-year-old Deaf students comparable to hearing 9-year-old students. Slower learning than of hearing students.
Instituto Valenciano de Audiofonía and educational centres in Valencia	1990s	Profound Deaf students: 28 of 10 years 12 of 13 years 53 older than 15 years	Average level of reading comprehension: 10 years. 15% above 15 years old: functional reading level.

formulation of hypotheses, in the planning of strategies, in abstraction and in verbal memory. These results also indicate important academic difficulties and a poor reading level (our translation).

12   See Villalba Pérez et al. (2005).

Authors	Period	Age	Results
University of Valencia Villalba, Ferrer and Asensio	1999	16 impaired undergraduates; 16 hearing undergraduates; 7 profound prelocutive Deaf in undergraduate age (who did not get access to university)	Undergraduates had a similar level to non-undergraduates. Deaf undergraduates took longer to read texts.
Cochlear implants and digital hearing aids open up new perspectives. So far, research has revealed that these users have a better level than the non-implanted Deaf and Deaf people from previous periods.			

Up to now, most of the Deaf have had lower levels of social and educational development than average levels that the rest of the population reaches, causing situations of social exclusion.[13]

Nevertheless, recent research on Spanish Sign Language (SSL) and language acquisition, as well as the passing of the law that recognised SSL as the Deaf people's language in Spain have led to new educational experiences in our country. Among these, we would like to highlight the following three:

1. In pre-school and primary school education: recent introduction to bilingual methodology in Deaf children, based on sign and oral language.

    This project stems from the consideration of SL as the natural language of Deaf people. This is why its introduction at an early age would aid the creation of a linguistic basis from which the Deaf child could access the rest of the curriculum and also the oral language used by the majority of the population.

    Thus, correct linguistic development at the beginning of education is fundamental to aiding balanced and harmonious general development, always with the final aim of reaching the best bilingual ability possible (sign language and oral language).

2. Secondary school and further education: incorporation of Sign Language interpreters, recognised by Royal Decree (2060/1995), in sec-

---

13 Special cases are the ones mentioned in the book *Sordo ¡y qué!* (2007). The book provides testimonies written by Deaf people who have overcome the obstacles imposed by their deafness and feel proud of their condition and way of life.

ondary schools, vocational training, and at some universities attended by a number of Deaf students. The interpreters' function is to serve as bridges for communication between hearing teachers and Deaf pupils/students, thus facilitating access to the curriculum and participation inside the classroom on equal terms (compared with the Deaf pupils'/students' hearing counterparts).

3. The new Advanced Technical Degree in Spanish Sign Language Interpreting.

The book *Libro blanco de la Lengua de Signos Española en el Sistema Educativo* (2004) insists on the importance of considering SSL not only as the language which can be used to access the curriculum but also as a new curricular area in the educational plans. It would be both a vehicle for teaching and an object of knowledge. If SSL becomes part of the educational plans, and the teaching and materials in oral language with which it coexists are adapted to the needs of the Deaf, we will be able to consider a form of bilingual education in which linguistic immersion may exist in both languages.

From the academic year 2008–2009 onwards, sign language will gradually be introduced into the educational system. The curricular proposal for Spanish Sign Language (SSL) was presented in January 2009 along with the specific didactic resources for the teaching of SSL at pre-school and primary school levels.

8. Conclusions

By way of conclusion, we would like to highlight the following findings:

1. In order to define the features of the Deaf groups of recipients for captions, we should start by taking into account not only the degree of loss of hearing but also whether the viewers use sign language as their first language. Signers are perfectly able to cope with visual linguistic communities because the linguistic systems of their communities are complete and self-sufficient. Translation from oral language into sign language would be enough to overcome any barrier that an oral society may impose.

2. Early intervention with the aim of developing the linguistic capacity of the Deaf children (in SSL and in oral language) at the same time as their hearing counterparts would allow the access to early reading, visual stimulation, etc. This is the foundation on which to consolidate bilingual development and such a foundation is necessary for the complete inclusion of Deaf people.

3. The poor success of imposing oral language on Deaf children was reflected in 91.9% of Deaf children having lower studies than secondary school level (Delgado & Bao, 2007). The complexity related to the acquisition of a spoken language is such that intelligent Deaf children (being exposed only to oral teaching) would obtain an average number of 50 words when they are five years old (Delgado & Bao, 2007). On the contrary, their hearing counterparts possess, at a similar age, around 2000 words and they are able to make up a whole story (López-Torres Hidalgo, López Verdejo, Boix Gras & del Campo del Campo, 2003).

4. The high correlation between reading level and the degree of loss of hearing has been stated by several researches in different countries. Kyle and Pullen studies (1985) carried out in Great Britain show that the reading speed of the Deaf spectator is about 90 to 120 words per minute. As there is no equivalent data in Spain, we are forced to plan without knowing in detail the actual needs of the Deaf recipients. This lack of information and research also makes the reduction of recipients to a certain number of groups difficult, although simplification of grouping is clearly necessary. Because of educational issues, the reading level of the Deaf users of SSL when reading Spanish written language is just like reading a second language (L2) or foreign language (FL). Their command of an L2 or FL in a written version does not allow them to read at the same rate found for users reading a first language (L1). This is why it will be essential to adapt the speed of the captions to their needs so that they can grasp the actual message of the captions.

5. The research by Lewis (cf. Pereira 2005: 23) points to 12 or 13 years as the age when Deaf prelocutive children acquire enough skills to be able to read. Consequently, the exposure time of captions on screen is clearly insufficient for them to read and truly understand.

6. The training of the Deaf as teachers for pre-school and primary education and strict research on SSL transcription systems, grammar, teaching, etc. that allows hearing people to become familiar with and learn SSL are some of the steps to follow.

7. Current subtitling for the Deaf in Spain should not be labelled as such. The differences with normal subtitling lie in the inclusion of references to environmental sounds, songs, etc. and in some cases, the assignment of colours to the main characters. Therefore, it will be necessary to improve the quality of subtitles and make the subtitles more suitable for the Deaf, taking into account important aspects such as the following: differences between languages, special features of sign languages, the need for appropriateness of each language: idioms, set phrases, synonyms, etc.

8. In order to improve this situation, we propose three groups to whom we can direct subtitles (although we count on the advantages that digital television offers). Even though the difficulties of grouping the Deaf population are still large, due to the special features of each individual, simplification is necessary if we want to achieve valuable captioning. There has been an important improvement in expectations as a result of a new situation brought about by the law passed in November 2007. Groups are extremely changeable and are determined by age but we think that in a period of time they could become more homogeneous and we can see the following three groups: profound prelocutive Deaf/users of SSL (for these Deaf recipients, the inclusion of a side window with simultaneous translation into sign language would be the ideal), hypoacusics/postlocutive Deaf (subtitles, maybe increasing the exposure time of the captions on screen), and implanted Deaf (they may be able to read unadapted captions, but we encourage more research in this field in the future).

References

Báez Montero, I., & Cabeza-Pereiro, C. (1997). El censo lingüístico de una lengua signada. *Proceedings of the First University of Vigo International Symposium on Bilingualism.* Vigo: Universidade de Vigo, 905–915. Retrieved 19 January 2009, from <webs.uvigo. es/ssl/actas1997/06/Baez.pdf>.

Buyssens, E. (1943). *Les langages et le discours: Essai de linguistique fonctionnelle dans le cadre de la sémiologie.* Brussels: Office de Publicité.

Delgado, J.A., & Bao, M. (2007). Apoyos educativos inclusivos en las dificultades de aprendizaje asociadas a discapacidad auditiva. In M. Deaño (Ed.), *XXXIII Reunión Científica Anual AEDES 2006* (pp. 151–168). Ourense: AEDES.

Escandell, M. V. (2005). *La comunicación*. Madrid: Gredos.

Gascón Ricao, A., & Storch de Gracia y Asensio, J. G. (2004). *Historia de la educación de los sordos en España y su influencia en Europa y América*. Madrid: Ramón Areces.

Herrero Blanco, Á. (2003). *Escritura alfabética de la lengua de signos española: once lecciones*. Alicante: Universidad de Alicante.

Kyle, J. G., & Pullen, G. (1985). *Young deaf people in employment*. Bristol: School of Education.

López-Torres Hidalgo, J., López Verdejo, M. A., Boix Gras, C., & del Campo del Campo J. M. (2003). Hipoacusia, *Guías Clínicas en Atención Primaria, 3(20)*, 1–7. Retrieved 19 January 2009, from <http://www.fisterra.com/guias2/PDF/Hipoacusia.pdf>.

Pereira, A. (2005). El subtitulado para sordos: estado de la cuestión en España. *Quaderns: Revista de traducció, 12*, 161–172. Retrieved 19 January 2009, from <http://ddd.uab.es/pub/quaderns/11385790n12p161.pdf>.

Pinedo, F.-J. (1989). *Una voz para el silencio*. Madrid: Fomento Empleo Minusválidos.

Serna, M. J. (1994). Prologue. In O. Sacks (Ed.), *Veo una voz: Viaje al mundo de los sordos*. Madrid: Anagrama.

Shannon, C. E., & Weaver, W. (1949). *The mathematical theory of communication*. Urbana: University of Illinois.

Villalba Pérez, A., Ferrer Manchón, A. M., & Asensi Barrás, M. C. (2005). *La Lectura en los sordos prelocutivos: Propuesta para un programa de entrenamiento*. Madrid: Entha Ediciones.

VV. AA (2007). *Sordo ¡Y qué!: Vida de persona sordas que han alcanzado el éxito*. Madrid: Lo que no existe producciones, S. L.

Carmen Cabeza-Pereiro

The development of writing and grammatisation: The case of the deaf[1]

Special attention should be paid to end users when drafting subtitles for the deaf and hard of hearing. Understanding the metalinguistic knowledge of deaf people, whose language has no written form, is a much needed point of departure when devising subtitles, so that the exercise becomes worthwhile for those whose first language has no fixed or standardised written representation. This paper revises the concept used in linguistic historiography, namely grammatisation *(Auroux, 1994), to explain the role played by the appearance, consolidation and democratisation of writing as an instrument for the development of an objective knowledge of language, with important practical consequences for the standardisation of languages.*

1. Introduction

This paper starts with a concept used in linguistic historiography, namely *grammatisation* (Auroux, 1994), to explain the role played by the appearance, consolidation and democratisation of writing as an instrument for

1   I wish to thank several individuals for the help that they provided. Firstly, María I. Massone for orienting me towards both Auroux's reading and his differentiation between metalinguistic and epilinguistic knowledge, applicable to the case of the deaf. Secondly, I would also like to thank Elena Cabeza, my sister, for her invaluable observations on linguistic conscience in language development, derived from her experience as a speech therapist with a solid linguistic training. And last but not least, I would also like to thank Irene Pazó for her contributions guided by her research focus on teaching written Spanish to deaf adults. This research has helped shed light on some specific issues in this article which had been maturing in my head for several years. My reflections are centred on a research project that has been supported in the form of a grant from the Spanish Ministry of Education and Science, reference: HUM2006-10870/FILO.

the development of an objective knowledge of language, with important practical consequences for the standardisation of languages. The grammatisation concept will then be applied to refer to the metalinguistic conscience settlement process that takes place in the linguistic development of an individual, through the acquisition of reading-writing skills.

Subsequently, the paper will explain how reading-writing skills are an instrument for conscious metalinguistic reflection since they provide the individual with mother tongue analysis categories. From these two perspectives, that is, historical and communal on the one hand, and the development of an individual on the other, the objective of the paper is to ascertain what linguistic knowledge the deaf have and the conditions under which the deaf access tasks of decoding subtitles that have been specifically created for them.

Although many of the considerations below may be applicable in a wider context, this paper refers to the Spanish deaf community and the current Spanish context whenever it describes linguistic situations in the deaf community.

2. The concept of grammatisation

The concept of grammatisation will be used as defined by Auroux (1994), who explains that the word *grammatisation* is a neologism created on the *alphabetisation* model. In order to explain the differences with the latter, Auroux (1994) adds:

> Within the use we suggest, to grammatise is also a transitive verb, though its object, instead of being necessarily the trace [+human] (a population is grammatised), is the language activity itself (a language is grammatised). (p. 12) (my translation)

Grammatisation is therefore a process through which objective knowledge of a language is consolidated within society, as a consequence of the appearance of a writing system. As mentioned above, this paper intends to extend the application of grammatisation not only to language but also to users, as learning to write leads to metalinguistic reflection during juvenile linguistic development. The concept will be later applied more specifically to the case of the deaf, who are users of a language for which no widely accepted written system has yet been developed.

The technological revolution, which – according to Auroux (1994) – enabled the introduction of writing, first manifested itself with the birth of the oldest writing systems and became established in Renaissance western Europe through the production of dictionaries and grammar books for neo-Latin languages, which resulted in the standardisation of and the provision of value (i.e., status consolidation) for these languages. The introduction of the printing press played a decisive role in the standardisation process (Auroux, 1994). Even though not all individuals necessarily acquire literacy, they do develop a culture for writing. In other words, a grammatisation process takes place.

From a historiographic point of view, Auroux (1994, p. 48) claims that the appearance of writing is an essential condition for the appearance of language sciences or for the appearance of metalinguistic reflection: "The process through which writing appears (I mean one particular writing) is a remarkable process of making objective with no previous equivalent" (my translation).

The earlier argument necessarily leads us to the following questions: If writing is an essential condition for the grammatisation process to occur, can we infer that grammatisation does not take place in oral cultures because there is no development of a written system? What consequences would we observe if this were to be the case?

Auroux (1994) refers to the case of the Dogon, a civilisation that has linguistic resources to differentiate between words taken from the language and other types of sounds. This, in turn, has given rise to myths related to the origin of language and linguistic diversity. Furthermore, the Dogon have (according to Auroux) an extremely rich oral literature.[2] However, the pictorial symbols that they draw cannot be considered a true writing system and they are also unable to explain the differences between normal language expressions and poetic expressions:

> Their [the Dogon people's] metalinguistic knowledge just enables them to claim that the latter [poetic language] has "more oil" than the former [common language] but not to explain how to create a strophe or a refrain, so the knowledge is reserved to the epilinguistic scope. (Auroux, 1994, p. 38)

---

2   Auroux (1994) cites Calame-Griaule (1965). Most of the Dogon live in Mali but there are some who live in the north of Burkina Faso. *Ethnologue* (Grimes, 2000) has identified ten varieties of the Dogon language.

3. The development of reading-writing skills
   and the consolidation of metalinguistic conscience
   in the individual

Citing Culioli, Auroux (1994) tells us of the acquisition of a first form of
linguistic 'knowledge' by an individual, termed as *epilinguistic*, which is
identified with the capacity to speak a language. This is unconscious knowledge and the following is said:

> Culioli uses the term to refer to the unconscious knowledge every speaker has of his
> own language and of the language nature: "language is an activity that involves in
> itself a permanent epilinguistic activity (defined as an "unconscious linguistic activ-
> ity"). (p. 23)[3]

Epilinguistic knowledge, for example, manifests itself as the ability to judge
whether a sequence is rightly or wrongly constructed but without being
able to provide reasons as to why it is so. From this we can gather that true
linguistic knowledge (in as far as its capacity to objectively represent language as an object) is metalinguistic. Language sciences are connected with
metalinguistics. Although Auroux (1994) applies the terms 'epilinguistic'
and 'metalinguistic' to the scope of historiography, the same will be applied here to the linguistic development of an individual because I believe
that these concepts can be transported without distortion and can be quite
useful for the objective of this contribution.

   In children with normal hearing, that is, children who develop their
language in natural contexts, the acquisition of reading-writing skills es-
tablishes the culmination of the development process because it provides
individuals with mother tongue analysis strategies. This is how, for example, a six-year-old child learns how to write. At first, the child probably
makes mistakes in the task of transforming phonic language units into
letters and words as is represented in Figure 1:

---

3   Without specific reference to Culioli's source in Auroux (1994).

Figure 1. A writing exercise carried out by a hearing child.

The child who wrote the expression above was six years and five months old and this written production is a good example of natural spelling, that is, the child was at a reading-writing stage at which it had still not fully assimilated the specific, arbitrary norms of spelling in a particular language but, nevertheless, it had incorporated some of the basic principles of correspondence between oral and written discourse. The written text in Spanish will now be reproduced and subsequently an explanatory gloss in English will be included:

madre	quieres	benir	<u>ala</u>	mar
mother	*want*.PRES.2SG	*come*.INF	*to·the*	*sea*

The example clearly shows that a part of the writing task has been successfully overcome (that is, the linking process between phonemes and graphemes), and that there is a need for further consolidation of issues related to language rules, which are sanctioned by usage considered to be correct. Since there is not much room for a detailed analysis in this contribution, two typical mistakes (which can be found in the example above) will be cited. Both mistakes are highlighted in bold and underlined in the reproduction of the text. The first mistake is that the letter chosen to represent the phoneme /b/ is not the one that the rule dictates. In this case, the word should be written as *venir*, since we are dealing with a case where two graphemes correspond to the same phoneme in written Spanish. The second mistake is the incorrect segmentation of the preposition *a* and the definite article *la* for feminine nouns in the singular. In this latter case, we must explain that if the definite article were used in its masculine form *(el)*, it would be written joined to the preposition (as is the case in the example *ala*) because the rule for writing states that there ought to be a contraction of the vowels *a + e(l)* resulting in the form *al.*

The mental correspondence between phonemes and graphemes is an essential requisite for the proper acquisition of reading-writing skills. Word identification is acquired by learning how to segment words and it is associated with blank spaces in writing.

This paper simply tries to illustrate that the reading-writing acquisition process is linked to the assimilation of linguistic analysis resources, which are not limited to phonic levels but extend to other, more complex, levels of grammar such as the segmentation of morphemes and words.

4. Where do the deaf stand: What is their linguistic knowledge like?

Following the previous approach, the question about deaf people's reading-writing acquisition will first be dealt with from a historical and social perspective. Let us start by explaining a fact which, although known, may still go unnoticed for those who do not consider the deaf as a linguistically coherent group. I refer to the fact that most countries do not actually have a normalised and general method for the transmission of the language and culture of the deaf.

In practice, schools for the deaf have, for decades, been the driving forces for the transmission of signed languages, in such a way that it can be stated that the linguistic variety used by a deaf person is largely determined by the school where that person was trained (see Parkhurst & Parkhust, 2000a). In Galicia, this is the case at the school for the deaf in Santiago de Compostela. Such schools do not necessarily teach Spanish Sign Language (SSL), nor is SSL an instrumental teaching language at the school since the usual objective in such schools is to teach Spanish and normal school curriculum subjects to students as part of the cultural knowledge acquired at school. However, the fact that deaf children mingle with other deaf children at school means that opportunities for learning and for the transfer of signed language exist, as is the case during break times.

Despite what has already been said, some exceptions to this absence of stable methods for language and culture transfer can be identified. The oldest centre for the teaching of deaf people's language and culture is in the USA,[4] where the University of Gallaudet (in Washington DC) fulfils the function of training future American Sign Language (ASL) teachers and professionals who will be working on tasks related to providing support to the deaf community in the entire country. Consequently, ASL is becoming a highly standardised language.

Since the 1990s there have been some initiatives in Spain aimed at introducing methods for teaching Spanish Sign Language (SSL) in certain education centres. Examples of such initiatives are the *Colegio Hispano-americano de la Palabra* and the *Colegio Público de Educación Especial de Sordos*, both located in Madrid. They employ a person called the counsellor for the deaf, whose function consists of both ensuring that students learn SSL and acting as an example of an adult signed language speaker (CNSE, 1997).

Another factor that has also been included since the 1990s is the introduction of SSL interpreters in secondary schools. The presence of such professionals in classrooms with deaf students may, over time, contribute to a change in the sociolinguistic situation of the deaf community, especially in as far as getting to know and value SSL, the deaf students' own language. In practice, the task of such interpreters is not limited to the transfer of subject content in SSL. Their task also extends, in many cases, to acting as linguistic reinforcement models for the deaf students for whom they interpret.

After describing the situation above, it should be easier to understand why there is no widely accepted written system for signed languages, even within deaf linguistic communities, which have had a long-term institutional history, that is, where the history of educating the deaf dates back centuries, as is the case in Spain (the sixteenth century), France or the United Kingdom (eighteenth century).

---

4   Denmark may be cited as another exception because for decades Danish Sign Language has been incorporated into school curricula as a vehicular teaching language. As explained by Hansen (2002), a bilingual education model was introduced in 1982 in Copenhagen, in a school for the deaf, where Danish Sign Language was the teaching language. It was considered to be the pupils'/students' first language. Danish was treated as a second language or foreign language. English was considered to be the third language (second foreign language).

Some notations and note-taking forms have been created in an attempt to write and transcribe the specific articulations of signed languages but with a linguistic description purpose in mind, like the one used by Stokoe and his team in their first ASL Dictionary (Stokoe, Casterline & Croneberg, 1965), or the HamNoSys, derived from Stokoe (Prillwitz, Leven, Zienert, Hanke &. Henning, 1989).

Worth mentioning is the proposal by Herrero-Blanco (2003) for an alphabetical writing system for Spanish Sign Language, which is viewed for use by the signed language user community. However, to date, it has not been widely accepted as the written form of SSL. The underlying idea is that of analysis of basic SSL units (i.e., signs) into sublexical components or *phonemes*, which are graphically represented using the letters of the Latin alphabet. Herrero-Blanco's system considers the sign as a sequential unit and its written reproduction is also sequential, since such is the nature of the letters of the alphabet.

However, Sign Writing, invented by Valerie Sutton, can fulfil all the requisites in order to function as a writing system adapted to sign languages of the deaf. The principal advantage of Sign Writing over other writing or sign-language notations is its visual nature, which tries to reproduce signs just as the signer would view them. It not only represents the relevant aspects of sign composition (*cheremes*, in Stokoe's nomenclature, see Stokoe et al., 1965), but also enables the reflection of some variations of elements considered 'phonemic' which may be relevant. For example, a sign articulated over the head is represented by a circumference and will simultaneously be followed by other symbols which will be the graphic image of aspects like the shape and orientation of the hand, type of movement and whether or not there is contact between the hand and the head, and if there is contact, at what point. If the signed language speaker produces a sign with a variation of its canonical form, this may also be represented by graphism (see Capovilla & Sutton, 2001; Sutton, 1995).

Let us now look at this simple example of written SSL using Sign Writing taken from Parkhust and Parkhust (2000b). This is the lexical unit *sordo* ('deaf') in its normal cited form, that is, as it would appear in a dictionary.

SORDO   Figure 2. The lexical unit for 'deaf' in Sign Writing.

Figure 2 shows a sign that is articulated with the active hand with the index finger stretched out and the rest of the fist clenched. The index finger first makes contact with the earlobe and then with the mouth.

The following two examples provide support to the argument that Sign Writing could fulfil the condition of writing being at the service of a linguistic community. Firstly, Sign Writing is apparently easy to learn, which is made evident through easy assimilation. It has been used, for example, in banners during *Deaf Pride* demonstrations, as a way of showing the identity of the deaf community.[5] Furthermore, there is the appearance during the past years of sign language dictionaries that use Sign Writing as a resource to transcribe the articulation of a lexical entry (Capovilla & Duarte, 2001). These are dictionaries that have been created to be used as supporting materials, and not as instruments for researchers, for the learning and the standardisation of a signed language.

Although these dictionaries are proof of the viability of Sign Writing as a signed language standardisation tool, this writing system has not yet been widely accepted by deaf people, as stated earlier. If it were introduced into the deaf community worldwide, it would be possible to verify whether it can effectively be consolidated as a written form of signed language.

The complexity of the natural acquisition process of signed language must be taken into consideration, from a deaf individual's perspective, when evaluating difficulties that deaf individuals experience when trying to access writing in oral languages. The diversity of situations for what can be understood as native language, if we have in mind the linguistic acquisition process, is huge and is determined by several factors, for example, the age at which loss of hearing takes place or the existence or non-exist-

---

5   The potential of Sign Writing as a written form of signed language that is easily adaptable to its viso-gestural peculiarities and its acceptance and assimilation by the deaf community have contributed to the appearance of proposals such as *The King James Bible in Sign Writing*, which is available online (<http://www.cyberjer.com/signbibl/>). This is an example of an evangelising application of this writing system.

ence of hearing vestiges. Another relevant factor is connected with the fact
that the percentage of deaf persons who actually acquire signed language
within a so-called native context, that is, within the family, is quite small
(not greater than five per cent of deaf children). This means that, in practice, the access age to signed language can be higher in comparative terms,
since linguistic input can be delayed until adolescence.

Deaf people's acquisition conditions usually result in fragility of linguistic categorisation, at least at the consciousness level. The earlier paragraphs have discussed the success possibilities of a writing system that is
characteristic of signed language: Sign Writing. I shall now talk about the
absence of learning a written form in deaf people's first or natural language (in as far as it is visible and therefore accessible to them), namely,
signed language.[6] The possibility of learning a system such as Sign Writing is surely not conceived of as part of the curricula for the deaf, that is,
it is not considered as something that a deaf child should learn during
its first years at school. The absence of such task definition in schools
leads to a lack of metalinguistic maturity described earlier by means of
the example of the six-year-old child's writing ability (see Figure 1 above
and the comments below). This succinctly shows that the acquisition of
reading-writing skills leads to the consolidation of conscious handling of
certain metalinguistic categories such as the phoneme or word and mor-
pheme.

The starting position, in as far as knowledge of the first language is
concerned, would be similar to that of the Dogon, as illustrated by Auroux
(1994) above. However, as deaf children become educated, they are subjected to an alphabetisation process, with all the inherent problems arising
from the fact that the language in which such a process occurs is not accessible to them in a 'natural' form, that is, through hearing. Consequently,
their knowledge of oral language is quite imperfect and they cannot form
a mental image of the phoneme category, as the one illustrated in section
2 with respect to a child with normal hearing.

The metalinguistic categorisation weakness of deaf people would lead
us to describe their linguistic knowledge as epilinguistic, just as described
by Auroux (1994). Some testimonies collected from alphabetisation courses
for deaf adults confirm this reality, as is evident from the deaf adults' ap-

6   The signed language learning situation being described here warrants the distinction
     between mother tongue and first language (in use).

parent difficulty to develop analytic formulas that would enable the deaf to refer to signed language categories. When teaching written Spanish, this would require the teacher to use strategies that fully avoid any references to usual linguistic categories.

Nevertheless, such a situation cannot be generalised to the entire deaf community. As can be envisaged, and in a similar manner to people with good hearing, the level of command of linguistic resources of the first language (signed language in the case of the deaf community) varies enormously from one individual to the next and notable differences can also be observed with regard to the ways in which metalinguistic categories are dealt with. Let us consider two cases which may generate controversy.

The first of these cases is related to individuals who, given their condition as language professionals (usually SSL teachers), have to face the challenge of making judgements about their language since they are required to develop strategies to teach the language. They receive further support via courses and other linguistic teaching methods. Some of these individuals are bilingual, that is, they have a good command of spoken Spanish, which, in turn, could contribute to the development of metalinguistic reflection, in as far as this stimulates contrast between signed language resources and the oral language resources.[7]

Another case would be that of deaf people who create poetry in signed language. Their poetic vocation and creative capacity lead them to another form of linguistic reflection. These people can develop a huge capacity for the lexical creation of abstract terms both in SSL and in Spanish, and in the latter case because they often wish to 'translate' their poetry into the spoken language (precisely to keep a written record). Their experience of poetic creation helps them enormously in learning written Spanish.

In both cases, and with only occasional specific exceptions, as the one referred in footnote 7, I believe that it would be far-fetched to affirm that we are witnessing an authentic case of metalinguistic reflection since such deaf people can hardly put together elaborate instances of discourse about their own language beyond declaring that an SSL expression is well or badly constructed or that one form has more poetic efficiency because it is 'more refined' or 'less refined'.

---

7   This is a case for one of the researchers involved in the signed language research group at the University of Vigo, namely Francisco Eijo, who is able to design exercises which work with a contrasting methodology. I believe that this is an absolutely exceptional case.

5. Final reflection

The situation that has been described in the paragraphs above leads us to consider that the models available for learning reading-writing skills are weakened in the case of the deaf. This applies to both the children's model, which incorporates a tool which enables them to develop a metalinguistic analytic process, and to the model for the adults, who access the learning of a foreign language in a written form, since they start off with metalinguistic knowledge, namely *grammatisation*, which is non-existent in the case of the deaf.

Therefore, whenever we think about reception conditions of a subtitle that is specific to the deaf, we should bear in mind the need to use linguistic strategies that reinforce the reading comprehension potential. In addition, we should try (in as far as this is possible) to relate the written language forms to the deaf perception formulas, that is, adapt them to the way typical signed language information is presented (see Pereira, this volume).

We should also understand the important role that subtitles can play for the deaf as an instrument capable of contributing to this grammatisation process. This process should be ideally complemented with another similar and parallel tool in the deaf people's own language, possibly by means of Sign Writing.

The situation may slowly change in Spain thanks to the changes that are being introduced in primary and secondary education. In this sense, it is quite important to highlight the role played by the passing of the act that regulates linguistic rights of deaf persons who use SSL as their means of communication.

References

Auroux, S. (1994). *La révolution technologique de la grammatisation*. Liège: Mardaga.
Calame-Griaule, G. (1965). *La parole chez les Dogons*. Paris: Gallimard.
Capovilla, F. C., & Duarte, W. (Eds.) (2001). *Dicionário enciclopédico ilustrado trilíngüe da língua de sinais brasileira*. São Paulo: Editora da Universidade de São Paulo.

Capovilla, F.C., & Sutton, V. (2001). Como ler e escrever os sinais da Libras: A escrita visual direta de sinais *Sign Writing*. In F.C. Capovilla & W. Duarte (Eds.), *Dicionário enciclopédico ilustrado trilíngüe da língua de sinais brasileira* (pp. 55–126). São Paulo: Editora da Universidade de São Paulo.

Confederación Nacional de Personas Sordas (CNSE) (Producer) (1997). *La educación de las personas sordas* [video]. Madrid: Confederación Nacional de Personas Sordas (CNSE).

Grimes, B.F. (Ed.) (2000). *Ethnologue: Languages of the world* (14th ed.). Dallas, TX: Summer Institute of Linguistics.

Hansen, B. (2002). Bilingualism and the impact of sign-language research on deaf education. In D.F. Armstrong, M.A. Karchmer & J.V. Van Cleve (Eds.), *The study of signed languages: Essays in honour of William C. Stokoe* (pp. 172–189). Washington DC: Gallaudet University Press.

Herrero-Blanco, Á. (2003). *Escritura alfabética de la lengua de signos española: once lecciones.* Alicante: University of Alicante.

Parkhurst, S., & Parkhurst, D. (2000a). La variación en las lenguas de signos: Un estudio de causas y una metodología analítica. In F. Martínez, et al. (Eds.), *Apuntes de lingüística de la lengua de signos española* (pp. 221–246). Madrid: Confederación Nacional de Personas Sordas (CNSE).

Parkhurst, S., & Parkhurst, D. (2000b). *SignoEscritura.* Madrid: Promotora Española de Lingüística (PROEL).

Prillwitz, S., Leven, R., Zienert, H., Hanke, T., & Henning, J. (1989). *HamNoSys. Version 2.0; Hamburg Notation System for sign languages: An introductory guide* (International Studies on Sign language and Communication of the Deaf; 5). Hamburg: Signum.

Stokoe, W.C., Casterline, D.C., & Croneberg, C.G. (1965). *A dictionary of American Sign language on linguistic principles.* Silver Spring, MD: Linstok.

Sutton, V. (1995). *Lessons in sign writing* (2nd ed.). La Jolla, CA: The Deaf Action Committee for Sign Writing.

Francisco Utray, Belén Ruiz, José Antonio Moreiro

Maximum font size for subtitles in Standard Definition Digital Television: Tests for a font magnifying application

This article discusses the results of the tests conducted by the Centro Español de Subtitulado y Audiodescripción *(CESyA) to establish the maximum acceptable font size for subtitles in standard definition digital television (SDTV).*[1] *The screen space taken up by texts was measured in pixels when establishing the specifications for a subtitle magnifying application. This application will allow users to optionally increase character size.*

1. Introduction

Subtitles provide access to audiovisual contents and are used by a wide group of viewers who require this service either because of hearing disabilities or to gain access to contents in a foreign language that they do not know or master (Díaz Cintas, 2003). But the size of subtitle fonts can be an obstacle to people who are unable to distinguish text on screen clearly. In digital television this problem can be addressed by developing a character magnifying application with the option of increasing character size in order to improve text legibility. This is a requirement that representatives of visually impaired people have been calling for worldwide (CERMI, 2006; RNIB-BBC, 2004) but the requirement also caters to the needs of a wider group of people who would benefit from it. The application is al-

---

1   The CESyA (Spanish Centre for Subtitling and Audio Description) is a Public Reference Institution dependent on the Royal Board on Disability – Ministry of Labour and Social Affairs. It was created to promote wider accessibility in the audiovisual media environment through the services of subtitling and audio description.

ready available in PC environments but has not yet been incorporated into European digital TV broadcasting systems.

Orero (2007) highlights the multidisciplinary nature of current studies covering content accessibility as well as the technology involved. Our article focuses on an extremely specific technological aspect, namely, the maximum size applicable in Europe to subtitle characters on 4:3 standard definition television screens. It describes the methodology followed and the results of the tests carried out by the CESyA.

In Europe, subtitles are currently broadcast on digital television via teletext services or in digital DVB sub format (ETSI, 2002, 2003; Martín Edo, Jiménez, Cisneros & Menéndez, 2007). In the case of teletext, the broadcaster transmits subtitles in text format, displaying the ASCII codes of the characters,[2] and the graphics are created in the receiver. However, in the case of the DVB sub format, subtitles are broadcast as a bitmap image, thereby ensuring a homogeneous graphical presentation on all receiver sets. In this case, typographical decisions are made by broadcasters and their subtitle production centres. Therefore, we are faced with two different scenarios for the specification of a font magnifying application, depending on whether subtitles are broadcast in text format or image format.

The first scenario deals with possible subtitles in text format: the font magnifying application needs to be developed by equipment manufacturers and it must be transparent for the broadcaster. In order to increase font size, receiver systems must be equipped with the necessary typeface options. Each receiver model will thus offer the user its own characteristics for subtitle display. The advantages of this method are that broadcast bandwidth is optimised and each manufacturer can differentiate itself from its competitors through the graphic features of subtitling.

The second scenario deals with possible subtitles in bitmap image format. In this case, typographical decisions are to be taken by broadcasters. In order to provide a font magnifying option, the broadcasters will need to broadcast two subtitle channels, one with the standard font size and another with magnified characters.[3] The advantage of this format is that it allows broadcasters to monitor the ways in which subtitles are displayed in

2   The ASCII code (American Standard Code for Information Interchange) is a code of characters used by computer systems to display texts.

3   Broadcasting of a subtitle channel in DVB Sub involves the use of a 50–120 kbit/s bandwidth, which is not always available for this purpose.

any receiver on the market. Subtitles in bitmap image format are also used for DVDs.

The following section analyses the conditioning factors that limit the possibility of increasing font size for PAL standard definition television in both scenarios referred to above.

2. Limits on increasing font size

The font magnifying application is subordinate to the main subtitle channel and must abide by the editorial decisions of the subtitler and observe the limits of the safe caption areas while ensuring interoperability with all receivers on the market. Each of these aspects is analysed below.

2.1. Safe Caption Areas

Digital television pictures for SDTV broadcasting are 720 pixels wide and 576 pixels high. According to the professional standards adopted by the industry (BBC, 2007; Ofcom, 2006), the text labelled on the image must be confined to a safe caption area, which decreases the available space by twenty per cent. Therefore, only 576 pixels are left horizontally for subtitles, as shown in Figure 1.

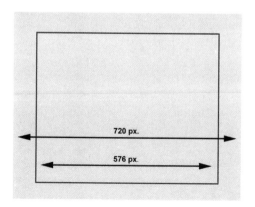

Figure 1. Safe caption area for a PAL SDTV image.

2.2. Structure of subtitle screens

During the subtitle production and editing processes, professionals comply with a number of criteria concerning reading speed (d'Ydewalle & Van Rensbergen, 1987) and grammatical arrangement of the sentences, depending on the space available (Díaz Cintas, 2003; Neves & Lorenzo, 2007). These criteria have resulted in the establishment of professional codes and standards of good practice that take into account the limitations of the Teletext system for analogue television (AENOR, 2003; ITC, 1999; Ofcom, 2006). In the digital environment, these codes and standards, which have already proved efficient in teletext, should be maintained to ensure compatibility with the catalogue of existing subtitles and with the receivers already installed in European homes. These standards establish a limit of 32 to 37 characters per line for teletext subtitling and recommend using only two lines of text on each subtitle screen (AENOR, 2003; ITC, 1999; Karamitroglou, 1998; Ofcom, 2006). This criterion is considered to set the limit for enlarging characters. Otherwise, when increasing font size, a point would be reached when three or four lines would be required to display the text, breaking the structure of the subtitle as designed during the production process.

2.3. Interoperability

Digital television reception is possible both on modern television sets with integrated digital receivers and on older television sets that require external set top boxes. The font magnifying application for subtitles should be available for all television sets in European homes. Therefore, it is important to comply with the safe caption areas, whether the subtitles are in an image format or a text format.

This requirement does not apply when the application is produced by a manufacturer for a specific screen, for example, in the case of a television set with a 16:9 flat widescreen and an integrated DTT receiver incorporating an application for magnifying subtitles in text format. The manufacturer is aware of the restrictions of these particular screens and can freely incorporate any changes to accommodate these restrictions, as the application will run only on that equipment and according to particular technical specifications. However, in the case of an external receiver, the manufacturer is unfamiliar with the characteristics of the screen to which the receiver will be connected and will therefore need to develop the application in accordance with the aforementioned specifications to ensure that the receiver will function properly on older 3:4 tube (CRT) television sets.

3. Technical tests to establish maximum font size

Technical tests were conducted to establish the maximum permitted font size, taking into consideration the different typographical styles available for subtitles. A reference text was selected for the tests, and measurements for each font were made in pixels.

3.1. Font selection

Regarding the choice of fonts, visually impaired user organisations recommend the use of fonts which are called sans serif fonts (Kitchel, 2006; ONCE, 2006; RNIB-BBC, 2004). Sans serif fonts eliminate all flourishes or serifs, which are the small decorative ornaments generally attached to the ends of the main character strokes. As pointed out by Ivarsson and Carroll (1998: 42), "embellishments like serifs might make the type more attractive and legible on paper, but tend to impair legibility on the screen". Figure 2 shows the difference between *sans serif* and *serif* fonts.

Figure 2. Example of *sans serif* and *serif* font types.

Of the sans serif fonts specifically designed to maximise legibility on electronic screens, the Tiresias font was created in 1998 by a team led by John Gill to meet the requirements of visually impaired people (Tiresias, 2007). It is the font recommended for digital television in the UK by the Royal National Institute of Blind People (RNIB) and by the regulator Ofcom (2006). A critical analysis of the Tiresias font performed by Clark (2005) points out a few flaws in its design and in the research conducted with users with a view to its validation.

In Spain, the national organisation for blind people (*Organización Nacional de Ciegos Españoles* (ONCE)) published a report in 2006 on captioning characteristics for visually impaired people, recommending the use of the Arial font (ONCE, 2006). Although the organisation fails to indicate how this conclusion was reached, it is along the same lines as the research on font legibility conducted by Bernard, Liao, Chaparro and Chaparro (2001), who consider Arial and Verdana to be the sans serif fonts best suited for computer screens. A major advantage of these typefaces is that they are available in most computer operating systems and on electronic equipment. However, the use of specific fonts for subtitles requires that the fonts be installed in production equipments and also in the receivers when broadcasting is performed in text format.

Four sans serif fonts were chosen for measurement: Arial Regular, Arial Narrow, Verdana and Tiresias. With the Arial Narrow font, letter spacing is substantially reduced and the shape of the characters is condensed so that the font also takes up less space on screen. In contrast, Verdana has wide interspacing. Tiresias was chosen because of its widespread use in the UK. The maximum permitted size was tested for each of these fonts in accordance with the aforementioned limitations.

3.2. Selection of a reference text for measurement purposes

The alphabet includes wide characters (such as M or W) that take up many pixels and narrow characters (such as I or L) that take up less room. Therefore, it is not possible to determine the exact length in pixels of a line of 32–37 characters as it depends on the arrangement of the characters that make up the subtitle line and on the language used for subtitling (Ivarsson & Carroll, 1998).

In the following examples, two lines of 37 characters were taken from the Latin text *Lorem ipsum,* which has been used for typographical tests since the invention of the printing press: *Lorem ipsum dolor sit amet, consectet* and *Quisque molestie cursus sem. Maecenas.* This text has been considered a useful reference for measuring the pixels required, since it contains the maximum number of characters permitted by the standards consulted (see 2.2) and an average combination of short and long letters.

3.3. Measurements in pixels of the reference text for each typeface

As mentioned above, in an SDTV image only 576 pixels are available horizontally (see 2.1) for subtitle texts. Measurements were carried out on the four selected fonts to establish the size beyond which the chosen text exceeds the 576 pixels available on the screen. The resulting figure for each of these fonts is the maximum font size recommended for a subtitle magnifying application in SDTV screens.

Figure 3 provides an example of subtitles in Arial Regular font. Above 31 points, texts may exceed the safe caption area. Therefore, 31 is the maximum size recommended.

Figure 3. Example of subtitles in Arial Regular 31.

As shown in Figure 4, Arial Narrow characters are narrower and the maximum size in this case is 39 points. It should be noted that the characters of this typeface are taller and thus take up a larger area of the picture.

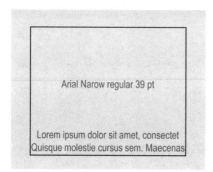

Figure 4. Example of subtitles in Arial Narrow 39.

Figure 5 shows the same example using Verdana typeface. In this case, the maximum recommended size for character magnification is 28 points.

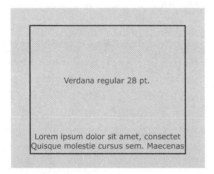

Figure 5. Example of subtitles in Verdana 28.

And lastly, the tests conducted using Tiresias typeface in Figure 5 point to a maximum recommended size of 30 points.

Figure 6. Example of subtitles in Tiresias 30.

4. Conclusions

Character magnifying applications for subtitles in digital television need to be compatible with all receivers installed in homes, including older television sets which cut off the edges of the picture. It is therefore necessary to comply with caption safety areas as defined by industry standards and quality standards of subtitling for people who are deaf and hard of hearing. In this respect, subtitles should take up fewer than 576 pixels horizontally.

Sans serif fonts, which have no ornamental details at the ends of the strokes, are the most legible fonts on screen. Arial, Tiresias and Verdana are examples of the fonts recommended by users for television screens.

According to the measurements carried out, the maximum recommended sizes for SDTV screens are as follows: Arial Regular 31, Arial Narrow 39, Verdana 28 and Tiresias 30. Above these sizes, there is a risk that the texts may not always fit on the screen.

The measurements were made on PAL Standard definition 4:3 screens. Therefore, they do not apply to future high definition television channels or to modern 16:9 screens. This is an important issue for the immediate future of television in Europe, which needs to be debated and researched, also paying attention to retrocompatibility for users who still have old television sets from the analogue era.

References

Asociación Española de Normalización y Certificación (AENOR). (2003). *Norma UNE 153010: Subtitulado para personas sordas y personas con discapacidad auditiva. Subtitulado a través del teletexto.* Madrid: Asociación Española de Normalización y Certificación.

Bernard, M. L., Liao, C. H., Chaparro, B. S., & Chaparro, A. (2001). Examining perceptions of online text size and typeface legibility for older males and females. *Proceedings of the 6th Annual International Conference on Industrial Engineering: Theory, Applications, and Practice.* San Francisco. Retrieved 6 April 2009, from <http://psychology.wichita.edu/mbernard/articles/IJIE%20Legibility%20for%20Older%20Adults.pdf>.

British Broadcasting Corporation (BBC). (2007). *BBC Technical Standards for Network Television Programme Delivery.* Retrieved 6 March 2008, from <http://www.bbc.co.uk/guidelines/dq/pdf/tv/tv_standards_london.pdf>.

CERMI. (2006). *Accesibilidad de la televisión digital para personas con discapacidad.* Retrieved 29 February 2008, from <http://www.infodisclm.com/documentos/accesibilidad/acces_tv_digital.html>.

Clark, J. (2005). What's wrong with Tiresias? Retrieved 6 April 2008 from <http://screenfont.ca/fonts/today/Tiresias/>.

Díaz Cintas, J. (2003). *Teoría y práctica de la subtitulación inglés – español.* Barcelona: Ariel.

Díaz Cintas, J. (2007). Por una preparación de calidad en accesibilidad audiovisual. *Trans. Revista de Traductología, 11,* 45–60.

d'Ydewalle, G., & Van Rensbergen, J. (1987). Reading a message when the same message is available auditorily in another language: The case of subtitling. In J. K. O'Regan & A. Lévy-Schoen (Eds.), *Eye movements: From physiology to cognition* (pp. 313–321). Amsterdam: Elsevier Science.

European Telecommunications Standards Institute (ETSI). (2002). *ETSI EN 300 743 V1.2.1. Digital Video Broadcasting (DVB): Subtitling systems.* Retrieved 6 March 2008, from <http://broadcasting.ru/pdf-standard-specifications/subtitling/dvb-sub/en300743.v1.2.1.pdf>.

— European Telecommunications Standards Institute (ETSI). (2003). *ETSI EN 300 472 V1.3.1 Digital Video Broadcasting (DVB): Specification for conveying ITU-R System B Teletext in DVB bitstreams.* Retrieved 6 March 2008, from <http:/broadcasting.ru/pdf-standard-specifications/multiplexing/dvb-txt/en300472.v1.3.1.pdf>.

Independent Television Commission (ITC) (1999). *ITC guidance on standards for subtitling.* London: Independent Television Commission.

Ivarsson, J., & Carroll, M. (1998). *Subtitling.* Simrishamn: TransEdit.

Karamitroglou, F. (1998). A proposed set of subtitling standards in Europe. *Translation Journal, 2,* 1–15.

Kitcherl, E. J. (2006). *Large print: Guidelines for optimal readability and APHont^{TM} a font for low vision.* American Printing House for the Blind. Retrieved 7 March 2008, from <http://ubceac.org/files/Large%20Print%20Guidelines%20for%20Optimal%20Readability.pdf>.

Martín Edo, C. A., Jiménez, D., Cisneros, G., & Menéndez, J. M. (2007). Implantación de la accesibilidad en la televisión digital: Situación actual y futuros desarrollos. In B. Ruiz & F. Utray (Eds.), *Accesibilidad a los medios audiovisuales para personas con discapacidad AMADIS 06* (pp. 115–129). Madrid: Real Patronato sobre Discapacidad.

Neves, J., & Lorenzo, L. (2007). La subtitulación para Sordos: panorama global y prenormativo en el marco ibérico. *Trans. Revista de Traductología, 11,* 95–113.

Ofcom. (2006). *Code on Television Access Services.* London: Office of Communication. Retrieved 14 April 2008, from <http://www.ofcom.org.uk/tv/ifi/codes/ctas/ctas.pdf>.

Orero, P. (2007) La accesibilidad en los medios: una aproximación multidisciplinar. *Trans. Revista de Traductología., 11,* 11–14.

Organización Nacional de Ciegos Españoles (ONCE) (2006). *Características de la rotulación para personas con discapacidad visual.* Retrieved 6 March 2008, from <http://wssa.once.es/crpdv/Senaletica.htm>.

RNIB-BBC. (2004). *Text on screen guidelines for television audience with sight problem.* Retrieved 5 April 2008, from <http://www.rnib.org.uk/xpedio/groups/public/documents/publicwebsite/public_TVprofessionals.hcsp#P8_658>.

Tiresias. (2007). *Guidelines: Television.* Retrieved 6 February 2008, from <http://www.tiresias.org/guidelines/television/>.

Eduard Bartoll, Anjana Martínez Tejerina

The positioning of subtitles for the deaf and hard of hearing[1]

This paper presents an empirical approach to the reception of subtitles for the deaf and hard of hearing. It is part of a more comprehensive project involving several researchers across Europe and dealing with different aspects of subtitles such as character identification and contextual information. The aim of the present study is to discover the most suitable font, size and position for subtitles for the deaf and hard of hearing. Once the pilot study was tested, the research followed the following four steps. Firstly, several clips from the film Stuart Little 2 *were subtitled using three parameters: three fonts (Arial, Tiresias, Verdana), several font sizes (ranging from 18 to 40) and three positions (top, bottom and mixed). Secondly, the audiovisual texts were shown to a selected audience consisting of individuals from various deaf associations all over Spain. These volunteers were chosen on the basis of a given set of criteria, namely, type of hearing disability and age. Thirdly, the members of the audience were asked to fill in brief questionnaires so as to enable the researchers to ascertain the degree of comprehension and enjoyment related to the different formats. Finally, relevant conclusions were drawn. Although, needless to say, more research will be carried out, taking into account other parameters such as tags or backgrounds, the study has already yielded some interesting insights into the most suitable font, font size and font position for subtitles taking into account audience members. It is argued that this type of research is particularly pertinent in the field of audiovisual translation and especially in the field of subtitling for the deaf and hard of hearing (SDH), in which research on the crucial area of reception is long overdue.*

---

1   This paper is part of the research project *La subtitulación para sordos y la audiodescripción: Primeras aproximaciones científicas y su aplicación* (Subtitling for the Deaf and Hard of hearing and Audiodescription: First scientific approaches and their application, reference HUM2006-03653FILO) funded by the Spanish ministry of education.

1. Introduction

In spite of living in today's mass media society, not everyone has full access to the media. A large section of the population – which includes disabled people – is being deprived of the right to full media access, which may lead to marginalisation, segregation and stigmatisation (Orero, 2007).

Needless to say, the quality of media accessibility is as important as accessibility itself. Obviously, subtitles that cannot be read by deaf people or that are read with difficulty are almost as bad as no subtitles at all. Therefore, monitoring the effectiveness and appropriateness of subtitles for the deaf and hard of hearing (SDH) is essential. Fortunately, there has been a great deal of development in accessibility research in the last few years as a result of both the increase in the number of publications and surveys (based mainly on research on reception or eye-tracking) and the existence of periodical conferences (e. g., *Media for All, Amadis*).[2]

One of the most relevant aspects of quality is standardisation. Its relevance has been stressed by deaf people for many years. In Spain, standards for the format of teletext subtitles were created in 2003 by the *Asociación Española de Normalización y Certificación* (AENOR) and with the aid of disabled people. These standards were called UNE 153010 *Subtitulado para personas sordas y personas con discapacidad auditiva. Subtitulado a través del teletexto* (Subtitling for the deaf and hard of hearing. Teletext Subtitling). The standards aim to specify the requirements for SDH teletext and they take into account colours, font size, number of lines, subtitle position, paging, text division, subtitle speed, subtitle synchronisation, spelling, grammar issues, subtitle editing, contextual information and information provided on the teletext pages. These standards are certainly a good starting point but, as many researchers have already stated (Pereira & Lorenzo, 2005, Fuertes & Martínez, 2007), we think that these standards should be the subject of monitoring and improvement.

Standardisation is a controversial and complex matter since the labels *deaf* and *hard of hearing* cover an extremely heterogeneous group, consist-

---

2   See the following websites: <http://www.cesya.es/estaticas/congreso/index.html>, <http://www.cesya.es/estaticas/amadis07/>, <http://www.cesya.es/estaticas/amadis 08/index.html>, <http://www.fti.uab.es/transmedia/> and <http://www.transmedia researchgroup.com/mediaforall.html> (Retrieved 1 May 2008).

ing of, for example, deaf children, cochlear implanted people, oralists, sign language users and prelingually and postlingually deaf people. All these individuals have very different needs and requirements. For example, while prelingually deaf people may benefit from reduced subtitles (which, conveying the same or very similar information, can be easily read), postlingually deaf people may be able to follow less edited subtitles. De Linde (1996: 181–182) explains that

> les premiers ont pour moyen principal de communication la langue des signes: leur aptitude à recourir aux sous-titres peut être gênée par leur faible capacité de lecture. [...] Les seconds ont pour la plupart reçu une éducation avec les bien entendants: leur vitesse de lecture peut être par conséquent assez élevée [...] la vitesse moyenne de lecture varie en fonction du dégrée de surdité.[3]

Moreover, hard of hearing people usually request verbatim subtitles for two main reasons: firstly, because reading something different to what is being heard is confusing and secondly, because, if information is being omitted or edited, hard of hearing people feel that some information has been withheld from them. Therefore, we believe that different subtitles should be developed for different audiences and we hope that the technological advances[4] offered by new platforms will allow users to choose the features of subtitles.[5] This choice would mean an important increase in SDH quality and would lead to true accessibility for the heterogeneous deaf community.[6]

3   The former use sign language as their main means of communication: their ability to resort to subtitles may be hindered by their weak reading ability. [...] The latter have mainly received an education with hearers: therefore their reading speed may be quite high [...] average reading speed changes according to the level of deafness (our translation).
4   The possibilities offered by digital Television are explained in Robson (2004).
5   It is important to take into account that the amount of increase is limited by the space available on the screen and by the structure of subtitle pages. Utray, Ruiz and Moreiro (this volume) determine the maximum font size for subtitles in standard definition digital television.
6   After an experiment on reception in which 200 volunteers collaborated, Kirkland (1999) reached the following conclusion: "Although there are certain areas of agreement [...] and certain feature combinations that may be inferred as being near agreement [...] no single model emerged that would fit the preferences of all caption viewers equally well. This suggests that some means of catering to individual differences in preferences should be considered by the television industry. A number of individually controllable features should be feasible with digital television, which would be a major step forward" (p. 258).

2. European project

As a result of a range of factors such as the limitations of platforms (that still do not allow users to modify subtitles parameters), the importance of SDH quality, the lack of standardisation and the shortage of research on reception, several researchers across Europe are participating in setting up a comprehensive project dealing with different aspects of subtitles such as character identification and contextual information. The aim of the project is to map SDH all over Europe in an attempt to harmonise different standards and to find the ideal SDH format according to the viewers.[7]

In the first instance, all the questionnaires are to be tested by a control group of AICE volunteers from the Spanish Association for Cochlear Implants to identify possible practical problems and to look for improvements using the volunteers' feedback. Once the surveys have been carried out, conclusions will be drawn and subsequent modifications will be made before starting the tests at the Spanish universities that are in contact with deaf associations all over Spain. These universities are the following: Universidad de Deusto, Universidade de Vigo, Universidad Carlos III, Universidad Rey Juan Carlos and Universitat Autònoma de Barcelona.

Once that stage of standardisation has been developed, the tests will be sent to the European universities that are taking part in the project: Copenhagen University (Denmark), Artesis University Antwerp (Belgium), Università di Napoli Federico II (Italy) and Roehampton University (UK).

---

7 Scholars such as Ivarsson and Carroll (1998), Karamitroglou (1998) and associations such as ESIST have worked towards the standardisation of subtitling practices. Díaz Cintas (2003) declares that "the ideal in this domain would be to be able to reach a consensus that could contribute to create a feeling of stability and homogeneity" (p. 70).

3. Positioning in ACAPPS

This contribution presents a practical survey that belongs to the comprehensive project mentioned above. As such, the survey took place after a pilot study. It is an empirical approach to the reception of subtitles for the deaf and hard of hearing and its aim is to find out the most suitable position for SDH, taking into account audience members' needs and requirements.[8] One of our hypotheses behind this survey was that the receptors' preferences would clearly be conditioned by conventions. Therefore, we expected that the conventional positions used in the most watched media would receive better results.

The survey was conducted in Catalonia, which has a community of approximately 12,000 deaf people and almost 300,000 hearing impaired people. Catalonia also has different organisations for the deaf, such as FESOCA, ACAPPS, APANSEC and AICE, which have been and still are committed to increasing (media) accessibility for the deaf and hard of hearing.

The topic of this paper, the positioning of subtitles, was tested following a four-step process. Firstly, a clip from the film *Stuart Little 2* was subtitled using different subtitle positions (top, bottom and mixed subtitles). Secondly, general questionnaires were filled in by a selected audience consisting of members taken from a Catalan organisation for the deaf (ACAPPS). The questionnaires were used to obtain general information about the profiles of the participating volunteers.[9] Thirdly, clips were shown to the audience members and they were asked to fill in two different questionnaires, with one of the questionnaires focusing on general features of the clip and a second questionnaire focusing on the specific topic of subtitle positioning. The aim of both questionnaires was to help us ascertain the degree of comprehension and enjoyment related to the different subtitle delivery formats. Finally, from the results obtained in step three, some relevant conclusions were drawn.

---

8   Positioning is the second parameter tested during the first stage of this project, which takes into account font and font size, positioning, speaker identification and paralinguistic and contextual information.

9   The participants were selected according to their degree of loss of hearing: five prelingually deaf people, five postlingually deaf people and five hearers.

4. The survey

The clips selected from the film *Stuart Little 2* were subtitled using different subtitle positions.[10] In Spain, subtitles may appear in three different positions: at the bottom of the screen (as is the case with most DVDs and Catalan TV programmes), at the top of the screen (as is the case with theatre plays and exhibitions), or in a mixed format, that is, contextual information at the top of the screen and dialogue at the bottom of the screen (as is the case with Spanish TV programmes with subtitles added following the aforementioned standard recommendation).

Once the clips were ready, we contacted ACAPPS (*Associació Catalana per a la Promoció de les Persones Sordes* (the Catalan Association for the Promotion of Deaf People), which kindly agreed to collaborate with us on the project and we arranged appointments with fifteen volunteers: five prelingually deaf people, five postlingually deaf people and five hearers.

We handed out a general questionnaire which had been designed to cover questions relating to most of the factors that could possibly influence the viewers' choices and that condition their preferences (from personal information such as age, academic achievements, occupation, and hearing disability to media usage and subtitle preferences). Despite the length of the general questionnaire, all the participants showed great interest in completing it.

The next stage was to show the same clip three times using different subtitle positions.[11] After each viewing, the volunteers were asked to complete short and specific questionnaires (see appendix), containing different statements that had to be evaluated on a scale from one to five.[12] This questionnaire was given to the participants after each viewing to ensure

---

10   The film *Stuart Little 2* was selected because it is one of the few films that was dubbed and subtitled in all the languages of the European countries taking part in the comprehensive project.

11   The order of the clips was changed in the survey carried out in other associations.

12   The pilot study showed us that a scale from one to ten led to a loss of accuracy. Statisticians and the creators of the questionnaire agreed that both a less elaborate scale and an explanation of the scale would probably simplify the results and avoid any disparity of answers. However, in order to make the interpretation of the results easier for the reader of this contribution, results shown in this article have been adapted to a scale from zero to ten.

that they would not forget the specific features of each clip or mix these features up.

After each viewing, three questions were asked to compare different positions. The aim was to give the volunteers the chance to express their opinions for each individual clip so as to allow them to compare the different possibilities. The following paragraphs show the opinions of the three groups of participants (prelingually deaf people, postlingually deaf people and hearers) about each of the three subtitle positions: at the top of the screen, at the bottom of the screen or a mixed format (dialogues at the bottom of the screen and contextual information at the top of the screen).

All questions on the questionnaires were related to the following three different features: legibility, understandability and the distinction between sounds and dialogues. In addition, the participants were also asked to provide general assessments of the subtitles that they had seen.

5. The results

The figures in brackets show the average rating given by the volunteers participating in the survey.

5.1. Legibility

According to the hearers, the position which was easier to read was the mixed one (7.6), followed by the bottom one (6), and then the top one (5.6). Among the prelingually deaf subjects, the mixed position and the bottom position obtained the same results (8.8), while the top position obtained a rating of only 5.2. Postlingually deaf subjects showed a preference for the mixed position (8.4), closely followed by the bottom position (8). The top position was given only an average rating of 5.6.

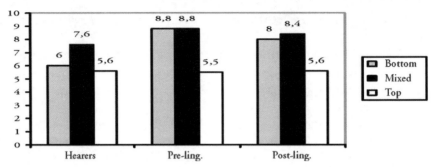

Table 1. Results on legibility

5.2. Understandability

Taking into account the ability to understand the different positions, the hearers gave the maximum rating to the mixed position (7.6), followed by the bottom position (7.2) and finally the top position (6.4). Prelingually deaf subjects gave the same rating to the mixed position and to the bottom position (9.2), and the lowest rating was given once again to the top position (6.4). The postlingually deaf participants in the survey gave the maximum rating to the mixed format (8.4), followed by the bottom option (8), and the lowest rating was given to the top option (6).

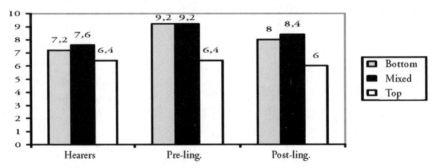

Table 2. Results on understandability

5.3. Distinction between sounds and dialogues

In terms of the distinction between sounds and dialogue, the hearers unanimously agreed that the clearer position was the mixed one (8), followed by the bottom position (6.8) and then the top one (6.4). According to the prelingually deaf subjects the option that presented a clearer distinction between sounds and dialogue was the bottom one (8.8), followed by the mixed position (7.2) and then the top position (4.8). Postlingually deaf subjects gave the same rating to both mixed and bottom positions (8), and only a 4 for the top position.

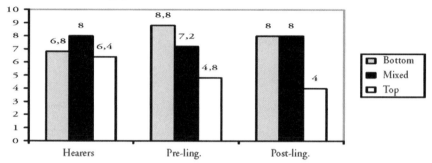

Table 3. Results on the distinction between sounds and dialogues

5.4. General assessment

Surprisingly enough, when asked to provide general assessments of the subtitles that they had seen, all participants showed a preference for the bottom position (9.2), despite the fact that the mixed format was the preferred positioning option when evaluating single features. The mixed format was given a rating of only 6.8, and the top position a rating of 4.8. Among the hearers, three out of the five subjects underlined their preference for the bottom position and two out of five preferred the mixed option. The prelingually deaf subjects also showed a preference for the bottom position (9.6), followed by the mixed position (7.6). The top position received a poor rating (2.8). Three out of the five prelingually deaf subjects chose the bottom position, while two out of five preferred the mixed format. Postlingually deaf participants shared the same opinion about bottom positioning (8.8), followed by the mixed positioning (8), and they gave the lowest rating to the top position (3.2). Nevertheless, three out of five subjects showed a preference for the mixed format while two out of five preferred the bottom position.

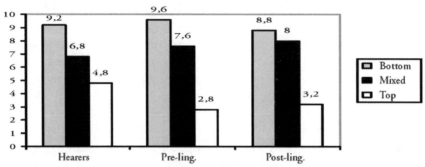

Table 4. Results of the positions of subtitles

6. Conclusions

The feedback from the participants in this survey allowed us to draw some interesting conclusions which will enable us to continue to work on further research.

The results for the mixed format and the bottom position present many similarities. This is possibly due to the fact that both options are currently widely used in Catalonia. While Spanish channels (TVE1, TVE2, Antena3, Cuatro, Telecinco, and La Sexta) use the mixed format option, Catalan channels (*Televisió de Catalunya*[13] broadcasting channels TV3, K3, C33, Canal 3/24, and 300) use the bottom position.[14] It is remarkable that many participants showed a preference for watching Catalan television, which could explain these balanced results as far as top/mixed positions are concerned. These results seem to confirm our hypotheses that viewers' prefer-

13   Televisió de Catalunya started using subtitles for the hard of hearing through the teletext system in 1990 (Matamala & Orero, 2009), according to the information provided by its document for private use *Subtitulació per a sords dels telenotícies de TVC. Orientacions per a l'edició de textos* (1993). Izard (2001) points out that TVE also started a subtitle service during the same year (1990).

14   Norms about the format and the contents of the subtitles are gathered in the booklets *Subtitulació per a persones sordes de programes enregistrats* and *Subtitulació per a sords dels telenotícies de TVC*.

ences are determined by conventions since the mixed and the bottom positions are used by the different channels watched by the volunteers who took part in the survey (the Spanish and the Catalan ones).

The fact that no participants chose the top position as a clear preference contrasts with the previous answers provided in the questionnaires, in which the top position was positively evaluated (the subjects graded it as acceptable (5.5/6 out of a maximum rating of 10) in aspects relating to, for example, legibility and understandability). This made us think that this preference may be due *not* to the quality of the position, but to frequency of the position (most viewers are used to the bottom position or the mixed format, but only some of the viewers have seen subtitles located at the top of the screen in the opera or at art exhibitions).

The results of the present study confirm not only our previous hypotheses but also what scholars such as Nootens (quoted by Díaz Cintas (2003)) or Luyken, Herbst, Langham-Brown, Reid and Spinhof (1991) have stressed: the audience's preferences are often influenced by habit/conventions.[15] Nevertheless, it is important to point out that these preferences are variable factors[16] and that they are not always the determining factor.[17] Considering the influence of daily habits and conventions in specific preferences for subtitle positioning, it would be interesting to invite volunteers who are not conditioned by conventions (that is, people who are not used to subtitles at all) to take part in subsequent surveys.

In addition, it is necessary to analyse other subtitling features. Positioning is simply one of the many parameters that must be taken into account when subtitling. That is why the first stage of the project takes into account other parameters such as font, font size, character identification and paralinguistic and contextual information.

This survey underlines the importance of studying subtitle positioning in depth and it may prove useful as a starting point for further re-

---

15 These authors refer mainly to the choice of modalities, but we consider that such influence could be extrapolated to the case presented in this contribution.

16 "Preferences may not be unalterable and that they might be transformed by familiarisation with other alternatives" (Luyken, 1991, p. 112). "It is obvious that habits can be modified, at least to a certain degree and for a specific audience" (Díaz Cintas, 2003, p. 55) (our translation).

17 Díaz Cintas (2003, p. 55) asks himself "otherwise, how could we explain that in a country like Spain, where the audience is used to dubbing, an increasing sector of the population prefers subtitling?" (our translation).

search. As the number of participants who took part in the survey is not large enough to be able to extrapolate the results to the deaf community, we consider it necessary to increase the number of volunteers in future surveys that will take place at the aforementioned Spanish universities. This should be done in an attempt to verify the results.

References

de Linde, Z. (1996). Le sous-titrage intralinguistique pour les sourds et les mal entendants. In Y. Gambier (Ed.), *Les transferts linguistiques dans les médias audiovisuels* (pp. 165–183). Paris: Presses Universitaires du Septentrion.

Díaz Cintas, J. (2003). *Teoría y práctica de la subtitulación inglés – español*. Barcelona: Ariel.

Fuertes, J. L., & Martínez, L. (2007). Media accessibility standards in Spain. *Translation Watch Quarterly, 3*(2), 61–77.

Ivarsson, J., & Carroll, M. (1998). *Subtitling*. Simrishamn: TransEdit.

Izard, N. (2001). La subtitulación para sordos del teletexto en Televisión Española. In L. Lorenzo & A. Pereira (Eds.), *Traducción subordinada inglés-español/galego II: El subtitulado* (pp. 169–194). Vigo: Universidade de Vigo.

Karamitroglou, F. (1998). A proposed set of subtitling standards in Europe. *Translation Journal, 2*, 1–15. Retrieved 26 April 2008, from <http://accurapid.com/journal/04stndrd.htm>.

Kirkland, C. (1999). Evaluation of captioning features to inform development of digital television captioning capabilities. *American Annals of the Deaf, 144*(3), 250–260.

Luyken, G. M., Herbst T., Langham-Brown J., Reid H., & Spinhof H. (Eds.). (1991). *Overcoming language barriers in television: Dubbing and subtitling for the European audience*. Manchester: European Institute for the Media.

Matamala, A., & Orero, P. (2009). L'accessibilitat a Televisió de Catalunya: Parlem amb Rosa Vallverdú, directora del departament de Subtitulació de TVC. *Quaderns de Traducció, 16*, 301–312

Orero, P. (2007). La accesibilidad en los medios: una aproximación multidisciplinar. *Trans. Revista de traductología, 11*, 11–14.

Pereira, A., & Lorenzo., L. (2005). Evaluamos la norma UNE 153010: Subtitulado para personas sordas y personas con discapacidad auditiva. Subtitulado a través del teletexto. *Puentes, 6*. Retrieved 23 July 2009, from <http://www.ugr.es/~greti/puentes/puentes6/03%20Ana%20M%20Pereira.pdf>.

Robson, G. (2004). *The closed captioning handbook*. Burlington, MA: Focal Press.

Televisió de Catalunya (1993). *Subtitulació per a sords dels telenotícies de TVC. Orientacions per a l'edició de textos*. Departament de subtitulació de TVC [document for private use only].

Televisió de Catalunya (1995). *Subtitulació per a persones sordes de programes enregistrats*. Departament de subtitulació de TVC [document for private use only].

Appendix

Answer each question by placing a tick in the selected box. The numbers stand for:

1. No.   2. A little.   3. So, so.   4. Quite.   5. A lot.

	1	2	3	4	5
Do you like clip number 1?					
Do you like subtitles at the bottom of the screen?					
Is it easy to read?					
Is it easy to know if there are sounds with all subtitles at the bottom?					
Is it easy to understand?					

	1	2	3	4	5
Do you like clip number 2?					
Do you like subtitles at the top of the screen?					
Is it easy to read?					
Is it easy to know if there are sounds with all subtitles at the top?					
Is it easy to understand?					

	1	2	3	4	5
Do you like clip number 3?					
Do you like subtitles at the top and at the bottom of the screen (as you see on TV)?					
Is it easy to read?					
Is it easy to know if there are sounds with subtitles at the top and at the bottom?					
Is it easy to understand?					

Which clip do you like the most?	
1	
2	
3	
Why?	
Would this always be your preference?	

Questionnaire

1) Personal details

a. Name: _____

b. Gender: ☐ Male   ☐ Female

c. Age: ____

d. Education (tick all the studies that you have completed):
    ☐ Primary School   ☐ High School
    ☐ Apprenticeship (Please specify which, if possible)   _____
    ☐ University degree (Please specify)   _____
    ☐ Other qualifications (Please specify) _____
    Type of education institution where you carried out your studies:
    ❒ Deaf school   ❒ Mainstream school   ❒ Other

e. Occupation:
    ☐ Student (Please specify)   _____
    ☐ Retired
    ☐ Professional (Please specify)   _____
    ☐ Other _____

f. Are you …?   ❒ Deaf   ❒ Hard of Hearing   ❒ Hearing

g. Do you use a hearing aid / an implant?   ☐ Yes   ☐ No

h. When did you start losing your ability to hear?
    ☐ From birth   ☐ + 2 years old   ☐ + 5 years old
    ☐ + 20 years old   ☐ + 50 years old

i. Language used to communicate:
    ☐ Only Spanish Sign Language / Catalan Sign Language
    ☐ Only Spanish / Catalan
    ☐ Preferably Spanish Sign Language / Catalan Sign Language
    ☐ Preferably Spanish / Catalan
    ☐ I am bilingual

j. Sight: ☐ I use glasses / contact lenses   ☐ No aid needed

k. Do you have difficulties seeing the screen or reading the subtitles?
    ☐ Yes   ☐ No   ☐ Sometimes

2.   *General information and preferences*

a.   How many Deaf or Hard of Hearing people live with you?
☐ 0   ☐ 1   ☐ 2   ☐ 3   ☐ 4   ☐ 5   ☐ 6

b.   How many hours a day do you spend reading (TV subtitles, newspapers, books…)?
☐ 0 h   ☐ 1–2 h   ☐ 2–3 h   ☐ 3–4 h   ☐ 4–5 h   ☐ 5–6 h

c.   What type of texts do you usually read?
☐ Newspapers ☐ Books ☐ Magazines ☐ TV ☐ DVDs ☐ Other

d.   Which of the following do you have at home?
☐ TV   ☐ Digital TV   ☐ Computer ☐ Laptop   ☐ VCR
☐ DVD player   ☐ Satellite TV   ☐ Internet   ☐ Telephone
☐ PDA   ☐ Mobile phone   ☐ Ipod   ☐ Other_____

e.   Who do you usually watch TV with?
☐ By yourself   ☐ Deaf friends/family   ☐ Hearing friends/family

f.   How many hours a day do you watch TV?
☐ 1h   ☐ 2h   ☐ 3h   ☐ 4h   ☐ 5h   ☐ +6h

g.   How many of those hours are subtitled?
☐ 1h   ☐ 2h   ☐ 3h   ☐ 4h   ☐ 5h   ☐ +6h

h.   When do you usually watch TV?
☐ 7:00 am – 12:00 am   ☐ 12:00 am – 5:00 pm
☐ 5:00 pm – 9:00 pm   ☐ 9:00 pm – 01:00 pm

i.   Do you choose the programmes you watch based on whether they are subtitled or not?
☐ Yes   ☐ No

j.   What do you use subtitles for?
☐ They help me understand   ☐ They are my only way to have access to the dialogue
☐ I use them for language learning   ☐ Other (specify) _____

k.   How do you know which programmes/films/DVDs include subtitles?
☐ Teletext   ☐ TV   ☐ TV guides   ☐ Friends   ☐ Other_____

l.   What do you do when a programme does not offer subtitles?
☐ Switch the TV off   ☐ Flick the channels and look for a subtitled programme
☐ Rely on lip-reading   ☐ Someone translates the programme for me
☐ Put the volume up (TV/hearing aid)   ☐ Guess by the context
☐ Use general subtitles (if available)

m. Do you think that subtitles are the best way to make audiovisual material accessible?
☐ Yes ☐ No ☐ Do not know / No comment

n. If you answered 'no' to the question above, please select the system that you think would be most useful?
☐ Interpreter ☐ Adapted subtitles ☐ A virtual interpreter

3) Subtitling

a. What do you think of subtitling in general (TV / DVD / cinema…)?
_____

b. What would you change / remove / add in subtitles?
_____

c. Are you aware of any regulations on how subtitles should be drawn up?
☐ Yes ☐ No

d. If the same type of subtitles was used for cinema / TV / DVD, would that make reading and understanding them easier?:
☐ Yes ☐ No ☐ Do not know / No comment

e. What difficulties do you think are involved in producing subtitles?
_____
_____

4) Subtitles on TV

a. Is it easy to find information on Teletext about which programmes are subtitled?:
☐ Yes ☐ No ☐ Don't know / No comment

b. Which channels offer the best subtitles?
(Rate them from 1 to 6: 1– best subtitles; 6 – worst subtitles)
☐ TVE1 ☐ TVE2 ☐ Antena 3 ☐ Tele 5
☐ Cuatro ☐ Sexta ☐ other (regional)

c. What channel offers the best subtitled news?
☐ TVE1 ☐ TVE2 ☐ Antena 3 ☐ Tele 5
☐ Cuatro ☐ Sexta ☐ other (regional)

d. Which aspects lead you to having that opinion?
☐ Programme offer available ☐ Subtitles quality ☐ Other_____

5) *Subtitles on DVD*

a. Is it easy to find information about which DVDs include subtitles for the Deaf and Hard of Hearing?:

☐ Yes　　　　　☐ No　　　　　☐ Do not know / No comment

b. If you answered 'yes' to the above question, where can you find that information?
_____

c. Do you choose the films you watch based on whether they offer subtitles for the Deaf and Hard of hearing people or not?

☐ Yes　　　　　☐ No　　　　　☐ Do not know / No comment

d. Finding subtitle options in DVD menus is:

☐ Easy　　　　　☐ Difficult

e. What type of subtitles do you find easier to read/understand?

☐ TV　　　　　☐ DVD

f. Why? _____

6) *Subtitling styles*

a. Do you find the font used in subtitles easy to read?

☐ Yes　　　　　☐ No　　　　　☐ Do not know / No comment

b. What type of font do you find easier to read?

☐ Normal TV　　　　　☐ Digital TV　　　　　☐ DVD subtitles

c. When characters need to be identified, what system do you prefer?

☐ Colours　　　　　☐ Positioning subtitles next to the characters
☐ Name tags　　　　　☐ Other _____

d. The number of colours used is:

☐ Sufficient　　　☐ We could do with a wider range　　　☐ Difficult to read

e. Where do you prefer subtitles to be shown?

☐ Bottom of the screen only　　　☐ Both top and bottom of the screen
☐ Top of the screen only　　　☐ Next to the character who speaks each time

f. For live events, you prefer that the subtitles are shown:

☐ Letter by letter　　　☐ Word by word
☐ Sentence by sentence　　　☐ All the text at once

g. How do you prefer descriptions of sounds to be reflected on the subtitles?
☐ Explaining where the sound comes from
☐ Using words reproducing the sound
☐ Describing what the sound is like

h. Where do you prefer that sound-related information to be shown?
☐ Top-right side of the screen
☐ Bottom of the screen next to the subtitles
☐ Next to the source of the sound

i. Regarding information about the mood of the characters, how do you prefer that to be shown?
☐ With emoticons   ☐ Explanation between brackets   ☐ Nothing

j. When there is music in a film/TV series, what do you prefer?:
☐ To have the title of the song on screen
☐ To have the words of the song subtitled
☐ To have information on what type of music it is
☐ An icon indicating 'music'
☐ Other _____

k. Which of the options below do you prefer?:
☐ Literal subtitles that contain absolutely all the information
☐ Not so literal but easier subtitles to read

l. If you chose 'literal subtitles' in the question above, can you explain why you prefer them?
_____
_____

m. When there is too much information for the space available in the subtitles and some-thing needs to be left out, what information do you prefer to be included?
(Please rate from (1) most important information to (4) least important.)
☐ Dialogue   ☐ Names   ☐ Sounds
☐ Mood or way of speaking (e.g.: 'shouting', 'whispering'…)
☐ Expressions like 'ok', 'well…'…

Ana Pereira

Criteria for elaborating subtitles for deaf and hard of hearing adults in Spain: Description of a case study[1]

The following contribution presents the materials, subjects, methodology and results of a study, the objective of which was to check the functionality and validity of a set of technical, orthotypographical and linguistic criteria for elaborating quality subtitles for deaf and hard of hearing adults in Spain.

1. Introduction

This contribution provides a full description of a case study, the objective of which was to check the functionality and validity of a previously established set of technical, orthotypographical and linguistic criteria for elaborating subtitles for deaf and hard of hearing (SDH) adults in Spain. In carrying out the study, we wanted to adjust, modify and/or assert the validity of these criteria in an attempt to produce functional quality subtitles. In order to achieve this purpose, a brief audiovisual document, which tells the story of Diego, a widower with three sons, and his wedding to Lucía, a divorced mother, who moves into Diego's house with her two daughters, was subtitled following the previously established set of criteria. A survey on the subtitled document was prepared and these materials were seen by two groups of deaf adults and a control group of hearers. This contribution is a detailed description of the technical and orthotypographical criteria, and of the reception study (materials, methodology and participants) and the main results of the study.[2]

---

1 This article is part of the ongoing research project *SDH and AD: First scientific approaches and their application* (reference HUM2006-03653FILO), financed by the Spanish Ministry of Education.
2 The linguistic criteria, which deal mainly with the incorporation of features of Spanish Sign Language (SSL) into subtitling, are explained in a second contribution by Pereira in this volume.

2. Proposal of criteria for producing subtitles for deaf and hard of hearing adult audiences

In this section, an explanation will be given regarding the criteria that were used to produce the subtitled material for the reception study. The main objective of this study was to contribute to making audiovisual products accessible with the highest standards of quality in a Spanish cultural context.

In order to determine these criteria, we took as a starting point preliminary studies on the reception of subtitles for the deaf and hard of hearing (Prada González, 2004), the research and experience of scholars and professionals in the field of subtitling (e.g., BBC, 1998; de Linde & Kay, 1999; ITC, 1999; Ivarsson & Carroll, 1998; Lorenzo & Pereira, forthcoming; Neves & Lorenzo, 2007; Pazó Lorenzo, forthcoming; Tercedor Sánchez, Lara Burgos, Herrador Molina, Márquez Linares & Márquez Alhambra, 2007), the nature of the deaf and hard of hearing audience in Spain (Alegría & Leybaert, 1987; Cambra, 2006; Moreno Rodríguez, 2000) and Spanish Sign Language (Chapa, 2001a, 2001b; Climent & Herrero, 2000; Herrero, 2005–2008; Minguet Soto, 2000; Rodríguez González, 1992; VV. AA., 2002). We also consulted Standard UNE 153010 (AENOR, 2003), the critical study of this standard (Pereira & Lorenzo, 2005) and the analysis of current practices in subtitling for the deaf and hard of hearing in Spain (Arnáiz Uzquiza, 2007; Méndez Brage, 2003; Pérez de Oliveira, forthcoming) and in other neighbouring countries (Justo Sanmartín, forthcoming; Moreira Brenlla, forthcoming; Neves, 2005).

In this paper we will ignore those aspects of subtitling for the deaf and hard of hearing to which the same criteria apply as to subtitles for hearers (e.g., cuts and shot changes, specific orthotypographical and punctuation conventions, synthesis strategies, subtitle segmentation). The interested reader may find additional information on these aspects in Díaz Cintas (2003) and Díaz Cintas and Remael (2007). Instead, we will focus on other aspects that are specific to the type of subtitling which concerns us here.

2.1. Technical criteria

In this technical section, we will deal with the marking of the speech-character relationship, the number of subtitle lines used, their position and justification, the length of display on the screen, and synchrony.[3]

2.1.1. Speech-character relationship

Of the three strategies usually employed to identify individual speakers in subtitles for the deaf and hard of hearing – positioning the subtitle under the speaker, using labels with the name of the speaker before the subtitle, and assigning a different colour to each speaker – we have chosen the last strategy. This is the strategy used by all Spanish television channels that provide subtitles for the deaf and hard of hearing. Therefore, it constitutes a technical feature with which deaf viewers are extremely familiar. We have followed the established colour conventions recommended by Standard UNE 153010, which also promotes the third strategy.[4]

Although viewers are used to and familiar with the use of colours to identify individual characters, we believe that for each programme the viewers must be provided with information regarding the colour assignment used, which, in the case of series, cartoons or programmes with generally the same characters, should always be the same. This information may be given on a teletext page or a site guide. Another option is to apply a strategy used in subtitling for the deaf and hard of hearing in Germany, which consists of indicating – at the beginning of the programme – the colour assigned to each character (name of the first main character: yellow, name of the second main character: green, etc.) (Moreira Brenlla, forthcoming). In any productions in which time is limited a single subtitle could be used, with the name of the main characters in the assigned colour, because such productions often begin by introducing the viewer directly to the action:

3   See Utray, Ruiz and Moreiro (this volume) and Bartoll and Martínez Tejerina (this volume) for all aspects relating to characters (size, font, spacing, effects, etc.).
4   The following colours are generally used: yellow on a black background for the main character or character with the greatest dialogue density; green on a black background for the second main character; cyan on a black background for the third main character; magenta on a black background for the fourth main character, and white for the rest of the characters or in news subtitling, documentaries and programmes with only one narrator.

First main character Second main character
Third main character Fourth main character

In the programmes that begin by introducing the characters, the colours assigned to the different main characters would be indicated when each character is introduced.

Even if the strategy chosen to indicate the speech-character relationship consists of assigning colours, it may sometimes be necessary to combine the strategy with the use of labels in upper-case letters, without brackets and followed by a colon.[5]

Regarding the use of the dash to introduce a dialogue, the following should be mentioned: given the variation observed among the different Spanish television channels, we used it only when it was absolutely necessary. When two different characters who had been assigned the colour white participated in the same subtitle, we introduced a dash in the second line to mark the speech of the second character.

2.1.2. Number of lines, position and justification

We used one or two lines for subtitles, positioned at the bottom of the screen, and one line for sound effects, positioned in the top right-hand corner of the screen. Whenever possible, we tried to avoid overlapping subtitles and sound effect indications. When subtitles reproduced a dialogue among several characters, each subtitle was assigned to one line. The subtitles were centred because the action usually took place in the centre of the screen. Consequently, the distance that the eye had to travel between the action and the text was kept to a minimum. Besides, deaf and hard of hearing viewers are used to this format since most television channels, following the Standard UNE 153010 recommendations, use this format for non-simultaneous subtitles.

---

5   The most common two cases are the following: 1) when several characters who have been assigned different colours say something at the same time. In this case, the subtitle will be white and the labels ALL: or BOTH: will be placed in front of the subtitle, and 2) in scenes in which one or more characters who have been assigned the colour white speak from a dark place, off-camera, with their backs to the viewer, etc., and there is consequently not enough visual information to determine who is speaking. In this case, a label with the name of the character will be added before the subtitle, for example, ANA:.

2.1.3. Length of display on the screen

As the results of studies on the reading speed of Spanish prelocutive[6] deaf viewers are still pending, we followed the six-second rule (Brondeel, 1994; d'Ydewalle & Van Rensbergen, 1987), which refers to the amount of time that the average hearing or postlocutive[7] deaf viewer needs to read and comprehend the information contained in two lines of subtitles with 35 characters each, for programmes aimed at an adult audience, increasing it whenever possible. For programmes intended for children or young viewers, we suggest the application of an eight-second rule. In any case, we disregarded the four-second rule suggested by Standard UNE 153010, which was probably developed as a result of a regrettable miscalculation (Pereira & Lorenzo, 2005).

2.1.4. Synchrony

As a general rule, subtitles should appear on screen when the characters begin to speak or any sound information is provided. They should disappear when the characters finish speaking or pause, and when the sound information has stopped. We have tried to be especially strict about this because the material chosen was filmed in the same language as the subtitles and, sometimes, deaf people with residual hearing or with technical hearing aids rely on synchrony between sound and lip movement to aid comprehension.

6   Prelocutive deaf viewers are viewers whose loss of hearing has taken place before the acquisition of spoken language. Regarding deaf viewers, some studies carried out in the United Kingdom (e.g., Kyle & Pullen, 1985) suggest that the reading ability of prelocutive deaf viewers is close to that of nine-year-old hearing children, that is, between 90 and 120 words per minute or, in other words, 1 or 2 words per second. In the case of prelocutive deaf children, a study by Lewis (referred to in Gregory & Sancho-Aldridge, 1997) indicates that prelocutive deaf children do not acquire adequate reading skills until the age of 12 or 13. Considering these figures, subtitles should be displayed between 1 and 5 seconds longer than for hearing viewers or postlocutive deaf viewers. We would also like to point out that subtitling for deaf and hard of hearing audiences began in the United Kingdom in the 1970s. As a result, British deaf viewers have been reading subtitles twenty years longer than Spanish viewers. Consequently, the figures about reading rates in both cultural contexts are probably not the same.
7   Postlocutive deaf viewers are viewers whose loss of hearing has taken place after the development of the basic skills in spoken language.

However, on some occasions, despite the synthesis strategies used, the message was still too dense. In these cases, since our priority was not to accelerate the reading rate, we allowed ourselves a certain margin of asynchrony and we made the subtitle either appear slightly before the character started speaking or disappear slightly after the character had finished. To avoid overlapping or the undesirable flash effect, we never used this technique when another character's intervention took place immediately before or afterwards.[8]

2.2. Orthotypographical criteria

In this section on orthotypographical criteria, we will explain how we marked suprasegmental features,[9] noises produced by the characters, sound effects and songs in the subtitles produced for this particular reception study.

2.2.1. Suprasegmental features and noises produced by the characters

In subtitling for the deaf and hard of hearing, suprasegmental information may be represented in the form of smileys,[10] didascalies[11] or different orthotypographical resources. The use of smileys is appropriate in subtitling for the deaf and hard of hearing because smileys save space and are easy to interpret. However, we believe that a young audience, which is used to using such symbols in e-mails and text messages, is able to interpret this strategy better than an adult audience, for whom we discourage the use of smileys. If smileys are used, we suggest replacing the smileys

---

8 The flash effect is produced when two adjacent subtitles are separated by fewer than 3 stills (or, in other words, under 1/6 of a second) (Díaz Cintas, 2003).

9 Suprasegmental information is information which is present in speech but not contained in the phonemes. In the case of this study, we are referring to mainly volume and tone of voice, accents, pauses, hesitation, stuttering, etc.

10 Smileys are graphical symbols that express a state of mind. Those recommended by Standard UNE 153010 are :-0 (shouting), :-x / :-• (whispering), :-; (ironic), :-) (happy) and :-((sad).

11 We are taking one of the meanings of the word *didascaly* – stage directions in a play, or instructions given by the author or director to the actors – and modifying it slightly. In this case, the word *didascaly* refers to an item of information that the subtitler provides the viewers. This is generally information about how the characters utter their speech.

represented by typographical signs with little faces,[12] which are clearer and easier to understand. In any case, the viewer must be informed of the symbols used and of what they represent.

The suprasegmental information represented by smileys and other information, for which there are no established popular emoticons, may be expressed through didascalies, placed in brackets before the corresponding subtitle, in the same colour and in upper-case letters.

Finally, different orthotypographical symbols may also be used to convey a variety of suprasegmental features (e.g., suspension points to indicate that a character is hesitating, upper-case letters followed by exclamation marks to indicate a rise in the volume of the voice).

Of the three possibilities described above, we gave priority to the use of didascalies, for two main reasons. Firstly, the use of didascalies is a more consistent strategy since all the suprasegmental information can be expressed consistently (there are not enough emoticons or orthotypographical symbols to express all the possible suprasegmental features). Secondly, the use of didascalies is more precise (for example, it allows different degrees of emotion to be expressed (elation, enthusiasm, happiness) and it avoids ambiguity (suspension points may indicate that the character is stuttering, having doubts, thinking, etc.).

Voice noises such as burping, coughing, grunting, etc., which are also uttered by the characters who take part in the audiovisual product, have been presented in the same way as suprasegmental features: upper-case letters, in brackets, before the corresponding subtitle and in the same colour as the colour used to represent the character on screen.

2.2.2. Sound effects

Regarding the music and the sounds that are produced in the background when the action takes place and which influence the characters' actions or provide necessary information to fully understand the product, we chose to describe these sounds rather than use onomatopoeic spellings. The reasons that led to this decision are related to uniformity and consistency. We can describe all sounds but not all of them can be represented by established onomatopoeic forms. Therefore, even if we were to use onomato-

12   (happy),   (sad),   (ironic), etc.

poeic spellings, we would find that, sometimes, we would have to turn to description.

The indications of background sound effects were positioned as recommended by Standard UNE 153010, that is, in the top right-hand corner of the screen, in red letters on a white box, without brackets and in lower-case letters, with the initial letter in upper case.

2.2.3. Songs

When the contents of the songs are related to the storyline of the programme, the songs must be subtitled because they are part of the script (this is the case, for example, in musicals) or provide information that complements the script.

We made a distinction between songs that were sung by the characters and songs that were not. For the latter, we used the format suggested by Standard UNE 153010, that is, blue characters on a yellow background. We followed this strategy since the viewers were already familiar with this format. For the former, we used the same font and colour assigned to the character, and we indicated that it was a song by placing a musical note (♪) at the beginning of each song subtitle and, in the case of the last subtitle, also at the end.

3. Checking the functionality of the criteria: the reception study

In the following section we will explain, on the one hand, the steps that we took to design and implement the reception study through which we checked the validity of the criteria, and, on the other hand, the main results that we obtained.

3.1. Elaboration of the materials

Once we had established the subtitling criteria, we selected the audiovisual material for the reception study. In the case of adult viewers, we chose the first ten minutes of the Spanish television series *Los Serrano*. For the reception study we selected the excerpt from the first episode of the first season. We chose this particular material because it was a successful programme among the population at the time that the field study was being prepared (2006–2007), and we selected the beginning of the series so that all the participants in the study would have the same information, since those who were following the series would probably not remember the first episode, even if they did recognise the characters, and those who had never seen it would be provided with the information that the others already had.

Los Serrano, produced by the Spanish television channel *Tele5*, was first shown in 2003. It tells the story of the Serrano family, who live in a Madrid neighbourhood on the banks of the Manzanares river and own a bar. The ninth and last season of the series was broadcast in 2008.

The scenes that we selected begin by introducing the Serrano family (Diego, the widowed father, and his three sons: Marcos, Guille and Curro), the neighbourhood, the bar, Lucía (Diego's second wife, divorced) and her two daughters, Eva and Teté. We see Diego's wedding to Lucía and how she and her daughters move into Diego's house, forming a big family.

The next step was to carry out the subtitling process (according to the established criteria) and to prepare the final copy. In order to do this, we used three types of free software: *Subtitle Workshop*, to localise and adjust the subtitles; *Sub Station Alpha*, to apply the colour labels and place the sound effects indications at the top of the screen; and, finally, *VirtualDub*, to insert the subtitles on the video stills permanently.

Subsequently, we designed the questionnaire which would accompany the audiovisual document which would survey the viewers about the functionality and usefulness of the criteria applied. The questionnaire was divided into three sections: the first section contained questions about the viewers' personal information and educational background. In the second section, which was given to the viewers after they had viewed the audiovisual material, the viewers were asked about the different technical aspects of the subtitles that they had seen (speech-character relationship strategy, length of display on the screen, number and position of the lines, format of the suprasegmental information and voice noises, background sound indications, songs, off-screen voices and colloquial register). Finally, in the third section, the viewers were given both comprehension questions and questions about the level of difficulty of the language used in the subtitles.

3.2. Selection of the participating subjects and the methodology of the field study

Besides the Universidade de Vigo, the following Spanish universities also took part in the study: Universitat Autònoma de Barcelona, Universidad de Deusto, Universidad Rey Juan Carlos I and Universidad Carlos III.[13] The materials were distributed to a total of 134 participants (76 women and 58 men) between the ages of 18 and 60. For the purposes of this study, we divided the group of participants into three groups: prelocutive deaf participants, postlocutive deaf participants and a small control group consisting of hearers.

The group of prelocutive deaf participants was the largest group, matching real-life statistics. It was composed of 78 participants (39 men and 39 women), 62% of whom were working, 26% of whom received unemployment benefits or other types of benefits, and 12% of whom were students.

The percentages regarding this group's academic background were as follows: 28% had completed primary education, 38% had completed secondary education or the first level of vocational training, 6% had completed the second level of vocational training, 13% had a university degree, and 15% did not answer this question.

The majority of the individuals in this group (87%) indicated that Spanish Sign Language (SSL) was the language with which they felt most comfortable. Only a minority (6.5%) preferred spoken language, and another minority (6.5%) felt comfortable using either language. When asked about their reading ability, 78% of the participants claimed to be able to read well or very well, and 22% admitted that they had difficulties reading. The same proportions were obtained when participants were asked about their use of subtitles: 78% used subtitles regularly while 22% did not.

13 We are grateful to the following student interns for their cooperation: Irene Pazó Lorenzo, Almudena Pérez de Oliveira and Santiago Rodríguez Bouzas (Universidade de Vigo), Verónica Arnáiz (Universitat Autònoma de Barcelona), Rubén Rojas (Universidad Rey Juan Carlos I) and José Luis Teigell (Universidad Carlos III). We are also indebted to Natxo Canto, Gonzalo Eguíluz (Universidad de Deusto), Mónica Souto (CESyA), Carmen Jáudenes and Begoña Gómez Nieto (FIAPAS). In addition, we would like to thank the following institutions for their hospitality: Asociación de Sordos de Vigo, Asociación de Sordos de Ourense, Instituto la Farisa de Ourense, ARANSBUR and MQD de Burgos, Asociación de Sordos de Alcorcón CODIAL, Centro Altatorre de Sordos de Madrid y Asociación de Personas Sordas de Bilbao y Bizkaia.

The group of postlocutive deaf participants was composed of 30 individuals (11 men and 19 women); 70% of whom were working, 20% of whom were students and 10% of whom received benefits.

The percentages regarding this group's academic background were as follows: 30% had completed primary education, 46% had completed secondary education or the first level of vocational training, 17% had completed the second level of vocational training, and 7% had a university degree.

As was the case with the group of prelocutive deaf participants, the majority of the individuals in this group (77%) preferred to use SSL while a minority (23%) felt more comfortable using spoken language. In terms of their reading ability, 70% claimed it was good, while 30% stated that it could be improved. In addition, 80% said that they used subtitles while the rest stated that they did not use them, or they simply did not answer this question.

The group of hearers was composed of 26 individuals (8 men and 18 women), 62% of whom were working and 38% of whom were students.

The percentages regarding their education were as follows: 19% had completed primary education, 39% had completed secondary education or the first level of vocational training, and 42% had a university degree. All of them claimed that they were able to read well.

3.3. Results regarding the technical aspects of the subtitles

As we will see below, in most cases, the results that we obtained with regard to the technical aspects of our subtitles supported and validated the criteria that we applied. In other cases, the results helped to define the criteria in a more precise way. On one occasion, the results surprised us because they contradicted working hypotheses and even previous reception studies.

In terms of the strategy chosen to mark the speech-character relationship (based on assigning colours), the majority of the participants surveyed (85% of the prelocutive deaf participants and 93% of the postlocutive deaf participants) stated that the strategy was functionally successful since the use of colours helped them to identify which speaker was saying what.[14]

When asked about the length of display of the subtitles on the screen (as we indicated before, we had rejected the four-second rule recommended

---

14   However, a significant number of participants admitted to having difficulties seeing the speech of the characters that had been assigned the colours cyan and magenta.

by UNE standards in favour of a six-second rule), a large number of the participants considered the length to be sufficient. However, there was a considerable difference between the percentages of the different groups: while 93% of the postlocutive deaf participants considered the length of display adequate, the number decreased to 77% among the prelocutive deaf participants. Therefore, the results obtained for the first group for this particular question were practically the same as those obtained for the group of hearers (96%). However, they differed significantly from those obtained from the prelocutive deaf participants since 23% of the prelocutive deaf participants considered that the time given to read (and understand) the subtitles was not enough. The difference can easily be explained if we bear in mind that postlocutive deaf viewers enjoy a great advantage: since they have fully (or almost fully) acquired the spoken language, their reading ability must be higher than that of prelocutive deaf viewers.

Regarding the position of dialogue subtitles on the screen, 86% of all the participants in the study stated that they preferred the subtitles to be positioned towards the bottom of the screen. However, the same unanimity in the responses was not found when the participants were asked about the number of lines that subtitles should consist of to be read more easily. While 58% of hearers claimed that they preferred two-line subtitles, 70% of the prelocutive deaf viewers and 80% of the postlocutive deaf viewers favoured single-line subtitles.

All the participants agreed, with virtually identical percentages in the three groups, on how suprasegmental information should be presented: 72% preferred the use of didascalies (e.g., JOKING), 26% preferred the use of little faces (e.g., 😊) and, finally, 2% preferred the use of emoticons represented by typographical signs (:-;).

Viewer preferences with regard to how background sound effects should be indicated (i.e., through description (e.g., bark) or onomatopoeia (e.g., woof)), provided unexpected results, which contradicted the researchers' hypotheses and the results from existing reception studies. Prada González (2004) reported that while half of the deaf viewers who watched a film *(Finding Nemo)* with subtitles chose the use of onomatopoeic spellings, arguing that they were familiar with them because they had heard them before and/or had read them in comics, the rest of the viewers (prelocutive deaf viewers) preferred description since they had never heard the sounds described before. In our reception study, 66% of the postlocutive deaf participants and 85% of the hearing participants chose the description of the sound. In contrast, 51% of the prelocutive deaf participants preferred the use of onomatopoeia (43% of this group selected description and 6% did not answer the question).

Once again, all participants agreed in almost identical percentages (approximately 74%) on the functionality of the criteria used to mark the songs sung by the characters: maintaining the colour assigned to each character and, at the same time, indicating that a song was being played through the use of a musical note.

Finally, a large number of the participants understood that the use of italics marked off-screen voices (85% of hearers, 70% of postlocutive deaf participants and 61% of prelocutive deaf participants) and that the presence of quotation marks signalled the use of informal language (90% of hearers, 73% of prelocutive deaf participants and 45% of prelocutive deaf participants). However, the lower percentages among the groups of deaf people confirmed the researchers' claim that there should be an explanatory page indicating the subtitling criteria used.

3.4. Results regarding comprehension and the level of difficulty of the subtitles

In order to find out if the subtitling drawn up according to the criteria of lexical and syntactical adaptation was fully understood by the viewers from a linguistic point of view, all participants answered questions about the level of difficulty that they had experienced when reading the subtitles.

When asked if the vocabulary used in the subtitles was easy, 100% of hearers and 87% of deaf participants (identical percentages among prelocutive and postlocutive deaf individuals) said yes. The results are the same as those obtained when the viewers were asked if they had understood all the words and sentences: 100% of hearing and 87% of deaf participants claimed to have understood everything.

However, when asked if they would like to receive explanations about the most difficult words and expressions before viewing any audiovisual document, all the hearing participants agreed that they would not like such explanations, while 49% of prelocutive deaf viewers and 54% of postlocutive deaf viewers stated that they would like such explanations and that such explanations would be extremely useful for them.

Besides the general questions, the questionnaire included specific questions about certain words and expressions in the subtitled extract that the researchers considered might present comprehension problems. The results in this case showed that, in fact, 100% of hearers understood all the words and expressions, as well as 87% of postlocutive deaf participants. However, in the case of prelocutive deaf participants, the percentage dropped to 75%.

4. Conclusions

Taking into account the viewers' evaluation of the criteria, we reached the conclusion that some of the issues under evaluation (the use of colours to mark the speech-character relationship, the length of display on the screen adapted to the six-second rule, the positioning of dialogue subtitles at the bottom of the screen, the use of a musical note to mark songs, and the preference of didascaly to little faces and emoticons) were confirmed by the reception study. Other issues under evaluation (the preference of sound description over the use of onomatopoeia) were not supported as clearly or as was expected, which requires further research into these aspects. Finally, some issues (the preference for single-line subtitles) were more clearly defined.

The fieldwork carried out revealed that adapted subtitles (simpler subtitles, with basic vocabulary, a slower reading rate, and the incorporation of features of SSL) are extremely useful for certain deaf adults, not only because they allow these adults to enjoy audiovisual documents but also because they help the adults to learn the spoken language, which, in some cases, is not their native language. In this sense, the incorporation of lexical and syntactical features of the viewers' native language (SSL) into the subtitles works as a tool for learning and understanding a different language. This is an original and innovative aspect of the research, which we believe should be developed further. In order to do this, collaboration among deaf and hard of hearing people and researchers and experts in this highly interesting field of research is essential.

We hope that the AENOR 153 committee, responsible for updating the subtitling standards, takes this study and other research into account, that television channels and subtitling companies adapt their products to these standards, and that the public administration continues to support research in this field to continue improving the quality of subtitling for deaf and hard of hearing people in this country.

References

Asociación Española de Normalización y Certificación (AENOR). (2003). *Norma UNE 153010: Subtitulado para personas sordas y personas con discapacidad auditiva. Subtitulado a través del teletexto.* Madrid: Asociación Española de Normalización y Certificación.

Alegría, J., & Leybaert, J. (1987). *Adquisición de la lectura en el niño sordo.* Madrid: Centro Nacional de Recursos para la Educación Especial.

Arnáiz Uzquiza, V. (2007). *El subtitulado para sordos en España.* Unpublished MA thesis, *Universitat Autònoma de Barcelona*, Spain.

British Broadcasting Corporation (BBC) (1998). *BBC Subtitling Guide.* London: British Broadcasting Corporation.

Brondeel, H. (1994). Teaching subtitling routines. *Meta, 34*(1), 26–33.

Cambra, C. (2006). Los subtítulos en la televisión: ¿facilitan a los adolescentes sordos la comprensión de programas? *Fiapas, 110,* 28–31.

Chapa, C. (2001a). Elementos no manuales (I): Los patrones labiales en la LSE. In A. Minguet Soto (coord.), *Signolingüística: Introducción a la lingüística de la LSE* (pp. 231–238). Valencia: Fundación Fesord.

Chapa, C. (2001b). El orden de los signos. In A. Minguet Soto (coord.), *Signolingüística: Introducción a la lingüística de la LSE* (pp. 283–290). Valencia: Fundación Fesord.

Climent, J., & Herrero, Á. (2000). La estructura sintáctica. In A. Minguet Soto (coord.), *Signolingüística: Introducción a la lingüística de la LSE* (pp. 57–65). Valencia: Fundación Fesord.

de Linde, Z., & Kay, N. (1999). *The semiotics of subtitling.* Manchester: St. Jerome.

Díaz Cintas, J. (2003). *Teoría y práctica de la subtitulación inglés-español.* Barcelona: Ariel.

Díaz Cintas, J., & Remael, A. (2007). *Audiovisual Translation: Subtitling.* Manchester: St. Jerome.

d'Ydewalle, G., & Van Rensbergen, J. (1987). Reading a message when the same message is available auditorily in another language: The case of subtitling. In J. K. O'Regan & A. Lévy-Schoen (Eds.), *Eye movements: From physiology to cognition* (pp. 313–321). Amsterdam: Elsevier Science.

Gregory, S., & Sancho-Aldridge, J. (1997). *Dial 888: Subtitling for Deaf children.* London: Independent Television Commission.

Herrero, Á. (2005–2008). La flexión verbal en español: La persona y el modo. Su realización en LSE. In *Gramática Contrastiva Español-LSE: Enseñanza virtual y autoevaluación de la escritura de personas sordas.* Retrieved 15 November 2008, from <http://www.cervantes virtual.com/seccion/signos/psegundonivel.jsp?seccion=signos&conten=linguistica& pagina=gram_contrastiva&tit3=Gram%E1tica+Contrastiva+Espa%F1ol+-+LSE>.

Independent Television Commission (ITC) (1999). *ITC guidance on standards for subtitling.* London: Independent Television Commission.

Ivarsson, J., & Carroll, M. (1998). *Subtitling.* Simrishamn: TransEdit.

Justo Sanmartín, N. (forthcoming). El subtitulado para sordos y personas con discapacidad auditiva en Inglaterra. In E. Di Giovanni (Ed.), *Entre texto y receptor: Accesibilidad, doblaje y traducción. Between text and receiver: accessibility, dubbing and translation.* Frankfurt: Peter Lang.

Kyle. J.G., & Pullen, G. (1985). *Young deaf people in employment.* Bristol: School of Education.

Lorenzo, L., & Pereira, A. (forthcoming). Deaf children and their access to audiovisual texts: school failure and the helplessness of the subtitler. In E. Di Giovanni (Ed.), *Entre texto y receptor: Accesibilidad, doblaje y traducción. Between text and receiver: accessibility, dubbing and translation.* Frankfurt: Peter Lang.

Méndez Brage, B. (2003). *El subtitulado para sordos.* Unpublished undergraduate thesis, Universidade de Vigo, Spain.

Minguet Soto, A. (coord.) (2000). *Signolingüística: Introducción a la lingüística de la LSE.* Valencia: Fundación Fesord.

Moreira Brenlla, E. (forthcoming). Subtítulos para sordos en la televisión alemana. In E. Di Giovanni (Ed.), *Entre texto y receptor: Accesibilidad, doblaje y traducción. Between text and receiver: accessibility, dubbing and translation.* Frankfurt: Peter Lang.

Moreno Rodríguez, A. (2000). *La comunidad sorda: Aspectos psicológicos y sociológicos.* Madrid: Confederación Nacional de Sordos de España.

Neves, J. (2005). *Audiovisual translation: Subtitling for the deaf and hard of hearing.* Unpublished doctoral dissertation, Roehampton University, United Kingdom.

Neves, J., & Lorenzo, L. (2007). La subtitulación para s/Sordos: Panorama global y preformativo en el marco ibérico. *Trans. Revista de Traductología, 11,* 95–113.

Pazó Lorenzo, I. (2006). *Propuesta de subtitulación para sordos de* La edad de hielo*: Búsqueda de la convergencia entre lenguas orales y signadas.* Unpublished undergraduate thesis, Universidade de Vigo, Spain.

Pereira, A., & Lorenzo, L. (2005). Evaluamos la norma UNE 153010: Subtitulado para personas sordas y personas con discapacidad auditiva. Subtitulado a través del teletexto. *Puentes, 6,* 21–26.

Pérez de Oliveira, A. (forthcoming). El subtitulado para sordos en las principales cadenas de televisión en España. In E. Di Giovanni (Ed.), *Entre texto y receptor: Accesibilidad, doblaje y traducción. Between text and receiver: accessibility, dubbing and translation.* Frankfurt: Peter Lang.

Prada González, M. (2004). Buscando a Nemo: *Propuesta de subtitulado para sordos a partir del análisis crítico de cuatro casos reales.* Unpublished undergraduate thesis, Universidade de Vigo, Spain.

Rodríguez González, M.Á. (1992). *Lenguaje de signos.* Madrid: CNSE/Fundación ONCE.

Tercedor Sánchez, I., Lara Burgos, P., Herrador Molina, D., Márquez Linares, I., & Márquez Alhambra, L. (2007). Parámetros de análisis en la subtitulación accesible. In C. Jiménez Hurtado (Ed.), *Traducción y accesibilidad. Subtitulación para sordos y audiodescripción para ciegos: Nuevas modalidades de TAV* (pp. 41–51). Frankfurt: Peter Lang.

VV. AA. (2002). *Apuntes de lingüística de la lengua de signos española.* Madrid: CNS.

Ana Pereira

Including Spanish Sign Language in subtitles for the deaf and hard of hearing[1]

The following article[2] describes the common rules and structures between Spanish Sign Language (SSL) and the Spanish language, which – because of their common features – can be incorporated into subtitling for the deaf and hard of hearing (SDH). The objective is to make subtitles more appropriate and to enable better comprehension of the subtitles by deaf audiences whose mother tongue is SSL.

1. Introduction

As is the case with subtitling for hearers, SDH is not, nor can it be, a complete written reproduction of the spoken language and the background sounds of an audiovisual document. The reasons are obvious to subtitlers, but viewers must also know and understand these reasons so that they are able to form a realistic idea of what can be expected of subtitles.[3] Subtitles represent a semantic account, which, in turn, allows the viewer to grasp the essence of a particular programme and enjoy that programme to the full. Consequently, one of the most characteristic features of subtitling, from a linguistic point of view, is the need for synthesis/reduction.

1   We are grateful to Irene Pazó Lorenzo, a Spanish Sign Language interpreter, for the information and knowledge provided for the production of the present article.

2   This article is part of the ongoing research project *SDH and AD: First scientific approaches and their application* (reference HUM2006-03653FILO), financed by the Spanish Ministry of Education.

3   Some of the most common reasons are the following: time and space limitations, maintaining a specific reading rate, the viewers' needs to read the subtitles and simultaneously assimilate any accompanying images.

However, even though many different reduction techniques are used in the production of subtitled material, we will not focus on this feature, which is not specific to subtitling for the deaf and hard of hearing. Instead, we will concentrate on the features of Spanish Sign Language (SSL) that can be incorporated into subtitles, to the degree that these features meet the rules and structures of the Spanish language. We think that including such features into subtitling will produce subtitles which will be better understood by deaf people whose native language is SSL. At the same time, people whose native language is Spanish will not detect anything strange because only the features that 'sound' natural in this language will be used. After providing a detailed analysis of studies on the nature of SSL (Chapa, 2001a/2001b; Climent & Herrero, 2000; Herrero 2005–2008; Minguet Soto, 2000; Rodríguez González, 1992; VV. AA., 2002), we will explain which syntactical and lexical characteristics of SSL we can incorporate into subtitling, as well as discuss the features of SSL that reinforce the understanding of verbal inflection for deaf viewers, since verbal inflection constitutes one of the greatest obstacles in deaf viewers' learning of the spoken language (Pazó Lorenzo, forthcoming).

2. The syntax of SSL in subtitles

At the syntactical level, subtitles can incorporate the correct order of elements in SSL. This correct order should meet the following two basic criteria: 1) ordering events chronologically (e. g., instead of using *I brushed my teeth after dinner*, *I had dinner and then I brushed my teeth* would be used) and 2) ordering information with the most general information appearing first and followed by more specific information (e.g., instead of using *The university doors are grey*, *The university has grey doors* would be used).

We can also try to preserve the Subject-Verb-Object (SVO) sentence structure and, although the tendency in Spanish is to leave out the subject, we can use the personal subject pronoun whenever possible because, sometimes, deaf viewers are unable to distinguish which person the verb in a particular sentence refers to. For example, in the Spanish sentence *Vivo en Alicante, pero trabaja aquí* (in English, *I live in Alicante but she works here*), the use of explicit pronouns to refer to the first-person subject of the verb form *vivo* (from the verb *vivir* (to live)) and the third-person subject of the verb form *trabaja* (from the verb *trabajar* (to work)) is unnecessary because the subject-related information is clearly contained in the inflected forms of the verbs. However, to avoid any possible confusion, we would make such pronouns explicit (*Yo vivo en Alicante, pero ella trabaja aquí*). We can apply the same strategy to object pronouns as long as time and space allows this. For example, instead of saying *Él la ama* (in English, *He loves her*, without the full object pronoun), we would say *Él la ama a ella* (making the full object pronoun explicit) or *Él ama a María* (in English, *He loves María*) because for deaf viewers it is not always easy to find the referent in the discourse.

We can also adapt the subtitles to other characteristics of SSL, such as placing the space and time indications at the beginning of the sentence and positioning the adjective after the noun, following the general-to-specific order (the object is introduced first and only then is it described). In addition, we can avoid the use of passive sentences and maintain the unmarked order of elements in the sentence in Spanish (subject/theme/given information → verb/focus/new information) because both characteristics contribute to better comprehension of the discourse by deaf and hard of hearing audiences.

As syntactical complexity increases, we must be more careful. In the table below, we present different types of sentences and the solutions that we recommend for the subtitles, which reflect the idiosyncrasy of SSL. The solutions have been provided with their English translations in parentheses:

TYPE OF SENTENCE	RECOMMENDED CONNECTIVES/MARKERS
Copulative coordination	*y* (and), *más* (plus), ni (*neither, nor*), *también* (also). We recommend avoiding the conjunction "e" (used instead of "y" when the following word begins with an i) by changing, for example, the order of the elements listed.
Disjunctive coordination	*o* (or)
Causal subordination The order of clauses in SSL is main clause+conjunction+subordinate clause, except in conditional sentences, where it is conjunction+protasis+apodosis.	*porque* (because), *el motivo* (the reason why)

TYPE OF SENTENCE	RECOMMENDED CONNECTIVES/MARKERS
Consecutive subordination	*por eso* (for that reason)
Final subordination	*para* (to, for), *objetivo* (objective) [*con el objetivo de que* (with the objective of)]
Adversative subordination	*pero* (but)
Concessive subordination	*da igual* (I don't care) (see box below), *aunque* (even if)
Conditional subordination	*si* (if), *por ejemplo* (for example) We recommend using conditional structures instead of concessive structures, because this avoids the use of the subjunctive. Including the expression *me da igual* (I don't care), we are adding the sense of concession, and this conjunction is easier to recognise than *aunque* (even if). *Aunque llueva,* iré a la fiesta. *Even if it rains,* I'll go to the party BETTER: *Si llueve,* me <u>da igual</u>, <u>iré</u> a la fiesta. *If it rains,* <u>I don't care, I'll go</u> to the party
Adjective subordination	*que* (that), *el mismo que* (the same that)
Closed questions	We suggest adding *¿...sí o no?* (real question tag) *¿...verdad?* (... right?) *¿Es tu hermano?* Is he your brother? BETTER: *¿Es tu hermano, <u>verdad</u>?* He is your brother, <u>right</u>?

3. The lexis of SSL in subtitles

SSL incorporates mouthings of words in Spanish, which can be used in all possible cases, since many deaf viewers use SSL and will understand those terms without any difficulty.[4] For example, when people are pleased when they see their family together, they may say *¡Qué estampa!* (in English, *What a sight!*). In this case, we can replace *estampa* (sight) with the vocali-

---

4   Mouthings of words are forms that constitute the spoken component of a sign, that is, the expression that accompanies the production of the sign, which is signed in the spoken language itself (Pazó Lorenzo, 2006).

sation corresponding to the sign SITUACIÓN (SITUATION), which gives us *¡Qué situación!* (in English, *What a situation!*).

At the lexical level, we can also use other strategies that do not belong specifically to SSL but that we consider appropriate for making subtitles accessible to the greatest possible number of viewers. These strategies include: choosing – in the case of synonyms – the most frequently used word (e. g., *avoid* instead of *circumvent*), negating the opposite (if it is more common) (e. g., *not sharp* instead of *blunt*) or using an adjective instead of an abstract noun (e. g., *good* instead of *goodness*), which is much more common in SSL.

4. SSL verbal inflection markers in subtitles

Sometimes, deaf people know the meaning of a verb, but do not recognise it when they read it with morphemes expressing tense, mood, aspect and person, which may all obscure the root. Even if they do recognise the verb, they do not perceive the nuances implied by those grammatical categories. For this reason, we suggest incorporating markers of the spoken component of SSL into the subtitles, which may help to retrieve the features that viewers miss when confronted with inflected verbs.

Before listing some of these markers, we would like to recommend avoiding, as far as this is possible, the use of irregular verb forms. Regarding the use of single or compound verb forms, we must say that although isolated studies (e. g., Dapoza, 2006) suggest that compound verb forms are easier to understand for deaf viewers, we believe that the data available at the moment do not provide sufficient evidence that would encourage us to use compound verb forms at the expense of single verb forms. More studies on the subject are required and until more results are available, from the point of view of subtitling, it goes without saying that simple verb forms allow for more space to be saved, and promoting the use of such verb forms is one of the reduction techniques recurrently employed by subtitlers.

4.1. Temporality: Tense and other temporal markers

Verbs in SSL do not include tense information. Therefore, even if verbs in subtitles include inflections, the inflections do not help all deaf viewers to locate the time at which the action takes place. For this reason, we could take advantage of the following temporal markers used in SSL to indicate the notion of temporality more clearly:

PAST	PRESENT	FUTURE
Ayer (yesterday)	*Ahora* (now)	*Mañana* (tomorrow)
Hace mucho tiempo	*Hoy* (today)	*Después* (then)
(a long time ago)	*Actualmente*	X
Desde hace muchos años	(currently)	*días/semanas/meses/años*
(for many years)	*Este mes, este año*	*después* (X
Desde hace tiempo	(this month, this year)	days/weeks/months/years later)
(for a long time)		
Hace poco (recently)		
Antes (before)		
X días/semanas/meses/años		
antes (X days/weeks/		*Vendrá en avión.*
months/years before)	*Viene en avión.*	He'll come by plane.
Tenía pesadillas por las noches.	He is coming by plane.	BETTER: *Vendrá en avión <u>mañana</u>.*
I had nightmares at night	BETTER:	He'll come by plane <u>tomorrow</u>.
BETTER: <u>*Antes*</u> *tenía*	*Viene en avión <u>hoy</u>.*	
pesadillas por las noches.	He is coming	
<u>Before</u> I had nightmares	by plane <u>today</u>	
at night		

4.2. Aspect markers

In addition to using tense and other temporal markers, we suggest applying the aspect markers in the overview below, which are used in SSL and whose mouthings correspond to Spanish. We believe that they can be extremely useful, especially for those deaf viewers who cannot glean enough information from the conjugated verb and have to make efforts to understand its meaning. In these cases, the inflection morphemes make it difficult for the viewers to associate a particular verb form with an infinitive. Consequently, these viewers do not recognise the nuances in terms of aspect conveyed by the different verb forms even if they know the verb.

ASPECT	MARKERS
Inchoative The action is about to start, but it has not started yet	*CASI* (ALMOST, the most common in SSL) *Llegué a casa y él estaba empezando a comer.* I arrived home and he was starting to have lunch. BETTER: *Llegué a casa y él <u>casi</u> estaba comiendo.* I arrived home and he was <u>almost</u> eating. *TODAVÍA* (YET): a very common marker used in SSL to indicate that the action has not started (yet = not yet), placed after the verb. *El niño aún no ha ido al colegio.* The boy still hasn't gone to school. BETTER: *El niño no ha ido al colegio <u>todavía</u>.* The boy hasn't gone to school <u>yet</u>. *IR + A + VERB* (TO BE GOING TO + INFINITIVE): This verb phrase marks inchoative aspect, but implies a different nuance: the action has not started yet, but attention is focused on the fact that it is highly likely to happen: *Si sigue así <u>va a</u> suspender.* (If he goes on like this, he's going to fail.) This verb phrase, which in SSL does not contain the preposition *a* ("to"), is used only in the third person. *ESTAR A PUNTO DE* (TO BE ABOUT TO)
Ingressive The action has already started, but it is at an initial stage.	*AL PRINCIPIO* (AT THE BEGINNING) *LA PRIMERA VEZ* (THE FIRST TIME) *EMPEZAR + A* (BEGIN TO)
Continuative It focuses on the intermediate stage of the action	*CONTINUAR* (CONTINUE). *El bebé sigue durmiendo.* The baby is still sleeping. BETTER: *El bebé <u>continúa</u> durmiendo.* The baby <u>continues</u> sleeping. *DURANTE, DURACIÓN* (FOR, LENGTH) *Los médicos estuvieron operándole 8 horas.* BETTER: *Los médicos estuvieron operándole <u>durante</u> 8 horas.* The doctors were operating on him <u>for</u> 8 hours. *La <u>duración</u> de la operación fue 8 horas.* The <u>length</u> of the operation was 8 hours. *MUCHO TIEMPO, MUCHAS HORAS, MUCHOS DÍAS* (A LONG TIME, MANY HOURS, MANY DAYS): We have chosen these expressions for those cases signed as "the hands of the clock turn repeatedly." *El bizcocho tardó mucho en hornearse.* The cake took long to bake.

	In this case, we would not use the verb *tardar* (take long to) because for deaf signers it implies delay. BETTER: *El bizcocho estuvo <u>mucho tiempo</u> horneándose.* The cake was baking <u>for a long time.</u> GERUND: the mouthing of the gerund is also used to mark the continuative aspect. *SEGUIR*: We recommend avoiding this verb in Spanish because although it can mean "continue", its most common meaning is *perseguir* (to chase) and it can lead to confusion.
Perfective It expresses the delimitation or completion of an action	*YA* (ALREADY): We especially recommend this marker. In Spanish, it is short, it does not take up too much space within the subtitle and, at the same time, implies that the action is in the past. *¿Has desayunado?* Have you had breakfast? BETTER: *¿Ya desayunaste?* Did you already have breakfast? *FIN* (END): Although this marker is constantly used in SSL, including it in this form in Spanish is difficult. In some cases, it might be possible to use *AL FINAL* (AT THE END) as a marker of the perfective aspect: *Nosotros esperamos en la cola del INEM, <u>al final</u> cerraron y no nos atendieron.* We waited in the unemployment office queue and, <u>at the end</u>, they closed and did not help us.
Gradual It focuses on the progressive development of an action	*POCO A POCO* (LITTLE BY LITTLE): *Progresivamente el niño irá aprendiendo.* Progressively the boy will learn BETTER: *El niño aprenderá <u>poco a poco</u>.* The boy will learn <u>little by little</u>.
Iterative Actions that repeat themselves several times in a period of time	*OTRA VEZ* (AGAIN): We should avoid the expression *volver a*, since in SSL the verb *volver*, in general, implies only returning to the point of departure, not repeating an action. In those cases, the notion of repetition is signed as *OTRA VEZ* (AGAIN). *Volví a fumar.*

	BETTER: *Fumo <u>otra vez</u>.* I smoke <u>again.</u> REPEATING THE VERB: This strategy could be used when its expressiveness (humour) is appropriate. *Es un poco torpe, se cayó una y otra vez.* He's a little clumsy, he fell once and again. BETTER: *Es un poco torpe, se cayó y se cayó.* He's a little clumsy, he fell and fell. *MUCHAS VECES* (MANY TIMES): *Es un poco torpe, se cayó una y otra vez.* He's a little clumsy, he fell once and again. BETTER: *Es un poco torpe, se cayó muchas veces.* He's a little clumsy, he fell many times.
Punctual Action as a point in time	*DE REPENTE* (SUDDENLY): We believe this is the best option in these cases. *Y así, sin más, se marchó.* And, just like that, he left. BETTER: *Se marchó <u>de repente</u>.* He left <u>suddenly.</u> *RÁPIDAMENTE* (RAPIDLY): This is not a specific SSL marker but we believe it is easily understood. However, in general, we recommend avoiding long adverbs ending in *-mente*.
Frequentative The action repeats itself habitually	*COSTUMBRE* (HABIT): *tener la costumbre, estar acostumbrado/a* (to have the habit of, be used to). *SIEMPRE* (ALWAYS) *HABITUAL* (HABITUAL)
Distributive It indicates multiple beneficiaries of an action	*CADA UNO* (EACH): *Le enviaron cartas a <u>cada socio</u>.* They sent letters to <u>each member.</u> *A DIFERENTES* (TO DIFFERENT): *Viajó a varios países.* He travelled to several countries. BETTER: *Viajó a <u>diferentes</u> países.* He travelled to <u>different</u> countries.

4.3. Mood markers

With regard to the attitudes of the speakers towards the fact that they are speaking or writing about, of the three moods (*indicative*: the speaker states a reality; *subjunctive*: the speaker is emotionally involved in that reality, looking forward to it, considering it improbable, unlikely, etc., and *imperative*: the speaker imposes that reality) the subjunctive is the mood that usually poses the greatest comprehension problems. However, in SSL there are markers that are constantly used to express subjunctive values, and we recommend using them. They are *EJEMPLO* (EXAMPLE), *CASO* (CASE) and *IMAGINA* (IMAGINE):

> *Y si saliese mal el plan, ¿qué hacemos?*
> What if the plan goes wrong? What do we do?
> BETTER: *Imagínate, sale mal el plan ¿Qué hacemos?*
> Imagine, the plan goes wrong. What do we do?
> *Por ejemplo, sale mal el plan ¿Qué hacemos?*
> For example, the plan goes wrong. What do we do?
> *En el caso de que salga mal el plan, ¿qué hacemos?*
> In case the plan goes wrong, what do we do?

As far as the imperative is concerned, some of the devices used to mark this mood in SSL and their possible counterparts in subtitling could be the following: the facial expression used in SSL could be represented through the use of exclamation marks, and the sign *mandar* (to command), which clearly indicates an order, the mood could be expressed by means of didascalies, avoiding terms such as *orden* and *ordenar* ('order' and 'ordering'), which in SSL have only the meaning of 'arranging things in the right place'.

5. Conclusions

In addition to a thorough knowledge of the deaf audience (characterised according to the degree of loss of hearing, the age at which the loss of hearing took place, the educational backgrounds, cognitive, linguistic, social and emotional alterations caused by deafness, etc.) and excellent skills in both the subtitling technique and the target language, the professional in charge of producing subtitles including features of SSL should – in an ideal situation – also be competent in sign language, the mother tongue of many audience members. As such, professionals in charge would be familiar with the features described above and would apply them naturally and without difficulty in their work.

However, this ideal situation is currently not the norm and, in general, not many subtitlers are competent in sign language. Studies such as the present one provide a contribution to fill this gap and establish a connection between two means of communication, subtitling and sign language, which generally occur and are studied separately.

References

Chapa, C. (2001a). Elementos no manuales (I): Los patrones labiales en la LSE. In A. Minguet Soto (coord.), *Signolingüística: Introducción a la lingüística de la LSE* (pp. 231–238). Valencia: Fundación Fesord.

Chapa, C. (2001b). El orden de los signos. In A. Minguet Soto (coord.), *Signolingüística: Introducción a la lingüística de la LSE* (pp. 283–290). Valencia: Fundación Fesord.

Climent, J., & Herrero, Á. (2000). La estructura sintáctica. In A. Minguet Soto (coord.), *Signolingüística: Introducción a la lingüística de la LSE* (pp. 57–65). Valencia: Fundación Fesord.

Dapoza, N. (2006). Necesidades comunicativas do receptor xordo e consecuencias para o traballo do subtitulador, lecture given on 1 December 2006 during the seminar *Accesibilidade nos medios audiovisuais. O papel do mediador en SPS e AD.* Vigo: FFT.

Herrero, Á. (2005–2008). La flexión verbal en español: La persona y el modo. Su realización en LSE. In *Gramática Contrastiva Español-LSE: Enseñanza virtual y autoevaluación de la escritura de personas sordas.* Retrieved 15 November 2008, from <http://www.cervantesvirtual.com/seccion/signos/psegundonivel.jsp?seccion=signos&conten=linguistica&pagina=gram_contrastiva&tit3=Gram%E1tica+Contrastiva+Espa%F1ol+-+LSE>.

Minguet Soto, A. (coord.) (2000). *Signolingüística: Introducción a la lingüística de la LSE.* Valencia: Fundación Fesord.

Pazó Lorenzo, I. (2006). *Propuesta de subtitulación para sordos de* La edad de hielo: *Búsqueda de la convergencia entre lenguas orales y signadas.* Unpublished undergraduate thesis, Universidade de Vigo, Spain.

Pazó Lorenzo, I. (forthcoming). La adaptación del subtitulado para personas sordas. In E. Di Giovanni (Ed.), *Entre texto y receptor: Accesibilidad, doblaje y traducción. Between text and receiver: accessibility, dubbing and translation.* Frankfurt: Peter Lang.

Rodríguez González, M. Á. (1992). *Lenguaje de signos.* Madrid: CNSE / Fundación ONCE.

VV. AA. (2002). *Apuntes de lingüística de la lengua de signos española.* Madrid: CNS.

LOURDES LORENZO

Subtitling for deaf and hard of hearing children in Spain: A case study[1]

This contribution presents a case study based on an episode of the television series Shin Chan *(subtitled for deaf and hard of hearing children) and the results of its viewing by several groups of Spanish children with hearing disabilities (and children with good hearing in order to establish a comparison between both groups). The focus of the study was on communicative efficiency of the subtitles. The intention behind such a study was to verify the functionality of the existing criteria in use in Spain and published by AENOR (*Standard UNE 153010* Subtitling for the deaf and hard of hearing. Teletext subtitling). At the end of the contribution proposals are made to complete the existing criteria and to focus on the areas for which the standard did not provide solutions (linguistic issues mainly). In addition, improvements are suggested for implementation into the existing standard, with a view to a possible revision of the standard for digital TV (DTV) in those areas in which it is clearly deficient.*

1. Background

As indicated in Pereira's contributions in this volume, we have taken Standard UNE 153010 and its critical analysis (Pereira & Lorenzo, 2005) as our basis in an attempt to produce the subtitles for our study. The study also departs from the following literature: on deaf viewers (Alegría & Leybaert, 1987; Cambra, 2006), on the deaf viewers' communicative skills in the

---

1   This article is part of the ongoing research project *SDH and AD: First scientific approaches and their application* (reference HUM2006-03653FILO), financed by the Spanish Ministry of Education.

oral and sign codes (Cabeza & Báez, 2005; Chapa, 2001; Dapoza, 2006; Minguet Soto, 2000; Pazó Lorenzo, 2006), on subtitling in general (Díaz Cintas, 2003, 2006; Ivarsson & Carroll, 1998), on subtitling for the deaf and hard of hearing in particular (Carrera, 2007; Carrera & Lorenzo, 2008; Gregory & Sancho-Aldridge, 1997; Lorenzo & Pereira, forthcoming; Neves & Lorenzo, 2007) and on the analyses of subtitling for the deaf and hard of hearing carried out in both Spain (Álvarez, 2006; Arnáiz Uzquiza, 2007; Martínez Ortiz, 2007; Pérez de Oliveira, forthcoming; Prada González, 2004; Tercedor Sánchez, Lara Burgos, Herrador Molina, Márquez Linares & Márquez Alhambra, 2007) and in neighbouring countries (Justo Sanmartín, forthcoming; Moreira Brenlla, forthcoming; Neves, 2005).

2. The reception study

In order to carry out the field studies that would allow us to measure the comprehension of subtitles by deaf and hard of hearing children, we were interested in selecting material that would be attractive to the children, that would not be too long (in order to attract the children's attention) and that would constitute a complete unit, that is, a single episode with a clear storyline and a definite beginning and end. With this as a starting point, any of the episodes of the television series *Shin Chan* fulfilled the requirements. *Shin Chan* is a Japanese series which is very well known in Spain, where it was dubbed into four official languages (Basque, Catalonian, Galician and Spanish) and broadcast by several television channels. Its main character is a small child (approximately seven years old), with whom young audiences can immediately identify since he reflects their own attitudes and behaviour. The usual length of a *Shin Chan* episode is under 10 minutes, and as such the episodes constitute independent units that can be understood as complete wholes, without any need to refer to the previous or following episodes.

The selected episode was entitled *We bathe in very hot water to take away the cold* and the analysis focused mainly on the linguistic level (lexical and syntactical difficulty, the presence of background sound effects, irony and metaphors, and the importance of intonation to understand the message) and the difficulties derived from the audiovisual context itself (for example, frames where we can see one character, but another character speaks off-camera).

The selected episode, which lasts approximately six and a half minutes, tells yet another anecdote in the daily life of the Nohara family. It is winter and Hiroshi, Shin Chan's father, comes home from work numbed by the cold outside. He wants to take a hot bath. Misae, his wife, has not cleaned the bathtub or heated the water, and this makes Hiroshi angry. When he is finally beginning to enjoy his hot bath, his wife tells him to bathe Shin Chan as well, to which he reluctantly agrees thanks to Misae's great 'powers of persuasion' (she is brandishing a knife because she is cooking dinner). Shin Chan brings several toys to the bath, including Mika, a very sexy doll. Taking advantage of the fact that Shin Chan has gone to have a pee, his father talks to the doll, imagining she is a very sexy and flexible woman. As the episode ends, Misae is furious when she comes into the bathroom and finds her husband playing with the doll.

3. Subtitling tools

The subtitles for this episode were produced using three types of free software and with the specific aim of carrying out the reception studies. *Subtitle Workshop*, created by the Uruguayan research group URUSOFT, is one of the most widely used subtitle simulators in use at Spanish universities. The program allowed us to localise and adjust the subtitles. *Sub Station Alpha* was used to apply colour labels (to identify the different characters) and to insert the background sound indications at the top of the screen. Finally, *VirtualDub* was used to insert the subtitles on the frames permanently.

4. The participants

The following universities participated in the reception studies: Universidade de Vigo, Universitat Autònoma de Barcelona, Universidad de Deusto, Universidad Rey Juan Carlos and Universidad Carlos III.[2] The subtitled chapter was distributed to 83 individuals (36 boys and 47 girls) with hearing disabilities of varying degrees and nature (30 postlocutive and 53 prelocutive deaf children). In order to be able to compare the answers given by the deaf individuals, the material and the questionnaire were also distributed to a group of 46 hearers (19 boys and 27 girls). Both the deaf and the hearing children were between the ages of 5 and 15. Within the group of participants the largest age-defined group consisted of 11-year-olds (58 participants), followed by the 12-year-olds, who formed the second largest age-defined group (19 participants). The number of participants in the other groups was as follows: 10-year-olds (14 participants), 9-year-olds (11 participants), 13-year-olds (9 participants), 7-year-olds (6 participants), 8-year-olds and 14-year-olds (4 participants in each group), 15-year-olds (2 participants) and 6-year-olds and 5-year-olds (1 participant in each group). Most of the participants had been born to hearing parents (87%). We were particularly interested in the case of a girl, born to deaf parents, who used only Spanish Sign Language (SSL) and always asked for an interpreter because she was not able to answer any of the questions. Thus, we assumed that her contact with spoken language was virtually non-existent.

In order to carry out the reception studies, student interns at the participating universities contacted schools and associations for the deaf, inviting them to participate in the experiment. In general, the response was positive, although some parents and educators were uneasy about the cho-

2   We are grateful to the following student interns for their collaboration: Irene Pazó Lorenzo, Almudena Pérez de Oliveira and Santiago Rodríguez Bouzas (Universidade de Vigo), Verónica Arnáiz (Universitat Autònoma de Barcelona), Rubén Rojas (Universidad Rey Juan Carlos I) and José Luis Teigell (Universidad Carlos III). We are also indebted to Natxo Canto, Gonzalo Eguíluz (Universidad de Deusto), Mónica Souto (CESyA) Carmen Jáudenes and Begoña Gómez Nieto (FIAPAS). In addition, we would like to thank the ass ociations for the deaf in Vigo, Ourense, Lugo (ANPANXOGA), Alcorcón (CODIAL), Bilbao and Bizkaia, the school Instituto La Farisa in Ourense, ARANSBUR and MQD in Burgos, and Centro Altatorre de Sordos in Madrid.

sen material, which they considered 'unsuitable' for children because of its contents. They did, however, understand the main reasons for selecting it: its complete success among children (98% of all those interviewed were already familiar with the series *Shin Chan*), appropriate language for children in that age range, and the children's ability to identify with the characters, who were children like themselves.

The groups of participants were created according to the availability of willing candidates. The group of prelocutive deaf individuals was, by far, the most numerous. This is not surprising, since prelocutive deaf individuals tend to develop a sense of 'belonging' to the deaf community and are present in the social spaces of deafness (education, health, leisure, associations). In contrast, postlocutive deaf individuals feel integrated among hearers and simply consider that they have a problem that requires a technical solution (e.g., hearing aids).[3] All of them attended integrated schools and, in general, claimed to be happy there.

Regarding their preferences in terms of communication codes, most prelocutive deaf individuals preferred SSL (72%), although a small group tended to choose oral language (16%) and another group felt comfortable in both languages (12%).[4] Postlocutive deaf individuals continued to prefer SSL (56%), but quite a high percentage (37%) claimed to feel more comfortable with oral language (especially those with cochlear implants), while the rest (7%) believed that they managed quite well in both languages.

---

3   Obviously, in the age range under investigation, individuals are not yet aware of this, but parents, following the advice of doctors and/or educators, guide children in the ways that they consider most appropriate. It is usually during adolescence that individuals become aware of their condition and decide to become involved, or not, in the deaf community (associations, groups of friends, etc.).

4   Some participants indicated that they preferred oral language because if they decided to use SSL, the other children "looked at them funnily" or "laughed at them." There was also one case that should make educational agents stop and think: a prelocutive deaf child born to hearing parents, with a clear preference for oral language, claimed to read well but not to understand what he was reading. Many sign language interpreters denounce this type of reading, similar to parrot language: in many schools, children undergo tedious speech therapy sessions in front of mirrors to get them to vocalise the words, and they manage to pronounce them (without having heard them), but in their minds those words are not associated with a meaning, which is really the point at which the reading process becomes significant.

The most interesting findings supported something that researchers have been claiming for a long time: exposure to oral language in subtitles undoubtedly improves the reading abilities of the deaf population. The results of the survey indicated that children who claimed to use subtitles regularly considered themselves good readers, while those who said that they seldom or never used subtitles admitted to having great reading difficulties.[5] At the same time, and as a logical result of this, the children who usually used subtitles and were able to read well thought that the subtitles were well done (marks from 7 to 10). On the contrary, those who seldom used subtitles and claimed to have great reading difficulties, gave subtitles extremely low marks (around 3). We were probably facing a vicious circle in that children who seldom or never used subtitles had reading difficulties and this, in turn, made them think that the subtitles had been badly done. That was then the reason why they did not understand the subtitles. Since they did not understand the subtitles, they used this service less and less, and this had a negative effect on their reading abilities. Among the group of hearers, almost all of those questioned considered themselves to have high reading skills.

5. Methodology

The subtitled copies were distributed among the participants in the study, together with a questionnaire that would allow us to evaluate in which aspects the subtitles were both functional and conducive to the comprehension of the audiovisual text. The questionnaire also allowed us to discover the aspects in need of improvement. The questionnaire was divided into three sections: (1) personal information related to the viewers and to the viewers' educational backgrounds, with a clear focus on their hearing disabilities (time of deafness acquisition, deaf or hearing parents, education in oral or sign language schools, self-evaluation of their reading

---

5   As might be expected, the youngest children (5–7 years old) did not use subtitles and
     were the ones who expressed the greatest reading difficulties. This fact, however, must
     be carefully interpreted since a significant part of those difficulties are similar to the
     ones encountered by hearing children of the same age.

skills, degree of satisfaction with teletext and Digital Terrestrial Television subtitles, knowledge of sign language); (2) questions related to the technical aspects of the subtitles (degree of satisfaction with the speech-character relationship strategies, length of display on the screen, number and position of subtitle lines, placement of suprasegmental information, voice noises, and background sound effects), and (3) questions related to the comprehension of the language and the contents (comprehension of the storyline, familiarity with the lexis, preference for onomatopoeic spellings or descriptions of the sounds, awareness of the function of certain oral language conventions in audiovisual texts, such as italics and quotation marks, etc.).

The subtitles were produced with child viewers in mind (the sample age ranged from 5-year-old to 15-year-old children and the mode (i.e., the most frequent age) was 11. We followed the basic aspects of Standard UNE 153010 *Subtitling for the deaf and hard of hearing. Teletext subtitling*,[6] supplementing the standard in those cases in which it did not offer solutions.[7] In addition, we decided to deviate from the standard with regard to its recommendations about the relationship between the number of characters and the length of display on the screen (4 seconds for 70 characters, compared with 6 seconds recommended for the same number of characters in subtitles for hearers). Our decision to deviate from the standard in this respect was based on our finding that the numbers suggested by the standard are a regrettable miscalculation, as was previously pointed out in another paper (see Pereira & Lorenzo, 2005).[8] Since a large number of the technical and orthotypographical criteria used to produce the subtitles are

6   Although it was actually published and meant to be applied to teletext, the standard is currently the only standard in Spain related to the area that concerns us here, and it is therefore often referred to by subtitlers working in any format and mode that implies hearing disabilities (DVD, cinema, etc.).

7   Standard UNE 153010 includes extremely vague statements. For instance, it indicates that for people with reading and writing difficulties "it is necessary to use more accessible and colloquial vocabulary. The verb forms must also be as accessible as possible" (AENOR, 2003, p. 237). How can the subtitler know which words and verb forms (simple, compound, tenses, modes) are more accessible?

8   If, as researchers claim (Cabeza & Báez, 2005; Dapoza, 2000; Delgado & Bao, 2007), many deaf individuals (especially prelocutive deaf people) have difficulties with oral language, it would be totally counterproductive to expose these individuals to subtitles that remain on the screen for a shorter period of time than subtitles for hearers.

common to subtitling for deaf and hard of hearing adults, we would like to refer the reader to Pereira's contributions in this book. The only differences emerged for a few technical criteria, more specifically, for the criteria that refer to the indication of sound effects (see subsection 6.2) and to the relationship between the number of characters and the length of display on the screen.[9] While we allowed 6 seconds per 70 characters in the subtitles for adults (the same proportion recommended in subtitling for hearers (Díaz Cintas, 2003), we used an eight-second rule (that is, 8 seconds for 70 characters, and the corresponding proportions as the number of characters decreases: 4 seconds for 35 characters, 2 seconds for 17 characters, etc.) for the subtitles for children. These two additional seconds provided the viewers with precious extra reading time without disturbing the necessary match between image, dialogues and subtitles.

6. Linguistic analysis

The treatment of the linguistic aspect of subtitles, seriously neglected (not to say ignored) by Standard UNE 153010, is worthy of special attention. Deaf children are at a double disadvantage when faced with subtitled audiovisual products in that subtitled audiovisual products probably confront them with lexical units, grammatical structures and cultural and intertextual references which they are not be familiar with but which they have to unravel with the help of the available context (Contreras, 1993; Dorr, 1986). Deaf children, whose natural language is sign language, experience these problems in a significantly more aggravated way as they are exposed to oral language in the subtitles. In the next section, we will offer a detailed description of the linguistic choices made for this study and the motivation behind these choices.[10]

---

9   When we speak of characters, we are referring to letters, spaces and orthotypographical signs.

10 See Lorenzo and Pereira (forthcoming) for further examples of linguistic adaptations in subtitled films for deaf children.

6.1. The treatment of oral language in subtitling for deaf children

The subtitling technique generally provides a semantic account of the dialogues, which enable viewers to follow the storyline (Díaz Cintas, 2003).[11] The purpose of subtitles is not to reproduce dialogues exactly but to provide a summary that allows the audience to enjoy the visual element. Consequently, one of the defining characteristics of the subtitled discourse is synthesis, both in the production of subtitles for the deaf and for hearers.

In the case of subtitling for people with hearing disabilities, this synthetic quality is complemented with other features that make the subtitles specific and different from subtitles for hearers. Subtitles for deaf and hard of hearing viewers are generally created from the dubbed version of the product (in the case of foreign films) since this allows individuals with residual hearing to follow the storyline more easily.[12] Subtitling for hearers, however, usually accompanies foreign language productions. Besides taking care of the dialogues, the written text also has to account for music, songs, background sound effects and states of mind (Díaz Cintas, 2006), especially in the two last cases (background sound effects and states of mind) when they are not obvious from the image (for example, when the sound of a storm is perceived from inside a room and the lightning is not visible, or when a character speaks off camera).

However, the specific characteristics of subtitling for the deaf and hard of hearing are not limited to those that we have just mentioned. Its most difficult aspect is probably not related to any of the characteristics that derive from the hearing disability itself (e.g., representing sound, music, states of mind or identifying characters) but to the need to deal with language in a special way. According to recent studies of subtitling for the deaf, this is the single most important matter still pending in this form of communication.

11   Subtitles may be used for a variety of purposes. The most common use is to accompany audiovisual texts in a foreign language and, in so doing, to allow comprehension. However, they may be applied in multiple ways: to learn languages (e.g., verbatim subtitles, which reproduce all the dialogues exactly in the same language as the film), as a karaoke effect, as a means of advertising (in the underground or on street billboards, etc.) or even as a tool at the service of a particular linguistic policy (bilingual subtitles, with one line in French and another in Flemish to satisfy the Walloon and Flemish communities in an area near the border in the region of Brussels (Díaz Cintas, 2003).

12   In this case, lip-reading, which many deaf people do, does not apply.

Subtitlers of audiovisual texts for deaf viewers cannot simply aim to provide a summary of the material in a way this would be done for subtitles for hearers. Without questioning in any way the intellectual capacity of deaf people, which is completely comparable to that of hearers, it is clear that, in Spain, oral language skills (in Spanish or any of the official languages of the autonomous communities) are much less developed among the deaf than they are among hearers.[13] Deaf children are at a disadvantage compared with hearing children and this because of two reasons. Firstly, they lack the reinforcement in the oral language that hearing children receive from the womb (a foetus is said to be able to hear the mother's voice sixth months into the pregnancy) and throughout their lives (continuous exposure to conversations, television, sound information in the street and means of transport, etc.). Secondly, the overall Spanish educational system currently displays serious shortcomings with respect to the education of deaf children,[14] which leads to poor development of both communicative skill in general and of oral language in particular. This, in turn, makes it much more difficult for deaf individuals to have access to culture.

In the episode that we subtitled to carry out the reception studies, we tried to be extremely careful with the linguistic choices. In addition, we based our work on a hypothesis that would mean a considerable step forwards in the much needed effort to create a single subtitling type that will satisfy a heterogeneous deaf audience (whose members range from individuals with a total lack of hearing from birth to individuals with progressive loss of hearing resulting from the ageing process):[15] aiming for the maximum possible convergence between oral language and sign language (in our case, Spanish Sign Language (SSL)). This can be achieved by strictly respecting the structure and the rules of the Spanish language but taking

13 We are obviously referring to prelocutive deaf people and not to those who have acquired deafness after reaching a high level of oral language skills.
14 See Dapoza (2000) and Delgado and Bao (2007) to learn more about the issue of education for deaf children in Spain. As a summary reflection on the situation, we can quote Dapoza (2000) here, who says that "while hearing children go to school with a language to learn, deaf children go to school to learn a language" (p. 19).
15 We speak of a 'much needed effort' because, although the ideal situation (Cambra, 2006) would be to create at least two different types of subtitling (a basic one for prelocutive deaf viewers and those that prefer simpler subtitles, and a more complex one for postlocutive deaf viewers and those that opt for subtitles with greater linguistic complexity), the reality of the present Spanish market seems to indicate that there will be only one type of subtitling for the deaf, which will obviously not satisfy everyone.

advantage of its freedom in terms of the position of the sentence elements, its flexibility in the use of pronoun forms (or their elision), etc.[16]

6.2. Examples from the analysis

In this section, we will present some of the most significant examples taken from the subtitles produced, in an attempt to illustrate both the process of synthesis that will facilitate reading and the linguistic choices and cases of convergence between SSL and Spanish. We will also provide examples of the ways in which we represented various types of music, sound effects and suprasegmental information, explaining when indications were considered necessary and when not.

6.2.1. Synthesis of the dialogues in the subtitles

As we stated before, subtitles must offer a summarised version of the dialogues so that viewers also have time to enjoy the image (Cambra, 2006). This type of synthesis is even more relevant in the case of subtitling for the deaf and hard of hearing since subtitlers are required to select the absolutely essential elements of the message and disregard additional elements (e.g., circumlocutions, discourse fillers, tags) that would make decoding the message more difficult. This procedure can be observed in the following examples, in which D refers to dubbing and SD refers to subtitling for the deaf:

(a) D: Y yo que venía con la ilusión de meterme en la bañera con agua bien caliente.
         [And, indeed, I was looking forward to getting into the bathtub with very hot water]
   SD: Yo quería darme un baño [I wanted to take a bath]
         con agua caliente. [with hot water]

(b) D: ¿Qué te parece si me ayudas a limpiar la bañera?
         [What do you think of helping me clean the bathtub?]
   SD: ¿Me ayudas a limpiar la bañera?
         [Will you help me clean the bathtub?]

16   This strategy has been applied before (Pazó Lorenzo, 2006, forthcoming) with reasonably satisfactory results among individuals with different degrees of loss of hearing and varying preferences (sign language users and oral language users). See also Pereira's contribution in this book.

(c) D: Ahora no puedo, papá. ¡Quién sabe! A lo mejor tendremos ocasión de hacer alguna cosa juntos otro día.
[I can't now, Dad. Who knows? Perhaps we'll have the opportunity to do something together another day]

    SD: Ahora no puedo, papá. [I can't now, Dad]
Otro día. [Some other day]

(d) D: Esta mujer es un peligro. Si quieres tener una vida familiar plácida sobre todo no hagas enfadar a tu mujer mientras tenga un cuchillo en la mano.
[This woman is dangerous. If you want to have a quiet family life, above all, don't make your wife angry while she's holding a knife]

    SD: Esta mujer es un peligro. [This woman is dangerous]
Para estar tranquilo [To be quiet]
no debes enfadar [you shouldn't anger]
a una mujer armada. [an armed woman]

(e) D: Pero no, claro, ella no quiere salir fuera porque hace un frío que pela.
[But no, of course, she doesn't want to go outside because it's freezing cold]

    SD: Ella no quiere salir [She doesn't want to go out]
porque hace mucho frío. [because it's very cold]

6.2.2. Linguistic choices

When producing subtitles for deaf children, one must be especially careful with the terms and structures chosen, and try to select the most precise way of communicating the information, avoiding indirect forms of reference (in example (a), "this woman" is replaced by "my wife") and circumlocutions (examples (b) and (c), especially if the image supplements the linguistic information (example (d)). It will also be necessary to select the most common and/or clear lexical items (in (e) 'very' instead of 'extremely' and in (f) 'lie down' instead of 'lie on her back'). In order to decide which words are well known and which are not, the advice provided by sign language interpreters may be extremely helpful:

(a) D: Al menos esta mujer podría limpiar la bañera, ¡que tiene todo el santo día!
[This woman could at least clean the bathtub, she has the whole day!]

    SD: Mi mujer podía limpiar la bañera, [My wife could clean the bathtub,]
¡tiene todo el día! [she has the whole livelong day!]

(b) D: ¡Cómo tarda en salir el agua caliente en invierno! Supongo que todavía hay para una media hora.
[The hot water takes such a long time in winter! I guess we still have another half hour to go]

    SD: ¡Qué lento va en invierno! [It's so slow in winter!]
Creo que tardará media hora. [I think it'll take half an hour.]

(c) D: Y me parece que también falta un buen rato para la cena.
        [And I think we still have a long way to go till dinner, too.]

    SD: Y también falta mucho [And we also have to wait]
         para la cena. [for dinner.]

(d) D: Has aprovechado que estaba fuera pelándome de frío para quitarme el sitio delante de la estufa.
        [You took advantage of the fact that I was out freezing to take my place in front of the heater]

    SD: Aprovechaste que estaba fuera [You knew I was out]
         para robarme el sitio.[and you took my place]

(e) D: Bueno, aún está demasiado caliente pero me aguantaré.
        [Well, it's still extremely hot, but I'll bear it.]

    SD: Aún está muy caliente [It's still very hot]
         pero aguantaré. [but I'll bear it]

(f) D: Pero, no, ella prefiere estar estirada.
        [But, no, she prefers to lie on her back]

    SD: (IRÓNICO) Pero ella prefiere estar tumbada.
         [(IRONIC) she prefers to lie down]

It is important to note that there are great differences between postlocutive and prelocutive deaf children. Let us look at some illustrative examples. In the episode, the water in the bathtub is described as *templada* (warm). The correct option in the questionnaire (= neither hot nor cold) was selected by 100% of the hearing children and 95% of the postlocutive deaf children, while only 46% of the prelocutive deaf children knew the word. The figures were similar when asked about the meaning of the word *tacaña* (stingy, not generous), which the father applies to the mother because she wants to save hot water in winter: 98% of the hearing children knew the word, while only 59% of the postlocutive deaf children and 36% of the prelocutive deaf children understood its meaning.

Knowledge of idiomatic expressions is also low among the groups of deaf participants in the study. While 100% of the hearing participants answered that *tratar como a un perro* (to treat like a dog, used by Shin Chan's father to describe how badly his wife treats him) means *to treat badly*, the percentage dropped to 91% among the postlocutive deaf participants and to a meagre 18% among the prelocutive deaf participants. The situation was similar when asked about the meaning of the sound effect indication 'romantic music' (played when Shin Chan's mother welcomes her husband, who is coming home from work, with a hug). The association with love is made by 100% of the hearing participants, 89% of the postlocutive deaf participants and 60% of the prelocutive deaf participants. An erroneous association with anger is made by 5.5% of the postlocutive deaf participants, and with sadness by the remaining 5.5%. The percentage of error increased in the case of the prelocutive deaf participants: 10.7% believed that the adjective 'romantic' was related to anger, 13.4% to sadness, and 15.9% did not answer the question.

6.2.3. Convergence between SLL and Spanish

One of the innovative features of our proposal is the search for common elements between sign languages and oral languages. They are obviously different codes and deaf people learn them as such. However, we believe that if we take advantage of what they may have in common, viewers will benefit. In order to do this, we suggest a type of lexical and syntactical convergence that will adapt the Spanish language to Spanish sign language (SSL) whenever possible. Thus, our proposal includes:[17]

Presenting events in chronological order:

> D: Me hacen salir fuera y llenar de combustible la estufa. [They make me go out and fill the stove with oil]
> SD: Debo salir fuera [I must go out]
>   y llenar de gasolina la estufa. [and fill the stove with oil]

Offering information from the most general to the most specific: "La casa de Shin Chan tiene una alfombra verde" ["Shin Chan's house has a green carpet"] instead of "Una alfombra de la casa de Shin Chan es verde" ["Shin Chan's house carpet is green"].

---

17   Whenever possible, we use examples from the subtitled episode. If no example from the subtitled episode is available, we offer illustrative examples from previous unpublished analyses.

Ordering the noun phrase according to the structure noun + adjective: "la cara triste del perro" [literally, following regular Spanish word order: the face sad of the dog] instead of "la triste cara del perro" [following the other possibility in Spanish: the sad face of the dog].

Ordering the sentence according to the structure adverbials (space and time) + subject + verb + object:

D: Ya no <u>me</u> quiero bañar. [I don't want to take a bath any more] (object pronoun before the verb)

SD: Ya no quiero bañar<u>me</u>. [I don't want to take a bath any more] (object pronoun after the verb)

Using closed questions, avoiding negative interrogation:[18]

D: "¡Eh! <u>¿No está</u> demasiado tibia? [Hey! <u>Isn't it</u> too lukewarm?]

SD: "Ahora está muy templada, <u>¿no?</u>". [Now it's very lukewarm, <u>right?</u>]

Using the spoken component[19] *that accompanies some signs* (e.g., ¡Esto es la gloria! ¡La gloria! [This is glorious! Glorious!] (SATISFECHO) ¡Qué gusto! [(PLEASED) This is heaven!] *or, if not available, the most frequently used term among synonyms, consulting frequency dictionaries or linguistic corpora* (e.g., CREA, Corpus de Referencia del Español Actual):

D: No parece que seamos padre e hijo este <u>crío</u> y yo. [We are not in the least bit alike, this <u>kid</u> and I]

SD: No parecemos padre e hijo [We are not alike]
     este <u>niño</u> y yo. [this <u>boy</u> and I]

D: Eso te pasa porque Misae te prepara las bañeras con agua <u>tibia</u>. [That's because Misae prepares your bath with <u>lukewarm</u> water]

SD: Eso te pasa porque Misae [That's because Misae]
     te prepara el baño <u>templado</u>. [makes your bath <u>warm</u>]

Repeating the word in order to indicate habits: "Todos los años igual, igual" [It is the same, the same every year] instead of "Todos los años pasa lo mismo" [It happens every year].

18   See Pereira (this volume) for recommendations for the convergence between SSL and Spanish regarding types of sentences (coordination and subordination) and verbal inflection.

19   An expression that accompanies the production of the sign, which is signed in the spoken language itself (Chapa, 2001).

Avoiding abstract nouns and metaphorical structures in as far as this is possible.
Regarding the latter, which are common sources of humour (Neves, 2007),
the loss of expressiveness tends to be significant, but it must usually be
sacrificed in favour of the intelligibility of the message:[20]

> D: Ahora <u>para acabarlo</u> [el día] <u>de redondear</u> solamente haría falta que entrasen por
>   la puerta un par o tres de chicas bien guapas. ¡Sería maravilloso! [Now all that's
>   missing <u>to round it off</u> [the day] is to see walking through the door two or three
>   really pretty girls. That would be wonderful!]
> SD: <u>Para ser perfecto</u> sólo falta [<u>To make it perfect</u> all that's missing]
>   que entren por la puerta [is to see walking through the door]
>
>   dos o tres chicas bien guapas. [two or three really pretty girls]
>   ¡Sería maravilloso! [It would be wonderful!]

6.2.4. Types of music

We limited the indications of types of music to the most easily recognisable
(e.g., happy music, sad music, horror music, action music, suspense music).

6.2.5. Sound effects and suprasegmental elements

The indication of sound effects and suprasegmental elements is specific to
subtitling for the deaf and it is included as such in Standard UNE 153010
(pages 233 and 238 to 240). However, Standard UNE 153010 is slightly
confusing in the following aspect: whereas on page 233 it is stated that "all
possible sound effects must be described", on page 238 Standard UNE
153010 indicates that "the maximum number of sound effects necessary
for the correct understanding of the programme must be described in one
line". Most of the individuals who participated in several reception studies
carried out to this date (Álvarez, 2006; Pazó Lorenzo, 2006; Prada González,
2004; the present study) disagree with the systematic description of background sounds because it reduces the time available to see the image. In
addition, such descriptions do not always provide relevant information.
Consequently, we avoided the indication of sound effects that can be 'visu-

---

20 Pazó Lorenzo (2006) also offers illustrative examples on how to substitute a non-
    metaphorical equivalent for a metaphor in her proposal of subtitles for deaf and hard
    of hearing in *Ice Age*. Instead of *Comprobaremos si la mente vence al músculo* [We will
    see if brains defeat muscles] (dubbed version), she suggests *Comprobaremos qué es
    mejor: ¿Ser fuerte o listo?* [We will see if it's better to be strong or smart].

alised' on the screen or that do not contribute to the comprehension of the storyline. For example, if viewers can see that it is raining, the sound of rain is not indicated. Likewise, the sound of the wind was not described in a scene in which the cartoonist represented it graphically (faded white) in the frame as is indicated in the picture below:

We also ignored the method of representing sound effects in children's programmes both through description and onomatopoeic spellings as is recommended by Standard UNE 153010. Even if indications such as *bark* (woof) or *telephone* (ring) have a didactic purpose, it is obvious that increasing the number of words will make reading more difficult and will take time away from watching the image. Therefore, we opted for the description of the sounds, which is possible in all cases, as opposed to the limited range of onomatopoeic expressions available in Spanish. We suggested placing those indications, as Standard UNE 153010 recommends, in the top right-hand corner of the screen, in red letters on a white background (we avoided using blue letters, which the Standard offers as an alternative, because, according to Prada González (2004) and Pazó Lorenzo (2006), viewers have expressed difficulties when reading this colour). The indications should be presented without brackets, in lower-case letters, and with an initial capital letter (e.g., Bark). The standard is not terribly clear about this issue either: whereas on page 238 there are examples completely in lower-case letters (e.g., (bark) woof), on the following page there is a picture with an initial capital letter: (Bark) Woof.

Regarding suprasegmental markers, that is, indicators of the conditions of speech (the character is happy, stutters, shouts, etc.), we followed the recommendations suggested by Standard UNE 153010: didascalies in upper-case letters, in brackets, in front of the character's speech and in the same colour. As in the case of indications regarding sound effects, we suggested limiting suprasegmental markers to those cases in which the image was not sufficiently clear, as in the following examples: in (a) Misae has her back to the audience and the deaf viewer would not perceive the anger conveyed by her tone of voice; in (b) the features of the cartoon drawing are not accurate enough to show his suspicion, which is revealed by the tone of his voice; in (c) there are no indications in the drawings nor moving images that would allow the viewer to know that Hiroshi is shivering, and the only sign of being cold is his tone of voice, with the lengthening of the 'o'; finally, (d) and (e) reveal the mood of Shin Chan's mother (whose face is not even visible) through the slow rhythm and the intonation, so the didascaly is necessary:

(a)   (ENFADADA) [ANGRY)]
      ¿Decías algo Hiroshi?
      [Did you say something, Hiroshi?]

(b)   (DESCONFÍA) [SUSPICIOUS]
      ¿Qué quieres? [What do you want?]

(c)   (TIRITANDO) ¡Ay, qué frío!
      [(SHIVERING) Ow! It's cold!]

(d) (CON FALSA AMABILIDAD)
     [WITH FAKE KINDNESS]
     ¿Decíais algo, chicos?
     [Did you say something, guys?]

(e) (CON RABIA Y DESPACIO)
     [ANNOYED AND SLOWLY]
     ¿Se puede saber qué haces?
     [What on earth are you doing?]

7. Results regarding the technical aspects of the subtitles

Below we will analyse the questionnaires to verify to what degree the technical criteria used are functional, and when they require adjustments. More specifically, we will study the marking of the speech-character relationship through colour labels, the length of display on the screen for each subtitle, the preference for presentation of the subtitles towards the bottom of the screen, the use of single-line or double-line subtitles, the marking of suprasegmental information, the indication of background sound effects, and the identification of the meaning of orthotypographical conventions, such as italics or quotation marks.

In general, the individuals surveyed agreed that subtitles helped them to understand the episode, and considered the assignment of colours to mark the speech-character relationship useful (82% of prelocutive and 90% of postlocutive deaf participants). There was, however, a general complaint regarding the use of the colour cyan, which makes reading the subtitles difficult. These data coincided roughly with those provided by the hearing participants, who watched the episode without sound.

Regarding the length of display of each subtitle on the screen, we used the ratio of 8 seconds per 70 characters, thus increasing the established length of display on the screen for deaf and hearing adults (6 seconds/ 70 characters). In this section of the analysis, significant differences can be perceived between the reading abilities of hearing children and those of deaf children: while only 21% of hearing children needed more time to read the subtitles,[21] over half of the deaf children (52%) required more time.

In relation to the placement of the subtitles on the screen and the presentation of the message as a single line or as two lines, both the group of hearers and the groups of deaf participants (97%) preferred single-line subtitles positioned at the bottom of the screen.

Much more considerable differences can be perceived between deaf participants regarding the marking of suprasegmental information: 53% of them claimed to understand little faces ( ) better, and only a small percentages preferred the other two methods (28% preferred didascalies and 19% preferred emoticons represented by means of typographical signs (:-;).

The indication of background sound effects pleased almost all the deaf participants, 60% of whom chose onomatopoeic spellings *(woof)* over the description of the sound *(bark)*. This result corroborated the findings of a previous study carried out by Prada González (2004) among deaf children from an integrated school in Vigo. Nevertheless, it was partly inconsistent with the findings of the reception studies among deaf adults included in this volume (see, for example, Pereira), in which the scales tilt slightly in favour of description. This difference might be explained if we consider that abstract concepts and certain lexical items *(bleat, drilling sound, slap)* are much easier for adults to grasp than for children. The latter, however, are used to 'seeing' the sound represented graphically (in, for example, comics and stories: baa!, brrrrr!, pow!).

As far typographical conventions were concerned, neither hearing nor deaf children seemed sure of their interpretations. The percentages of difficulty are similar in the interpretation of italics and quotation marks;[22] only 48% of the hearing participants and 45% of the deaf participants understood that italics signal off-screen voices; for 82% of the hearing

---

21 That fact that not all of the hearing children were able to read the subtitles is perfectly understandable if we consider that some of the participants were between 5 and 8 years old.

22 Italics and quotation marks were clearly associated with these meanings in the context of the episode. Naturally, they may have different meanings in other contexts.

participants and 71% of the deaf participants, quotation marks indicated the imitation of other people's voices:

Use of italics:
Sinosuke, di a tu padre
que te lave la cabeza
[Sinosuke, tell your father/ to wash your head]

Use of quotation marks:
"Pero yo puedo hacer cosas que
las personas no pueden hacer".
[But I can do things/ other people can't]

8. Results regarding the comprehension and the level of difficulty of the subtitles

Through a series of questions regarding language and contents, we attempted to verify whether the subtitles produced according to the criteria described in section 2.2.1 did, in fact, allow children to understand what was happening in the *Shin Chan* episode, which was the object of study. Obviously, we cannot be as naive as to think that comprehension of the episode depended only on the subtitles. It is clear that, even relying only on the image, any child, hearing or deaf, would be able to understand the basic elements of the story provided that the rest of the child's cognitive abilities are intact. However, certain questions about specific aspects not directly revealed by the frames can provide us with a wealth of information about the aid given by the subtitles.

For the great majority of the hearing participants (98%), the vocabulary was easy and the participants were able to understand all the words and sentences. As a logical result, almost none of the participants (9%) were interested in receiving any explanation of the vocabulary before viewing the episode. The results derived from the answers of the deaf children are rather more disheartening: only 69% of the prelocutive deaf participants and 68% of the postlocutive deaf participants described the vocabulary as easy. 55% of all the deaf participants expressed a desire to receive explanations of the words and sentences prior to watching the episode. As might be expected, those participants who considered the vocabulary most difficult and were not able to understand everything were, for the most part, those who never used subtitles and believed that they read badly.[23]

9. Conclusion

So far, the case study has shed light on the requirements for subtitling for deaf and hard of hearing children. Though more research in that field (on different audiovisual genres (Agost, 1999), among other age groups, with several degrees of deafness, etc.) would be advisable, we think that the present sample – 83 individuals with hearing disabilities and 46 hearers (for purposes of comparison) – is significant enough to establish subtitling for deaf and hard of hearing protocols as far as technical, linguistic and cultural dimensions are concerned. Such protocols will be the core of the next contribution in this volume.

References

Agost, R. (1999). *Traducción y doblaje: Palabras, voces e imágenes*. Barcelona: Ariel.
Asociación Española de Normalización y Certificación (AENOR). (2003). *Norma UNE 153010: Subtitulado para personas sordas y personas con discapacidad auditiva. Subtitulado a través del teletexto*. Madrid: Asociación Española de Normalización y Certificación.

23 The great differences between hearing and prelocutive deaf children with respect to their command of oral language can be clearly seen in the answers to questions on plot comprehension. Hearing children answered more or less precisely depending on the ages, but always using correct Spanish. On the contrary, deaf children's explanations showed the children's huge problems with respect to using oral language. To the question 'Why did Shin Chan's mother get angry?', the answers were "El padre se fadado porque eres muy bajo"/"porque lengaña a moñena y son peligroso"/"porque yo no quiere trabajar" [multiple mistakes regarding lexical and structural levels].

Alegría, J., & Leybaert, J. (1987). *Adquisición de la lectura en el niño sordo*. Madrid: Centro Nacional de Recursos para la Educación Especial.

Álvarez, M. (2006). *Encomenda de tradución simulada: subtitulación para xordos do filme Pocahontas*. Unpublished undergraduate thesis, Universidade de Vigo, Spain.

Arnáiz Uzquiza, V. (2007). *El subtitulado para sordos en España*. Unpublished master's thesis, Universitat Autònoma de Barcelona, Spain.

Cabeza-Pereiro, C., & Báez, C. (2005). En la senda del conflicto lingüístico: La literatura infantil para niños sordos. In C. Vázquez, V. Ruzicka & L. Lorenzo (Eds.), *Mundos en conflicto: Representación de ideologías, enfrentamientos sociales y guerras en la literatura infantil y juvenil* (pp. 567–579). Vigo: Universidade de Vigo.

Cambra, C. (2006). Los subtítulos en la televisión: ¿facilitan a los adolescentes sordos la comprensión de programas? *Fiapas, 110*, 28–31.

Carrera, J. (2007). *La subtitulación para sordos: El caso de las variedades del español*. Unpublished master's thesis, Universidad de Valladolid, Spain.

Carrera, J., & Lorenzo, L. (2008). Variedades de español en subtitulación para sordos: Análisis de casos y propuesta de marcadores. In C. Jiménez & A. Rodríguez (Eds.), *Accesibilidad a los medios audiovisuales para personas con discapacidad AMADIS '07* (pp. 79–89). Madrid: Real Patronato sobre Discapacidad.

Chapa, C. (2001). Elementos no manuales (I): Los patrones labiales en la LSE. In A. Minguet Soto (coord.), *Signolingüística: Introducción a la lingüística de la LSE* (pp. 231–238). Valencia: Fundación Fesord.

Contreras, E. (1993). *Televisión y niños, niños y televisión: Aproximación al estado del arte en la investigación empírica*. Retrieved 15 December 2007, from <http://sdbaro.org.ar/files/formacion/pedagogia/documentos/la_tele_y_los_ninos.pdf/>.

Dapoza, N. (2000). Problemática de la educación de las personas sordas. In X. Rodríguez López, et al. (Eds.), *Primeras Jornadas Provinciales sobre la Educación Bilingüe del Sordo* (First Provincial Conference on the Bilingual Education of the Deaf) (pp. 19–35). Vigo: Asociación de Sordos de Vigo.

Dapoza, N. (2006). Necesidades comunicativas do receptor xordo e consecuencias para o traballo do subtitulador, lecture given on 1 December 2006 during the seminar *Accesibilidade nos medios audiovisuais. O papel do mediador en SPS e AD*. FFT: Vigo.

Delgado, J.A., & Bao, M. (2007). Apoyos educativos inclusivos en las dificultades de aprendizaje asociadas a discapacidad auditiva. In M. Deaño (Ed.), *XXXIII Reunión Científica Anual AEDES 2006* (pp. 151–168). Ourense: AEDES.

Díaz Cintas, J. (2003). *Teoría y práctica de la subtitulación inglés – español*. Barcelona: Ariel.

Díaz Cintas, J. (2006). *Competencias profesionales del subtitulador y el audiodescriptor*. Report written in September 2006 at the request of the Centro Español de Subtitulado y Audiodescripción (Spanish Centre for Subtitling and Audio Description, CESyA). Retrieved 6 May 2008, from <http://www.cesya.es/estaticas/jornada/documentos/presentacion_CESyA.pdf>.

Dorr, A. (1986). *Television and children: A special medium for a special audience*. Beverly Hills, CA: Sage.

Gregory, S., & Sancho-Aldridge, J. (1997). *Dial 888: Subtitling for Deaf children*. London: Independent Television Commission.

Ivarsson, J., & Carroll, M. (1998). *Subtitling*. Simrishamn: TransEdit.

Justo Sanmartín, N. (forthcoming). El subtitulado para sordos y personas con discapacidad auditiva en Inglaterra. In E. Di Giovanni (Ed.), *Entre texto y receptor: Accesibilidad, doblaje y traducción. Between text and receiver: accessibility, dubbing and translation.* Frankfurt: Peter Lang.

Lorenzo, L., & Pereira, A. (forthcoming). Deaf children and their access to audiovisual texts: school failure and the helplessness of the subtitler. In E. Di Giovanni (Ed.), *Entre texto y receptor: Accesibilidad, doblaje y traducción. Between text and receiver: accessibility, dubbing and translation.* Frankfurt: Peter Lang.

Martínez Ortiz, M. (2007). *Subtitulado para sordos: análisis, procedimiento y problemática del subtitulado de Harry Potter y la Cámara Secreta.* Unpublished undergraduate thesis, Universidad de Valladolid, Soria.

Minguet Soto, A. (coord.) (2000). *Signolingüística: Introducción a la lingüística de la LSE.* Valencia: Fundación Fesord.

Moreira Brenlla, E. (forthcoming). Subtítulos para sordos en la televisión alemana. In E. Di Giovanni (Ed.), *Entre texto y receptor: Accesibilidad, doblaje y traducción. Between text and receiver: accessibility, dubbing and translation.* Frankfurt: Peter Lang.

Neves, J. (2005). *Audiovisual translation: Subtitling for the deaf and hard of hearing.* Unpublished doctoral dissertation, Roehampton University, United Kingdom.

Neves, J. (2007). There is research and research: Subtitling for the deaf and hard of hearing (SDH). In C. Jiménez Hurtado (Ed.), *Traducción y accesibilidad. Subtitulación para sordos y audiodescripción para ciegos: Nuevas modalidades de traducción audiovisual* (pp. 27–40). Frankfurt: Peter Lang.

Neves, J., & Lorenzo, L. (2007). La subtitulación para s/Sordos: Panorama global y prenormativo en el marco ibérico. *Trans. Revista de Traductología, 11,* 95–113.

Pazó Lorenzo, I. (2006). *Propuesta de subtitulación para sordos de* La edad de hielo*: Búsqueda de la convergencia entre lenguas orales y signadas.* Unpublished undergraduate thesis, Universidade de Vigo, Spain.

Pazó Lorenzo, I. (forthcoming). La adaptación del subtitulado para personas sordas. In E. Di Giovanni (Ed.), *Entre texto y receptor: Accesibilidad, doblaje y traducción. Between text and receiver: accessibility, dubbing and translation.* Frankfurt: Peter Lang.

Pereira, A., & Lorenzo, L. (2005). Evaluamos la norma UNE 153010: Subtitulado para personas sordas y personas con discapacidad auditiva. Subtitulado a través del teletexto. *Puentes, 6,* 21–26.

Pérez de Oliveira, A. (forthcoming). El subtitulado para sordos en las principales cadenas de televisión en España. In E. Di Giovanni (Ed.), *Entre texto y receptor: Accesibilidad, doblaje y traducción. Between text and receiver: accessibility, dubbing and translation.* Frankfurt: Peter Lang.

Prada González, M. (2004). Buscando a Nemo: *Propuesta de subtitulado para sordos a partir del análisis crítico de cuatro casos reales.* Unpublished undergraduate thesis, Universidade de Vigo, Spain.

Tercedor Sánchez, I., Lara Burgos, P., Herrador Molina, D., Márquez Linares, I., & Márquez Alhambra, L. (2007). Parámetros de análisis en la subtitulación accesible. In C. Jiménez Hurtado (Ed.), *Traducción y accesibilidad. Subtitulación para sordos y audiodescripción para ciegos: Nuevas modalidades de TAV* (pp. 41–51). Frankfurt: Peter Lang.

Lourdes Lorenzo

Criteria for elaborating subtitles for deaf and hard of hearing children in Spain: A guide of good practice[1]

The purpose of the present contribution is to provide a series of recommendations to guide subtitlers in the production of subtitles for deaf and hard of hearing children in a Spanish context. In order to establish such criteria, this contribution has taken as its starting point several reception studies of a children's product subtitled for the deaf and hard of hearing. The product is an episode of the cartoon series Shin Chan, *whose subtitles were specifically produced for this study (see previous contribution in this volume) according to the existing criteria in Spain (Standard UNE 153010 Subtitling for the deaf and hard of hearing. Teletext subtitling, published by AENOR), corrected (Pereira & Lorenzo, 2005) or implemented when necessary (see previous contribution in this volume). The recommendations offered here may also serve as points of departure for future analyses of subtitling for deaf and hard of hearing children, using different methodological tools such as eye-tracking or any other cognitive technology. The recommendations will also serve as a guide which can be taken into consideration when drafting the Spanish Standard for Subtitling for Deaf and Hard of Hearing (Children) for digital television.*

1. Subtitling for the deaf and hard of hearing in Spain: a three-dimensional protocol

In light of the findings of the reception study described in the previous contribution, and on the basis of Standard UNE 153010, its critical study (Pereira & Lorenzo, 2005) and the studies mentioned in the introduction

1   This article is part of the ongoing research project *SDH and AD: First scientific approaches and their application* (HUM2006-03653FILO), financed by the Spanish Ministry of Education.

of the previous contribution, we offer below a series of recommendations to guide subtitlers of audiovisual texts for children with hearing disabilities. All of the recommendations will be discussed and placed into one of three levels of interest: the technical level, the linguistic level and the cultural level.

1.1. The technical level

Speech-character relationship

Whenever technical tools allow it, we recommend using colour labels to identify each character, as suggested by Standard UNE 153010. The only exception in this respect is the use of the colour cyan, which should be replaced by a clearer shade of blue since it is generally accepted to be a colour which is difficult to read.

Length of display on the screen

For the time being, it seems appropriate to apply a ratio of 8 seconds/70 characters (4 seconds/35 characters, 2 seconds/17 characters, etc.), though further studies on this issue should be carried out and larger sample groups should be used. In order to apply such a ratio, and thus facilitate easier reading, subtitlers must show a certain degree of flexibility in terms of synchrony. If the rhythm of the dialogue permits it, subtitlers should try to introduce the subtitle slightly before the character begins speaking and withdraw it slightly after the character has finished speaking. An increase in the number of subtitled programmes will be a significant tool in improving the reading abilities of deaf children since, as the answers to the questionnaire indicate, the greater the exposure to subtitles, the greater the development of the deaf children's reading skills. In any case, reading speed is also strongly related to the ability to understand what is being read, and in order for deaf children to make progress in the use of oral language, educational methods must be refocused according to suggestions put forward by many specialists (see Delgado & Bao, 2007), that is, combining the learning of oral and signed codes. This bilingual system of education would also be extremely useful in any attempt to increase the cultural knowledge of deaf children in general.

Presentation on the screen

Deaf children show a clear preference for single-line subtitles located at the bottom of the screen.

Background sound effects

Not all of the background sound effects should be systematically indicated since doing so would create communicative noise. Only those effects that help to create a specific atmosphere or are essential to understanding the storyline should be considered. If the programme specifically targets children, the use of sound descriptors placed in the top right-hand corner of the screen is recommended. They should be presented in red letters on a white background, without brackets, in lower-case letters, and with an initial capital letter (e. g., Bark).

Types of music

In subtitling for children, it is more appropriate to avoid specific types of music such as sinister music, romantic music or melancholy music. We recommend more commonly used terms, which appeal to basic feelings: happy/sad/horror/action/suspense music. Obviously, this list should be expanded to include other feelings but, in that case, we suggest the creation of a glossary available to all television channels and DVD industries, similar to the one created by the Australian channel SBS, one of the few channels that has an ample database to describe musical types in subtitling for the deaf (Prada González, 2004). A good way to share this glossary and guarantee access to it in Spain would be to publish it on the CESyA website (Spanish Centre for Subtitling and Audio Description).

Suprasegmental elements and information regarding the states and conditions of the characters

Of the three options suggested by Standard UNE 153010 (symbols, emoticons or descriptions of the situation [didascalies] in upper-case letters, within brackets, located before the character's intervention and in the same colour), most children clearly prefer representation of states and conditions using little, symbolic faces (e. g., ☺), probably because images are more attractive to children. This could be an appropriate solution as long as graphic designers are able to offer enough symbols to represent the basic emotions most frequently found in audiovisual texts. Didascalies constitute another quite successful method, although we would like to point out the need to produce unified lists and avoid divergent notations (e. g., SUSPICIOUS vs. SUSPECTIN). As we suggested above with regard to the types of music, it would be useful to publish such lists (which could be expanded as the need arises) on a website accessible to subtitlers (e. g., the CESyA website). Avoid the use of typographical emoticons, (e.g., :- O), whose meanings are difficult to infer, and limit suprasegmental markers to those cases in which the image is not clear enough.

Typographical conventions

While hearing children can rely on sound elements that help them to interpret messages correctly (they understand the off-screen voice indication – italics and/or quotation marks – because they can hear sounds from far away, and because they can identify the characters' voices and their tones even though the characters may not be visible on the screen), deaf children find themselves at a greater disadvantage. There are no sound clues to help deaf children to shape messages (intonation, rhythm, strength of voice). Therefore, special efforts must be made to make the audience aware of the conventions used in subtitled programmes in general (e. g., extra information on DVDs or pages with specific information for deaf viewers in television programmes, where the meaning of each typographical symbol is explained).

1.2. The linguistic level

Spanish deaf children are at a disadvantage compared with their hearing peers. Whereas the latter receive a continuous stream of oral feedback in their foetal period and throughout their lives (exposure to television, conversations, sound information in the street, etc.), the former lack such reinforcement and, consequently, the learning of vocabulary and structures turns out to be a hard process. Moreover, the actual shortcomings of the Spanish educational system as far as the education of deaf children is concerned (see Dapoza (2000) or Delgado & Bao (2007) for more information) make the acquisition of communicative abilities and cultural elements seem like unattainable issues.

For all these reasons, subtitlers must pay special attention to the choices that they make in terms of structures and lexis, continuously asking themselves if the chosen elements will be understood by deaf viewers (especially if they are children). This does not mean, of course, that subtitlers must always limit themselves to a restricted range of grammar and lexis. It means that deaf children must be able to carry out what educators refer to as 'significant learning' (Ausubel, 2000), that is, relate new knowledge (lexis, structures, cultural referents, etc.) to the knowledge that they already have.

We recommend using words and structures that deaf children are likely to know, consulting specific dictionaries for deaf children, corpora such as CREA, or frequency dictionaries. In this sense, the guidance of experts in sign language or professionals specialised in communication with deaf people could be of great use. New terms or less frequent synonyms may (and should) be used, as long as they can be clearly understood by means of the context or the image, so that the linguistic range of young viewers may be gradually increased. At present, the findings of this study and the previous studies analysed seem definite about the following specific points.

Linguistic variation

Any form that deviates from the standard (lexis from a different time period or geographical area, slang, teenage expressions, etc) should be avoided. If any of these elements are included because they are considered necessary for the construction of a character, it must be done in such a way that meanings are made clear through paraphrasing or close synonyms. Expressions such as *flipar* (flip out), *mola, tronco* (cool, dude), *bellaco* or *pelotudo* (jerk in Argentinian Spanish) frequently become barriers that make comprehension of the scenes more difficult.

Ad-hoc neologisms/foreign expressions

Neologisms created specifically for a particular case (e.g., fishicide) and expressions in other languages (e.g., *C'est la vie!, Sayonara*) should generally be avoided unless the context makes them very clear.

Taboo vs. euphemism

Oral and signed languages are not equivalent in terms of taboo words. Generally, we recommend the use of taboo words whenever trying to avoid indirect forms of giving the message, which may increase difficulty for deaf children. For example, in the film *Ice Age* there is a sequence where Sid puts his foot in a rhinoceros's faeces and exclaims (in the dubbed version): *Te habrás quedado a gusto, ¿no?* (You are fine now, aren't you?). Pazó Lorenzo's reception study (2006) proves that it is advisable to avoid this indirect act of speech and, instead, use a subtitle such as: *¡Caga a un lado, por favor!* (Shit out of the road, please!).

Metaphors

Metaphors constitute one of the elements of greatest difficulty for deaf viewers, both those included in dictionaries (e.g., *No veo un burro a tres pasos* (I'm as blind as a bat) and newly created ones (e.g., *No quiero estirar la aleta* (I don't want to be pushing up the seaweeds (instead of *daisies*)). Their use in subtitles is generally discouraged. However, because of their expressiveness and humour, they could be used in subtitled products with didactic aims in an educational context (for example, in collections of audiovisual texts designed for teaching deaf children, together with written materials for prior work on the oral language).

Abstract nouns

We recommend, as Dapoza (2006) does, to avoid the use of abstract nouns as far as this is possible. It is advisable to use *la mujer es feliz* (the woman is happy) instead of *la felicidad se refleja en su cara* (she is beaming with happiness).

Nouns vs. pronouns

Contrary to the recommendations of Standard UNE 153010, comprehension of the message seems easier if nouns are used instead of pronouns although this goes against the economy of the language desired in subtitles. It is, for example, advisable to use *lee el periódico* (he reads the newspaper) instead of *lo lee* (he reads it).

Qualifying adjectives

Qualifying adjectives can be used in subtitling for the deaf and hard of hearing whenever the meanings of the adjectives are clear thanks to the image. If this is not the case, another option must be chosen (e.g., *el perro con pelo* (the dog with hair) is better than *el perro peludo* (the hairy dog) (Dapoza, 2006).

Possessives

Possessive adjectives must be used (*ese es su coche* (that is her car) instead of pronouns (*el coche es suyo* (the car is hers) (Dapoza, 2006).

Quantifiers

According to Dapoza (2006), deaf children do not seem to have problems understanding some quantifiers (e.g., *todo/-s* (all), *poco/-s* (little), *alguno/-s* (some) but they do have problems with forms such as *bastante/-s* (enough) and *unos cuantos* (a few).

Verbs

Avoid the passive voice and participles (Dapoza, 2006).

Affirmative versus negative sentences

Affirmative sentences are easy to understand *este chico está triste* (this boy is sad) is better than *este chico no está content* (this boy is not happy) (Dapoza, 2006).

Comparative sentences

Some studies (Dapoza, 2006) show that most deaf people understand *más … que* (more … than) better than *menos … que* (less … than).

Convergence between oral language and sign language

We recommend choosing, as far as this is possible, those features that are common to both codes (placing sentence elements in chronological order and from the most general to the most specific; ordering the noun phrase according to the structure noun + adjective and the sentence according to the structure adverbials + subject + verb + objects; using closed interrogative sentences; employing the spoken component and repeating a word to indicate habits). In so doing, the decodification of the message will be made easier for habitual users of sign language, without hindering comprehension for oral language users. For a detailed proposal, see Pereira's contribution in this volume.

1.3. Cultural level[2]

Cultural and intertextual referents in audiovisual texts must be closely examined by subtitlers, who will have to evaluate their intelligibility and act accordingly. Ideally, the referent should be maintained, because this will broaden the audience's cultural knowledge. However, this can be done only if the referent is explained through the image, the surrounding subtitles or the general context of the programme.

2. Conclusion

It is obvious that overall comprehension of a subtitled audiovisual text does not rely only on subtitles. For deaf children, image is probably the main way to build meaning. However, subtitles for deaf and hard of hearing children must be seen not only as an aid to understanding the audiovisual text but also as an enjoyable system to learn oral languages. Indeed, one of the interesting findings of this case study points to a better command of oral languages by those deaf children who use subtitles regularly in comparison to those children who seldom or never use them.

References

Asociación Española de Normalización y Certificación (AENOR). (2003). *Norma UNE 153010: Subtitulado para personas sordas y personas con discapacidad auditiva. Subtitulado a través del teletexto.* Madrid: Asociación Española de Normalización y Certificación.

Ausubel, D. P. (2000). *The acquisition and retention of knowledge.* Dordrecht: Kluwer.

Dapoza, N. (2000). Problemática de la educación de las personas sordas. In X. Rodríguez López, et al. (Eds.), *Primeras Jornadas Provinciales sobre la Educación Bilingüe del Sordo* (First Provincial Conference on the Bilingual Education of the Deaf) (pp. 19–35). Vigo: Asociación de Sordos de Vigo.

2   For examples of the cultural level see Prada González (2004), Pazó Lorenzo (2006) and Lorenzo and Pereira (forthcoming).

Dapoza, N. (2006). Necesidades comunicativas do receptor xordo e consecuencias para o traballo do subtitulador, lecture given on 1 December 2006 during the seminar *Accesibilidade nos medios audiovisuais. O papel do mediador en SPS e AD*. Vigo: FFT.

Delgado, J.A., & Bao, M. (2007). Apoyos educativos inclusivos en las dificultades de aprendizaje asociadas a discapacidad auditiva. In M. Deaño (Ed.), *XXXIII Reunión Científica Anual AEDES 2006* (pp. 151–168). Ourense: AEDES.

Lorenzo, L., & Pereira, A. (forthcoming). Deaf children and their access to audiovisual texts: school failure and the helplessness of the subtitler. In E. Di Giovanni (Ed.), *Entre texto y receptor: Accesibilidad, doblaje y traducción. Between text and receiver: accessibility, dubbing and translation.* Frankfurt: Peter Lang.

Pazó Lorenzo, I. (2006). *Propuesta de subtitulación para sordos de* La edad de hielo*: Búsqueda de la convergencia entre lenguas orales y signadas*. Unpublished undergraduate thesis, Universidade de Vigo, Spain.

Pereira, A., & Lorenzo, L. (2005). Evaluamos la norma UNE 153010: Subtitulado para personas sordas y personas con discapacidad auditiva. Subtitulado a través del teletexto. *Puentes, 6*, 21–26.

Prada González, M. (2004). Buscando a Nemo: *Propuesta de subtitulado para sordos a partir del análisis crítico de cuatro casos reales*. Unpublished undergraduate thesis, Universidade de Vigo, Spain.

CLARA CIVERA, PILAR ORERO

Introducing icons in subtitles for the deaf and hard of hearing: Optimising reception?[1]

Although the field of subtitling for the deaf and hard of hearing is perhaps the most widely researched field – and the field which has captured the interest of both broadcasters and postproduction media industry – there is still much research to do to validate the already existing services, and to suggest new and attractive ways to improve these mature services. This contribution proposes a new approach to the creation of subtitles, borrowing ideas from mobile technology and the internet, and applying popularly accepted iconography to subtitles for the deaf and hard of hearing in an attempt to enhance the reception of contextual information.

1. Introduction

In today's Western society we are surrounded by icons and pictograms which are the elements of efficient, and almost universal, semiotic communication. There is no need for any written message to understand what most symbols mean (see Figure 1), although there are still some exceptional cases, in which the message is not always clear (see Figure 2). However, on the whole, when symbols are used, they are used with the aim of optimising the reception of the message. Hence, symbols can be a powerful tool when thinking of ways to offer information in a synthetic manner.

1   This article is part of the ongoing research project *SDH and AD: First scientific approaches and their application* (reference HUM2006-03653FILO), financed by the Spanish Ministry of Education.

Figure 1. International symbols

Figure 2. Photograph taken in Phnom Penh Khmer Rouge
Genocide Museum (Cambodia)

This contribution proposes a new approach to subtitle creation, borrowing ideas from mobile technology and the internet, and applying already popularly accepted iconography to subtitles for the deaf and hard of hearing to enhance the reception of contextual information. After a short introduction to iconography in new ways of communication, general introductions to both subtitling for the deaf and hard of hearing (SDH) and to the representation of contextual information will be provided. In addition, an introduction to the opportunities offered by digital television will also be provided. Subsequently, two different types of icons will be presented: on the one hand, icons which can be used to represent sound context and, on the other hand, icons which can be used to represent characters and moods, a proposal based on a technology called Face Alive Icons (FAIs).

2. New ways of communication: Iconography in mass media

Nowadays, and thanks to the expansion of new communication platforms such as mobile phone technology and the internet, the symbols which represent emotions are commonplace in virtual communication. The word *emoticon* is a compound – portmanteau word – formed by combining the terms *emotion* and *icon*. Although emoticons may be used more frequently now, they have been around for centuries (Zimmer, 2007). In the text below a 19th-century emoticon can be found: the snigger point proposed by Ambrose Bierce.

While reforming the language I crave leave to introduce an improvement in punctuation—the snigger point, or note of cachinnation. It is written thus ‿ and represents, as nearly as may be, a smiling mouth. It is to be appended, with the full stop, to every jocular or ironical sentence; or, without the stop, to every jocular or ironical clause of a sentence otherwise serious—thus: "Mr. Edward Bok is the noblest work of God ‿." "Our respected and esteemed ‿ contemporary, Mr. Slyvester Vierick, whom for his virtues we revere and for his success envy ‿, is going to the devil as fast as his two heels can carry him." "Deacon Harvey, a truly · good man ‿, is self-made in the largest sense of the term; for although he was born great, wise and rich, the deflection of his nose is the work of his own coat-sleeve."

For Brevity and Clarity (Bierce, 1887)

The first emoticon on the internet dates from 1982, more accurately from 19 September 1982 at 11:44 a.m., when Scott Fahlman posted this electronic message to a computer science bulletin board at Carnegie Mellon University:

19-ep-82 11:44 Scott E Fahlman :-)
From: Scott E Fahlman <Fahlman at Cmu-20c>
I propose that the following character sequence for joke markers: :-)
Read it sideways. Actually, it is probably more economical to mark
things that are NOT jokes, given current trends. For this, use :-(

Since then emoticons have been developed and increasingly adopted and nowadays millions of users resort to emoticons to express various moods and feelings. Thanks to online chat programs, blogs and text messaging, people are getting used to expressing themselves, using emoticons and pictograms such as the following:

:-) ☺ (happiness)   :-(☹ (sadness)

Or more sophisticated images such as the following:

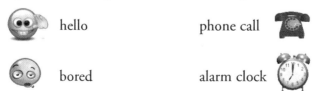

hello   phone call

bored   alarm clock

The use of emoticons in computer-mediated communication is now the subject of various lines of investigations in many fields ranging from linguistics, with available dictionaries (Godin, 1993) and sociolinguistic studies (e. g., Marcoccia, 2000) to pragmatics (Torres Vilatarsana, 2001) and psychology, where, for example, the efficacy of distinct non-verbal cues (Kalyanaraman & Ivory, 2008) and semiotics (Fullwood & Martino, 2007) are examined.

3. Subtitles for the deaf and hard of hearing

One of the main features of subtitling for the deaf and hard of hearing is that sound, which is an integral part of the audiovisual message, has to be represented in some way to make it available for those with hearing problems. Different proposals have been made, as will be described in section 3.2, but technical issues must not be forgotten since such issues can offer explanations as to why some subtitling traditions are so pervasive in the new digital era.

3.1. Analogue and digital subtitling

In analogue television, subtitles are created in text format, using the ASCII codes of the characters,[2] which are transmitted on Line 21 data area found in the vertical blanking interval of the television signal. Teletext has no support for block graphics or multiple pages but it can reproduce up to eight different colours, the use of an italic typeface and also the different icons which can be formed with the combinations of characters such as ;-).

Figure 3.
Teletext subtitles with character identification

2   The ASCII code *(American Standard Code for Information Interchange)* is a character code that uses computer systems to represent texts.

In digital television (DTV) subtitles are sent in separate streams and are displayed as bitmap images. Any image which can be digitised can appear encrusted on the screen as a subtitle. Consequently, the possibilities are endless. Bitmap subtitles offer the possibility of improving legibility and readability of texts displayed on the screen. They also open up new avenues for research (see Arnáiz Uzquiza, Pereira, and Lorenzo, in this volume) with regard to the ways in which images can provide sound context information, which characterise subtitles for the deaf and hard of hearing.

Figure 4.
Bitmap subtitle created and developed by Clara Civera

3.2. Subtitling sound in SDH

Sound is an integral part of the audiovisual message and it has to be represented in some way to make it available for those with hearing problems. Sound may have different sources: apart from the words spoken by characters, subtitles may also represent noises for which there is no typographical representation (e. g., grunting, yawning). Characters may speak with accents or have speech impediments such as lisps. Sound also comes from background music and special effects such as the slamming of a door. These days special effects such as sound blasts in news programmes or laughter and cheering are also added to enhance reception. People may utter sentences with irony or hatred. All these sounds, noises, and music should be represented in subtitles.

Figure 5. TV screen in the UK advertising SDH

According to de Linde and Kay (1999) there are three different strategies to provide sound in subtitles:

1. The use of text labels with the name of the character who is speaking

Figure 6. Label identifying the name of the character: Patrice.

2. The use of icons (such as ♪ ♫) to show that there is music playing or the use of a symbol (such as a ☎) to show a telephone ringing.

Figure 7. Label identifying the lyrics of a song

3. The use of colours to identify speakers, rather than use of text labels

As is visible in the following examples where, in the first screen, we can see two different speakers having a conversation and, in the second screen, we can see three speakers.

Figure 8. Identification of characters using colour

It seems as if the third strategy is the one which has the widest acceptance, even though there are inherent problems (see Pereira, in this volume) and other possibilities such as icons should be researched (de Linde & Kay, 1999; Neves 2005).

All the audible information which must be represented in subtitles can lead to overloading the screen with more text, which, on the one hand, has the benefit of offering valuable information while, on the other hand, may burden viewers with more text to be read, thus reducing the time to search for visual clues. Indeed, subtitles for the deaf and hard of hearing pose a thorny challenge to viewers as far as reading speed is concerned. Spontaneous speech rate in English is believed to be in the range of 140wpm (words per minute) and 160wpm (Kelly & Steer, 1949; Steinfield, 1999; Wingfield et al., 2006) hence verbatim subtitles should reproduce that rate. Recent research (Romero-Fresco, 2009) on TV programmes broadcast by the BBC in the United Kingdom points to the existence of different speeds for different genres. In sports, the average speed would appear to vary from 124wpm to 182wpm, with an average of 160wpm. News seem to be spoken faster, between 161wpm and 198 wpm, with an average of 180wpm. Interviews and weather reports are spoken even faster, and the speed varies from 211wpm to 245wpm, with an average of 230wpm. But viewers read from the screen and they must also look for visual clues. The reading speed of some viewers with hearing problems are also an issue (Neves, 2008). Some studies carried out by organisations such as Ofcom (ITC, 1999) and the Spanish Subtitling Standard (AENOR, 2003) recommend high-speed subtitles, and user associations also insist on verbatim subtitles. More scientific studies and validations are required to ascertain the optimum reading speeds for people with hearing impairments, and ways to offer contextual sound information in a more synthetic manner.

If, on top of the text, there are written labels which inform the speaker of the sound or the mood of the scene, these will add increased numbers of characters which must be read, adding further stress to readers. We shall not delve into any other problems associated with long subtitles but a few of these problems are related to issues such as screen pollution, covering the part of the screen where action takes place, or covering the lips of the speaker, thus hindering comprehension for those who resort to lip-reading (Neves, 2005, 2008).

Watching the visual channel while reading text makes the experience of watching a film or TV programme a stressful and tiring exercise, so the next question would be: how can we make subtitles shorter?

5. Icons

Icons can represent almost anything, and to enhance subtitle reception we would like to propose three possibilities: the use of icons to represent the sound context, the use of icons to represent characters, and the use of icons to represent the characters' moods. However, we would like to attempt to combine the last two types of icons.

5.1. Icons to represent sound context

Internet and mobile phone users are accustomed now to understanding symbols which represent feelings, moods or even opinions. Using these types of symbols in conjunction with subtitles would be a possible solution (Civera, 2005).

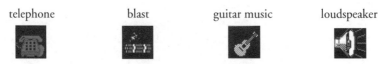

telephone   blast   guitar music   loudspeaker

Figure 9. Symbols developed by Clara Civera

Our proposal would be to develop an iconography which could be used in any subtitling software and which would represent these sounds in an attempt to shorten the written text in the subtitle, hence, optimising reading speed and comprehension. An icon will be seen by itself and will represent the sound.

Figure 10. Icon inserted in substitution for text

In Figure 10 a siren was inserted to represent the sound which can be heard and which was used to announce the arrival of the police cars. In the following figure subtitles have been combined with an icon.

Figure 11. Icon and subtitles created by Clara Civera

In the frame above the text *caminen por los bordes* (walk through the side of the road) is spoken through a loudspeaker.

5.2. Icons to represent the speaker and the mood

The old saying 'an image is worth a thousand words' can easily be confirmed though the use of miniature pictures to signal speaker recognition. This idea was used by the Spanish broadcaster Cuatro in the political debates leading to the general elections in 2008 in Spain. As we can see in Figure 12, two different approaches were taken, both based on the same principle: speaker identification by a photograph.

Figure 12. Speaker identification by photograph of the speaker in the subtitles

The problem with using real-life human faces, as can be seen in the examples above, is that a fixed face with its expression was used for all types of messages. This could be misleading since we could view the fixed smiling expression of the conservative candidate, who is simultaneously saying that the economy is plummeting or that the country is falling apart. Facial expressions are one of the most powerful communication tools, sometimes even more expressive than words, and hence the solution arrived at in the Spanish debate was interesting but it still requires further research.

At present, using real human faces is not possible for three main reasons (Li, Chang & Chang, 2008):

1. Acquisition. Real human faces are hard to acquire. In addition to the privacy issue, it costs too much effort to take photos of each expression.
2. Transference. Real human faces are too big to transfer. The users may use portable devices with limited processing power and network bandwidth.
3. Display. Real human faces are too large to display. There are only small display areas in the portable devices such as mobile phones and PDAs.

For these reasons Xin Li, Shi-Kuo Chang and Chieh-Chih Chang have developed a technology called Face Alive Icons (FAIs) at the Industrial Technology Research Institute in Taiwan. FAIs are a hybrid of existing warping and morphing software. The researchers' approach consists of two processes. A front-facing portrait of the user is first decomposed into static facial features such as the nose, ears, and hair, that is, features that remain the same regardless of emotion (Noh et al., 2008).

The icon is then synthesised with combinations of certain expressional features (such as changes in the eyes and mouth that typically evoke feeling) to create a Facial Icon Profile (FIP).

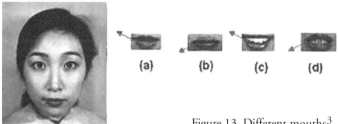

Figure 13. Different mouths[3]

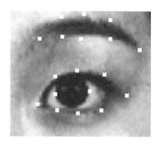

Figure 14. The eye area with 18 landmark points

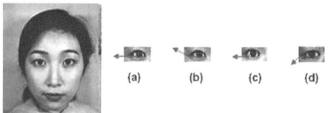

Figure 15. Four different eyes

The software modifies key points, also known as landmark points, of the expressional features to denote different emotions such as happiness, sadness, surprise, anger, disgust and fear.

3   All FAI images have been taken from Noh et al., 2008.

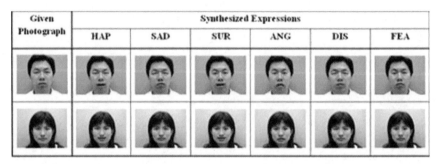

Figure 16. Six different expressions using FAIs

FAIs are still being tested for accuracy at the University of Pittsburgh,[4] where 93 per cent of people were able to recognise a Face Alive Icon for 'Surprise'. However, a lower percentage of people (69%) recognised the icon for 'Disgusted'. FAIs could also have broader applications than mobile communication. Because the icons are actually small files (64×64 pixels), they are well-suited for portable devices but also for accompanying subtitles. This innovative suggestion is in need of much research but as is visible in the next two frames there is scope for its application since mood and character are simultaneously combined in the same image. Though we lack the technology to produce such type of subtitle, we have simulated two frames (see Figure 17) to indicate what our proposal may look like.

Figure 17. Two screens simulating a face alive icon along a subtitle

---

4   For more information regarding tests at University of Pittsburgh, see <http://www.digitalcamerainfo.com/content/U-of-Pittsburgh-Tests-Face-Emotion-Icons.htm>.

6. Conclusion

Subtitles are a complex text structure in which many factors are at play (see other articles in this volume). Subtitles have been on display for decades now, yet little research has been carried out to analyse their reception and possible ways to improve them. While in the past (with analogue broadcasting) there was little room for manoeuvre and improvement, the situation has changed dramatically. Digital broadcasting and bitmaps have provided possibilities for fruitful lines of research and various improvements. Such possibilities are a focus of the research which is being carried out in the European project DTV4ALL,[5] in which we are identifying options both to improve existing access services, such as subtitling for the deaf and hard of hearing and to study emerging access services and the many possibilities there will be on offer to optimise the inclusion of all citizens to broadcasted media in Europe. This article has presented a possible solution for reducing subtitle text and optimising the production of reader-friendly subtitles through the use of icons.

Acknowledgements

We would like to thank both Anna Matamala and Pablo Romero-Fresco for excellent comments on earlier drafts of this contribution.

References

Asociación Española de Normalización y Certificación (AENOR). (2003). *Norma UNE 153010: Subtitulado para personas sordas y personas con discapacidad auditiva. Subtitulado a través del teletexto*. Madrid: AENOR.
Bierce, A. (1912). For brevity and clarity. *The Collected Works of Ambrose Bierce, Vol. XI: Antepenultimata*. New York: Neale.

5   See <http://www.psp-dtv4all.org/> (Retrieved 15 May 2009).

Civera, C. (2005). Introducing emoticons and pictograms in SDHH. Paper delivered at Media For All Conference, Universitat Autònoma de Barcelona, June 2005. Retrieved 1 April 2008, from <http://www.fti.uab.es/transmedia/abstracts/ccivera.htm>.

de Linde, Z., & Kay, N. (1999). *The semiotics of subtitling.* Manchester: St. Jerome.

Fullwood, C., & Martino, O. (2007). Emoticons and impression formation. *Applied Semiotics, 19,* 4–14.

Godin, S. (1993). *The smiley dictionary.* Berkeley: Peachpit.

Independent Television Commission (ITC) (1999). *ITC guidance on standards for subtitling.* London: Independent Television Commission.

Kalyanaraman, S., & Ivory, J. (2008). The face of online information processing: effects of emoticons on impression formation, affect, and cognition in chat transcripts. Paper presented at the annual meeting of the International Communication Association, Dresden International Congress Centre, Dresden, Germany. Retrieved 1 April 2008, from <http://www.allacademic.com/meta/p93286_index.html>.

Kelly, J., & Steer, M. (1949). Revised concept of rate. *Journal of Speech and Hearing Disorders, 14,* 222–226.

Li, X., Chang, S., & Chang, C. (2007). Face Alive Icons. *Journal of Visual Language and Computing, 18(4),* 440–453.

Marcoccia, M. (2000). Les Smileys: Une représentation iconique des émotions dans la Communication Médiatisée par Ordinateur. In C. Plantin, M. Doury &. V. Traverso (Eds.), *Les émotions dans les interactions* (pp. 249–263). Lyon: P.U.L.

Neves, J. (2005). *Audiovisual translation: Subtitling for the deaf and hard of hearing.* Unpublished PhD Thesis. Roehampton University, London. Retrieved 1 April 2008, from <http://roehampton.openrepository.com/roehampton/handle/10142/12580>.

Neves, J. (2008). 10 fallacies about Subtitling for the d/Deaf and the hard of hearing. *The Journal of Specialised Translation, 10,* 128–143.

Noh, J., Fideleo, D., & Neumann, U. (2008). Gesture driven facial animation. Retrieved 1 April 2008, from <http://www.cs.usc.edu/Research/techreports/papers/02-761.pdf>.

Romero-Fresco, P. (forthcoming). More haste less speed: Edited vs. verbatim respoken subtitles, *VIAL (Vigo International Journal of Applied Linguistics), 6.*

Steinfield, A. (1999). *The benefit to the deaf of real-time captions in a mainstream classroom environment.* Unpublished PhD Thesis. The University of Michigan.

Torres Vilatarsana, M. (2001). Funciones pragmáticas de los emoticonos en la comunicación mediatizada por ordenador. *TEXTOS de la CiberSociedad, 1.* Retrieved 1 April 2008, from <http://www.cibersociedad.net>.

Wingfield, A., McCoy, S. L., Peelle, J. E., Tun, P. A., & Cox, L. C. (2006). Effects of adult aging and hearing loss on comprehension of rapid speech varying in syntactic complexity. *Journal of the American Academy of Audiology , 17,* 487–497.

Zimmer, B. (2007). The prehistory of emoticons. Retrieved 1 April 2008, from <http://itre.cis.upenn.edu/~myl/languagelog/archives/004935.html>.

Verónica Arnáiz Uzquiza

SUBSORDIG: The need for a deep analysis of data[1]

SUBSORDIG analyses the subtitling parameters currently used on the Spanish audiovisual market, and, more specifically, compares these subtitling parameters to the different subtitling conventions adopted in other European countries. All the data analysed in the SUBSORDIG project were obtained from detailed interviews with different groups of users and answers provided by these groups in questionnaires, following a bottom-up methodology. Results from the project reveal tendencies that might question the validity of these data. These tendencies are the result of the possible influence of local subtitle conventions on individuals' reading habits and, consequently, on the individuals' subtitling preferences. In order to remove any subjective information from our study, it was essential that we adopt scientific tools such as eye-tracking technologies, which are currently used in other disciplines such as psychology, marketing and medicine, to enable further studies based on objective analysis, and to provide a basis for comparison and proper definition of the technical aspects involved in subtitling. This contribution describes the application of eye-tracking to the study of subtitling and will focus on the steps taken to evaluate and to update many of the technical parameters involved in the process.

1. Introduction

Since its early days, subtitling has evolved in a number of forms and styles into what is now a heterogeneous landscape worldwide. Different factors – economic (Gottlieb, 2005), human (Díaz Cintas, 2000) or technical

1   This paper is part of the research project *La subtitulación para sordos y la audiodescripción: Primeras aproximaciones científicas y su aplicación* (Subtitling for the Deaf and Hard of Hearing and Audiodescription: First scientific approaches and their application) (reference HUM2006-03653FILO) funded by the Spanish ministry of education.

(Ivarsson & Caroll, 1998; Kirkland, 1999)[2] – have progressively and simultaneously reconfigured today's uneven subtitling panorama, turning it into little more than a collection of various – and differing – styles and guidelines available on the market. Having said that, most of these guidelines are the result of arbitrary conventions 'coined' through practice and, in many cases, as is the case with the 6-second rule,[3] the guidelines are based on unknown or, for the most part, non-existent research.

Subtitling for the deaf and hard of hearing (SDH), currently one of the most relevant disciplines aimed at achieving accessibility, is directly affected by such a heterogeneous panorama. In Spain, SDH first appeared on television screens in the 1990s. Yet, it was not until 2003 that the first initiatives for harmonising this growing industry came into effect with the issuing of a non-binding UNE Standard.[4] However, due to its non-binding nature, to the fact that it was restricted to analogue television, and to the lack of empiric validation of all parameters gathered, the accuracy and validity of this subtitling standard has been questioned since its conception (Arnáiz Uzquiza, 2008; Pereira & Lorenzo, 2005).

Similarly, as Kirkland (1999) points out, current SDH standards throughout the world are based on relaxed and open criteria for the application of specific parameters relating to character identification, context information description, colour definition, orthotypographical conventions or reading speeds. Now that analogue television is progressively being replaced by digital television and we are moving towards new technological possibilities and audiovisual products, traditional subtitling standards also need to be revisited since they were specifically developed

2 Kirkland (1999) summarises the current state-of-the-art as follows: "[…] The current style of captions is affected by the limitations of analog television technology and decoder capabilities. Within these technical limits, various captioning practises and policies evolved, creating a "style" of captioning that utilizes a subset of the features provided by the technology. […] there are several options that relate to these matters of style that could be varied to best meet the needs of people who are deaf, hard of hearing, learning English, learning to read, or otherwise able to benefit from captions." (p. 251)

3 "[…] This rule [6-second rule] is being applied in all countries that use subtitles, although no one seems to know why." (Gielen & d'Ydewalle, 1992, p. 248).

4 UNE 153010: *Subtitulado para personas sordas y personas con discapacidad auditiva. Subtitulado a través del teletexto* (Subtitling for Deaf and Hard of hearing People. Subtitling by teletext) issued by AENOR (Spanish Association for Standardisation and Certification) (2003).

for teletext production and the ongoing adoption of these standards seem outdated and vague.

Under this distorted panorama, institutions, professionals, scholars and users have continuously put forward a set of initiatives to update and review the SDH production scene, including surveys, training and regulatory bodies.[5] Finally, in 2005 the Spanish National Centre for Subtitling and Audiodescription (CESyA) was created and its aim was to promote and harmonise accessibility in Spain. But much has yet to be done and research is still being carried out to try to establish a basis for more standardised development in the near future.

It is this context into which the SUBSORDIG project fits. The project tries to look for the necessary framework to analyse current styles by following a bottom-up methodology. A close look at the results obtained, first from a pilot study, and then from the body of research, highlights the importance of data collection and analysis.

The growing evolution of multidisciplinary studies and the need for further research on perception studies within audiovisual translation and accessibility have led us to new technologies. New tools such as eye-trackers can now help us bridge the gap between long-lasting subjective SDH practices and increasing calls for empirically based, standardised guidelines.

2. SUBSORDIG: The project

The SUBSORDIG project was initially envisaged for the research and development of criteria for subtitling for the deaf and hard of hearing in digital television. Its aim is to analyse current subtitling production, comparing examples from the Spanish scene with different practices and styles which are used in other countries. Examples of subtitling guidelines were taken from Australia, Belgium, Canada, France, Ireland, Italy, Spain, Swit-

---

5   Some examples of these initiatives were the issuing of the subtitling standard UNE 153010 (AENOR, 2003); state-of-the-art studies by CMT (Pardina i Mundó, 2000), and the *Real Patronato sobre Discapacidad – "Estudio de Viabilidad del Centro Español de Subtitulado: FASES I y II"* (RPD, 2004–2005).

zerland, the United Kingdom and the United States (see Appendix 1), whereas further information or real production was found in the *Comparative Subtitling* project carried out by the European Association of Studies in Screen Translation (ESIST).[6]

The project, designed for implementing SDH for digital television, focuses on the most important parameters involved in current SDH production on the audiovisual market. It examines the adequacy of a set of local, national and foreign conventions applied to some technical, stylistic and linguistic parameters in subtitling. Examples of parameters are font type and font size, character identification, subtitle placement, linguistic strategies in use – verbatim subtitling versus condensation or reduction –, etc.

Once the desired parameters have been identified, they are applied to the subtitling of different short videos that are presented to three different groups of users – twenty deaf, hard of hearing and hearing viewers per group – for both adult and child audiences. Volunteers are subsequently asked to fill in different personal questionnaires and preference and comprehension questionnaires. This procedure, repeated in a number of cities across Spain (Barcelona, Madrid, Vigo and Burgos), aims to detect and analyse whether differences can be identified depending on the local development and social reality of deaf users within their local communities. Bilingual communities such as Catalonia (Barcelona) and Galicia (Vigo) were represented in the test together with monolingual ones, such as Madrid or Castile.

3. SUBSORDIG: Pilot study

All the data gathered in the SUBSORDIG project aimed to shed light on the formula for the elaboration of perfect – non-customised – subtitles. Therefore, in order to outline the final test and avoid unexpected results, it was first necessary to launch a pilot study with the goal of identifying general mistakes and weak areas within the tests to be conducted.

6   For more information on the *Comparative Subtitling* project and ESIST turn to <http://www.esist.org/projects.html> (Retrieved 7 May 2008).

The pilot study – 'control group' in our research – was carried out with a sample audience – five users per group – in Barcelona and the *Asociación de Implantados Cocleares en España* (AICE).

The three groups[7] which participated in the pilot study were shown the videos and given the questionnaires. Their answers, together with their feedback, were vital in detecting problems and preventing further disruptions in our study. At the same time, new areas of interest concerning SDH elaboration and perception arose when examining the data.

The first problem that arose, and a basic example of subsequent reorganisation which was carried out, concerned the identification of age groups. Throughout our pilot study we were able to confirm the differences between younger and older audiences in terms of subtitling preferences – and even perception – already exposed in previous research projects.[8] Adult viewers – aged 21 to 65 – showed particularly varied choices for the first visible part of subtitles: characters and fonts.[9] Deaf, hard of hearing, and hearers under 50 showed their preference for Verdana whereas older viewers – 50 to 65 – preferred Arial or Tiresias in all three groups. This fact, unexpected when the project was first outlined, led us to redefine age groups within the existing categories. Was this difference caused by habit, cultural or perceptual – sight – reasons? Questionnaires, previously thought to provide useful background information on each viewer's socio-cultural profile, revealed vague answers that frequently did not match results derived from comprehension or preference tests. It was by analysing and processing all the data gathered that the second main difficulty came to light: subjectivity and sociocultural inference.

The direct influence of subjective responses in data collection is perfectly described by Schiessl, Duda, Thölke, and Fischer (2003), who sum-

---

7   Each group consisted of five deaf, five hard of hearing and five hearing adults.

8   D'Ydewalle and Gielen (1992), Kirkland (1999) and Peli, Goldstein and Woods (2005) conducted different experiments to trace reading and perception patterns in young and old audiences. In all cases, common patterns and differences were identified between the major age groups.

9   Technologically restricted by analogue teletext restrictions, font types have traditionally been taken for granted and their application has been limited without questioning their functionality. New audiovisual technologies have brought new possibilities, making further analysis essential. Furthermore, the great differences implied in font type variations make the study of such variations compulsory for any possible modification of current SDH parameters.

marise the problems that these sort of studies encounter when dealing with people's reactions as follows:

> Another well known major validity problem using conventional usability methods arises when testing subjects in an artificial environment, such as a usability lab. Subjects are aware of the test situation. The description and verbalisation of their own behaviour might be biased in terms of social expectations, political correctness or simply to give a good impression. (p. 9)

Although in our case subjects were not confined to a proper usability lab, conditions were far from being those found in real life. This might also have influenced their responses.

As we can see, the presence of subjective thinking might condition research output, making it essential to develop scientific tools that help us to differentiate between instinctive and acquired – or pretended – behaviour in subtitle reading. However, further research is still required to determine the steps and methodologies to be applied for obtaining 'sterilised' data.

4. Further research: Perception studies and eye-tracking

As early as 1992 Gielen and d'Ydewalle (1992) confirmed that

> [...] this strategy [information processing: subtitles + images] is already being developed in childhood and because of long-standing experience it is largely based on automatic processes. Some observations, however, indicate that the reading of subtitles should not be considered as a purely automatically elicited type of behaviour [...] (p. 257)

Thus, taking into account a partly automatic nature, it is then essential to analyse common patterns in reading behaviours to determine a set of basic elements in further research on the topic.

Some other researchers also remark on the lack of information on this abnormal type of 'reading'. Jensema (2000) claims the following that

> [...] Over the last 20 years, closed captioning has evolved from a PBS engineering development project to an established part of the overall television system in the United States. Millions of dollars are spent each year providing captioning services,

but it is still not known exactly where people are looking when they watch captioned television (e.g. at the captions, at the picture) and how their eyes scan the screen to absorb the information. (pp. 275–276)

This statement, also valid for most European countries in which SDH ('captioning' overseas) is practised, describes the real situation of the SDH practice. It becomes essential to adopt technologies that enable researchers to make complete recordings of the viewers' perceptions of the audiovisual product. Nevertheless, ongoing projects are still trying to define successful procedures that help to remove all subjective, individualised, conditioned or acquired behaviours that have progressively marked the subtitling produced today.

This was traditionally questioned, first in film, then in psychology, and now in accessibility studies, and has allowed scientific tools such as eye-tracking technologies – currently used in other disciplines such as psychology, gerontology, marketing and medicine – to enable further research based on objective analysis. Its long-lasting presence in such diverse fields of study provides us with a reliable example of its potential application in SDH. In our project, eye-tracking technology formed the basis for confronting existing SDH parameters with real objectives and instinctive reading behaviours.

Eye-tracking studies date back to 1890 (Jacob & Karn, 2003), although technological developments in search of an accurate methodology for data collection did not make their effective application to subtitle reading possible until the 1970s (Jensema, 2000).

As De Graef, Van Rensbergen and d'Ydewalle (1985) describe:

[...] The eye movement pattern and the attention shift between the image and the subtitles are measured with the use of the pupil-center corneal-reflection method. This method allows the determination of the subject's point of regard by employing a vector, which is continually being calculated between the center of the pupil and the corneal reflection. (p. 5)

Nowadays eye-tracking technology may be found in many different areas and in recent years different fields of research have turned their attention to the use of this technology in perception studies. Publicity, computing, psycholinguistics, medicine and usability are some of the areas to have recently adopted such an accurate tool and applied its results in a number of ways. Within the field of psychology and its psycholinguistic variant, a number of studies have been conducted with a focus on the reading and perception of simple stimuli with ordinary texts or pictures. Within audio-visual disciplines, there have been several projects that have applied eye-tracking to different studies in film perception, revealing frequency patterns in TV and film viewing (e. g., d'Ydewalle, Warlop & Van Rensbergen, 1989; Peli, Goldstein & Woods, 2005).

But, as eye-tracking studies evolve and their research possibilities increase, studies are multiplying, adapting and adopting various stimuli into their projects. Different authors such as Chapdelaine, Gouaillier, Beaulieu and Gagnon (2007), d'Ydewalle & Van Rensbergen (1987), d'Ydewalle, Warlop & Van Rensbergen (1989), d'Ydewalle, Praet, Verfaillie & Van Rensbergen (1991), Jensema (2000) and Kirkland (1999) have applied this tool to analyse SDH perception in recent decades. However, the amount of information derived from all these pilot studies makes further research necessary in the field. Whereas in 1987, d'Ydewalle & Van Rensbergen (1987) claimed that "[…] switching between the visual image and the subtitle obscures to a certain extent the normal patterns of eye movements in reading" (p. 321), three years later Jensema (2000) stated that "[…] In general, people who view a particular video segment have similar eye movement patterns. The addition of captions to a video results in a major change in eye movement patterns, and the viewing process becomes much more of a reading process" (p. 284). Furthermore, later studies based on eye-tracking application to SDH subtitling and conducted by CRIM[10] in Canada have revealed that

> […] Impaired viewers had different strategies not only for reading caption but also for watching the visual content […] We found that they spent significantly less time reading caption than hearing viewers and time allocated would vary not only upon caption rate, but also motion level in images. So any assessment made by hearing human on caption rate while captioning may be inaccurate if based on reading speed only (quoted in Chapdelaine, Gouaillier, Beaulieu & Gagnon, 2007, p. 10)

So, as we can see, although perception, comprehension and reading behaviours have traditionally been the principal key to this type of studies, differences emerging from these projects reinforce the idea that further research is still necessary, especially with regard to SDH and deaf audiences.

---

10   For further information consult http://www.crim.ca/fr/index.html

5. Conclusions

The current international scene for SDH is the result of a wide range of different styles and practices in use. Research projects such as the SUBSORDIG project are highlighting how these practices, however diverse, (in)adequate or (il)logical they may be, are always preferred – within their specific areas of influence – to other possible implemented styles.

Previous and ongoing research methodologies applied to test subtitle reception have traditionally been based on personal interviews and questionnaires on user preferences, but, as we have seen, results derived from such data collection methods cannot be over-analysed as a result of the imprecise nature of the data. The tight bond between practices and preferences, the lack of accuracy and certainty in conventional usability research methods, together with the generalised lack of empirical evidence behind any of the isolated parameters configuring the different subtitling guides, make it essential that we harmonise production styles by following identical guidelines based on parameters obtained through scientific research.

In recent years, the growing inter- and multidisciplinarity and the emergence of new technological methodologies have provided the fields of audiovisual translation and accessibility with empirical tools that can help eradicate subjectivity from the existing SDH guidelines. Eye-tracking, tracing perception through the analysis of eye movements, offers the possibility of gathering accurate and precise data that could help us to maximise – and to increase – reading speeds; to identify 'best practises' in subtitling; to adjust existing parameters, and for the most part, to standardise a practice which, at the time of writing this contribution, remains arbitrary.

References

Asociación Española de Normalización y Certificación (AENOR). (2003). *Norma UNE 153010: Subtitulado para personas sordas y personas con discapacidad auditiva. Subtitulado a través del teletexto.* Madrid: Asociación Española de Normalización y Certificación.

Arnáiz Uzquiza, V. (2008). La objetividad en el subtitulado: Justificación de los parámetros formales mediante *eye tracking*. In Á. Pérez-Ugena & R. Vizcaíno-Laorga (Eds.), *ULISES: Hacia el desarrollo de tecnologías comunicativas para la igualdad de oportunidades. Retos y perspectivas para sordos signantes* (pp. 73–84). Madrid: Observatorio de las Realidades Sociales y de la Comunicación.

Chapdelaine, C., Gouaillier, V., Beaulieu, M., & Gagnon, L. (2007). Improving video captioning for deaf and hearing-impaired people based on eye movement and attention overload. Retrieved 20 April 2008, from <http://members.e-inclusion.crim.ca/files/articles/SPIE-6492.pdf>.

d'Ydewalle, G., & Van Rensbergen, J. (1987). Reading a message when the same message is available auditorily in another language: The case of subtitling. In J. K. O'Regan & A. Lévy-Schoen (Eds.), *Eye movements: From physiology to cognition* (pp. 313–321). Amsterdam: Elsevier Science.

d'Ydewalle, G., & Van Rensbergen, J. (1989). Developmental studies of text-picture interactions in the perception of animated cartoons with text? In H. Mandl & J. R. Levin (Eds.), *Knowledge acquisition from text and pictures* (pp. 233–248). Amsterdam: Elsevier Science.

d'Ydewalle, G., Warlop, L., & Van Rensbergen, J. (1989). Television and attention: Differences between young and older adults in the division of attention over different sources of TV information. *Medienpsychologie: Zeitschrift für Individual- und Massenkommunikation, 1*, 42–57.

d'Ydewalle, G., Praet, C., Verfaillie, K., & Van Rensbergen, J. (1991). Watching subtitled television: Automatic reading behavior. *Communication Research, 18*, 650–666.

d'Ydewalle, G., & Gielen, I. (1992). Attention allocation with overlapping sound, image, and text. In K. Rayner (Ed.), *Eye movements and visual cognition* (pp. 415–527). New York: Springer.

De Graef, P., Van Rensbergen, J., & d'Ydewalle, G. (1985). *User's manual for the Leuven Eye Movement Registration System* (Psychological Reports No. 52). Leuven: University Press of Leuven.

Díaz Cintas, J. (2000). *La traducción audiovisual: El subtitulado*. Salamanca: Almar.

Gielen, I., & d'Ydewalle, G. (1992). How do we watch subtitled television programmes? In A. Demetriou, A. Efklides, E. Gonida, & M. Vakali (Eds.), *Psychological research in Greece: Vol. 1, Development, learning, and instruction* (pp. 247–259). Thessaloniki: Aristotelian University Press.

Gottlieb, H. (2005). Texts, translation and subtitling: In theory, and in Denmark. In H. Gottlieb (Ed.), *Screen translation: Eight studies in subtitling, dubbing and voice-over* (pp. 1–40). Copenhagen: University of Copenhagen.

Ivarsson, J., & Carroll, M. (1998). *Subtitling*. Simrishamn: TransEdit.

Jacob, R., & Karn, K. (2003). Eye tracking in human-computer interaction and usability research: Ready to deliver the promises. In J. Hyöna., R. Radach & H. Deubel (Eds.), *The mind's eye: Cognitive and applied aspects of eye movement research* (pp. 573–605). Amsterdam: Elsevier Science.

Jensema, C. J. (1998). Viewer reaction to different television captioning speeds. *American Annals of the Deaf, 143*(4), 318–324.

Jensema, C. J. (2000). A study of the eye movement strategies used in viewing captioned television. Retrieved 20 May 2008, from <http://www.dcmp.org/caai/nadh7.pdf>.

Kirkland, C.E. (1999). Evaluation of captioning features to inform development of digital television captioning capabilities. *American Annals of the Deaf, 144*(3), 250–260.

Orero, P. (2007) La accesibilidad en los medios: una aproximación multidisciplinar.. *Trans. Revista de Traductología, 11,* 11–14.

Pardina i Mundó, J. (2000). *Estudio sobre el servicio audiovisual de subtitulación para personas sordas o con pérdidas auditivas en el mercado televisivo español.* Retrieved 23 July 2009, from <http://www.cmt.es/es/publicaciones/anexos/subtitula.pdf>.

Peli, E., Goldstein, R. B., & Woods, R. L. (2005). Scanpaths of motion sequences: Where people look when watching movies. *Computers in Biology & Medicine, 37*(7), 957–964.

Pereira, A., & Lorenzo, L. (2005). Evaluamos la norma UNE 153010: Subtitulado para personas sordas y personas con discapacidad auditiva. Subtitulado a través del teletexto. *Puentes, 6,* 21–26.

Real Patronato sobre Discapacidad (RPD) (n. d.). *Estudio de viabilidad del Centro Español de Subtitulado: FASES I y II.* Retrieved 23 July 2009, from <http://www.cesya.es/en/actualidad/documentacion/01>.

Schiessl, M., Duda, S., Thölke, A., & Fischer, R. (2003). Eye tracking and its application in usability and media research. *MMI-interaktiv Journal, 6,* 41–50.

Appendix I

Subtitling guidelines analysed in the SUBSORDIG project

AUSTRALIA: Deafness Forum of Australia (2004). Retrieved 23 July 2009, from <http://www.deafnessforum.org.au/pdf/Position%20Statements/Captioning%20Quality%20V2.pdf>.

BELGIUM: Arte G.E.I.E. (2004) *Consignes pour la preparation du materiel de difusión destiné à ARTE G.E.I.E..* Retrieved 23 July 2009, from <http://www.cst.fr/IMG/pdf/ARTE_2003-12-20.pdf>.

CANADA: Canadian Association of Broadcasters (2004) *Closed Captioning Standards and Protocol for Canadian English Language Broadcasters.* Retrieved 23 July 2009, from <http://www.cab-acr.ca/english/social/captioning/captioning.pdf>.

FRANCE: FRANCE 3 "Un code des couleurs pour comprendre les dialogues". Retrieved 8 March 2007, from <http://www.france3.fr/teletexte/soustitrage/7156388-fr.php>.

IRELAND: Broadcasting Commission of Ireland (2005) "BCI Guidelines Subtitling". Retrieved 23 July 2009, from <http://www.bci.ie/documents/BCI_Guidelines_Subtitling.rtf>.

ITALY: RAI (2002) "Scripta Volant: La Rai per i Sordi", Secretariato Sociale e Rapporti con il Pubblico.

SPAIN: AENOR (2003). *Subtitulado para personas sordas y personas con discapacidad auditiva. Subtitulado a través del teletexto*. AENOR (UNE153010), Madrid.

UNITED KINGDOM: Ofcom (2003) *Guidance on Standards for Subtitling*. Retrieved 23 July 2009, from <http://www.ofcom.org.uk/tv/ifi/guidance/tv_access_serv/archive/subtitling_stnds/itc_stnds_subtitling_word.doc>.

UNITED STATES: DCMP (2007) Captioning Key. Retrieved 23 July 2009, from <http://www.dcmp.org/captioningkey/captioning-key.pdf>.

PABLO ROMERO-FRESCO

D'Artagnan and the Seven Musketeers: SUBSORDIG travels to Europe[1]

The imminent analogue switch-off and the move to digital TV in Europe have pushed an increasing number of audiovisual translation scholars to work closely with broadcasters and users in projects aimed at providing accessible contents in the digital medium. This is the case of DTV4ALL, a EU-funded project involving broadcasters, providers and universities that attempts to facilitate the availability of access services on digital television in Europe. The aim of this article is to present D'Artagnan, the part of DTV4ALL dealing with subtitles for the deaf and hard of hearing (SDH). First of all, a description is provided of the rationale, methodology and timescale of the project, which attempts both to ascertain the viewers' preferences in relation to a given set of subtitling parameters and to obtain objective data through the use of eye-tracking technology. This contribution also includes a discussion of the first results obtained in the UK and Spain, where groups of Deaf, hard of hearing and hearing viewers were shown excerpts from the film Stuart Little 2 *with different types of SDH and were asked to express their opinions regarding formal parameters such as font, size, position and character identification. These preliminary findings point to the existence of some common patterns but also to the existence of many discrepancies between viewers, both across and within countries, which highlights the difficulty involved in the harmonisation of SDH in Europe.*

1   This paper is part of the EC research project DTV4ALL (<http://www.psp-dtv4all.org/>).

1. Introduction: From SUBSORDIG to DTV4ALL

The analogue switch-off and the imminent move to exclusively digital TV in Europe, to be completed by 2012, have prompted a quick reaction on the part of researchers working in the field of audiovisual translation (AVT) and accessibility. Many of these researchers are now working closely with broadcasters and users to examine the possibilities of the digital medium to offer fully accessible contents for people with disabilities. A case in point is SUBSORDIG, a state-funded Spanish project involving six universities and aimed at the development and assessment of a set of appropriate criteria for the creation of subtitles for the deaf and hard of hearing (SDH) in Spain.[2]

At a European level, a similar idea can be found in the *Digital Television for All* project, also known as DTV4ALL. Classified within the Competitiveness and Innovation Framework Programme as an Information and Communication Technologies Policy Support Programme (ICT PSP), DTV4ALL is aimed at facilitating the availability of access services on digital television in Europe mainly, though not only, for people with physical, mental or age-related impairments. Indeed, people with disabilities constitute about 15% of the European population, and the current demographic shift means that whereas 18% of the European population was aged over 60 in 1990, this number is expected to rise to 30% by 2030.[3] Yet, the users of access services such as SDH and audio description belong not only to these groups, as shown by independent user research conducted for Ofcom in the UK in 2006.[4] According to the Ofcom survey, 7.5 million people use subtitles to watch television, of whom 6 million do not have any hearing impairments. It is for this reason that in the written declaration issued by the European Parliament on 26 February 2008,[5]

2   Further information on the SUBSORDIG project can be found in both Arnáiz Uzquiza's and Pereira and Lorenzo's articles in this volume.
3   Communication from the Commission to the Council, the European Parliament and the European Economic and Social Committee of the Regions eAccessibility [SEC(2005)1095] Brussels, 13.9.2005 COM(2005)425 final.
4   For a review of television access services see <http://www.ofcom.org.uk/consult/condocs/accessservs/summary/>.
5   Written declaration pursuant to Rule 116 of the Rules of Procedure by Lidia Joanna Geringer de Oedenberg on the subtitling of all public-service television programmes in the EU.

which calls on the European Commission to put forward "a legislative proposal requiring public-service television broadcasters in the EU to subtitle all of their programmes", specific mention is made of the potential of subtitles to "help with foreign-language learning". In the face of this reality and the above-mentioned imminent analogue switch-off, DTV4ALL is seeking to promote the provision of access services on digital television across the European Union. In addition to providing access services such as SDH and audio description, recommendations to EBU, NEM and other bodies representing stakeholders in the access service value chain should be made so that these bodies can take appropriate action in relevant standardisation bodies and forums.

To meet these targets, DTV4ALL consists of a heterogeneous group of partners, ranging from broadcasters (e.g., RAI, Danish Broadcasting Corporation, Institut für Rundfunktechnik, Rundfunk Berlin-Brandenburg and Televisió de Catalunya) to providers (e.g., Red Bee Media) and the Universitat Autònoma de Barcelona, which is responsible for collating the work of a consortium of universities, including researchers from more than ten European universities. The whole project is being coordinated by Brunel University. The work of the consortium of universities is divided into three subprojects: the Pear Tree Stories, which is looking into audio description, an audio subtitling study and the D'Artagnan project dealing with SDH. It is the D'Artagnan project which will form the focus of the present contribution.

2. The D'Artagnan project

Over two years, the D'Artagnan and the Seven Musketeers project will have researchers from seven European countries working to create one SDH standard, that is, one standard for all viewers, hence its name. In the following sections, an outline will be provided for the rationale behind the project, the project participants, the methodology, the timescale and the initial project results.

2.1. Rationale

As was the case with SUBSORDIG, the rationale behind the D'Artagnan project is, first of all, what Díaz Cintas (2003) describes as a "lack of harmonised consensus when it comes to implementing formal parameters to regulate the provision of subtitles on the screen" (p. 138; my translation). This lack of consensus can be found not only between individual countries but also at a national level and a regional level in the individual countries, and even in different products commercialised by the same broadcaster or TV channel (Díaz Cintas 2003). Scholars such as Ivarsson (1992), Gottlieb (2005) and Neves (2005) concur with this view, which is also highlighted by the European project entitled Comparative Subtitling. Launched by the European Association for Studies in Screen Translation (ESIST) in 2000,[6] this project has contributed to identifying the heterogeneity of the subtitling landscape in Europe with regard to formal parameters such as font, spacing, placement, number of characters, etc.

However, the state of affairs described above cannot be equated with a total lack of active subtitling guidelines. As explained by Arnáiz Uzquiza (this volume), Belgium, France, Ireland, Italy, Spain, Switzerland and the United Kingdom all have a set of more or less official subtitling standards at their disposal. Yet, these standards do not seem to be applied regularly (Arnáiz Uzquiza, 2007) and, most importantly, many of the guidelines have been questioned by scholars (Pereira & Lorenzo, 2005, in the case of the Spanish standards), not least because they are not backed by empirical research (Gielen & d'Ydewalle, 1992). Taking into account that these guidelines have been devised for analogue TV, Neves's (2007) plea for urgent research on this issue in the face of the imminent move to exclusively digital TV seems all the more justified:

> [...] it is worth considering deeper research into issues such as reading speed, readability, legibility (fonts, use of colour, positioning...), character identification, conveyance of sound effects or music, or at a yet more detailed approach, of the importance of conveying paralinguistic information in subtitle form. (p. 30)

In order to carry out this much-needed research, the SUBSORDIG project opted for survey-based reception studies. Data were obtained from inter-

---

6   For further information on the European Association for Studies in Screen Translation, see <http://www.esist.org/> (Retrieved 7 May 2008).

views and questionnaires, in which groups of Spanish users gave their views on different subtitling parameters. Although extremely useful for gauging the viewers' preferences, this approach may err, as pointed out by Arnáiz Uzquiza (2008), on the side of subjectivity, with participants often choosing what they are used to (from habit), as opposed to what is more adequate on different accounts. According to Arnáiz Uzquiza (2008) a possible solution to this problem is the application of eye-tracking technology, which can provide

> accurate and precise data that could help us maximise – and increase – reading speeds; identify "best practises" in subtitling; adjust existing parameters, and for the most, standardise a practise which, up to date, is still arbitrary. (pp. 78–79)

In light of this, the D'Artagnan project presented in this contribution attempts to reconcile both approaches, gathering the viewers' preferences with regard to a given set of subtitling parameters and checking these views against the objective data obtained with eye-tracking technology. Led by the Universitat Autònoma de Barcelona, the D'Artagnan project consists of researchers from seven European countries: Denmark, Italy, Poland, Spain and the United Kingdom.

2.2. Methodology

The methodology of the D'Artagnan project draws heavily on the SUB-SORDIG project, using the tests carried out as part of the SUBSORDIG project in Barcelona and Madrid to identify potential problems that may arise when applying similar tests in the different European countries. Although subject to availability, the aim is to have three groups of 15 deaf, hard of hearing and hearing participants in every country. Given the key role played by age in both the pilot study and previous research (d'Ydewalle & Gielen, 1992; Kirkland, 1999; Peli, Goldstein & Woods, 2005), the participants' ages were restricted to 20–45 years for the deaf and hearing groups and 65+ for the hard of hearing group, as it is mainly the elderly individuals that make up the hard of hearing group. The initial tests carried out in Barcelona and Madrid also stressed the need to gather as much information about the participants' backgrounds as possible, and to take this information into consideration when analysing the results.

The D'Artagnan project is divided into two main project phases. The aim of the first phase is to ascertain the viewers' preferences with regard to a given set of formal subtitling parameters, namely font, size, position, character identification and justification. The film chosen for this purpose was *Stuart Little 2*, based on the fact that it is one of the few films available with dubbed and subtitled versions in the languages of the countries involved in the project. Participants were shown clips with three different variables for each of the parameters referred to above. The choice of these variables was based on a careful analysis of the different subtitling practices currently in use in the countries involved, and especially of their national guidelines. Thus, Arial, Verdana and Tiresias were the three fonts tested; the font sizes were 28, 32 and 36. The positions were bottom, mixed (dialogue at the bottom and extralinguistic information in the upper right corner, as is usually the case in Spain) and top. Finally, characters were identified using colours, tags and displacement. After viewing the clips, participants were asked to fill in specific questionnaires about the different types of subtitles as well as a brief general questionnaire designed to gather background information.

As an intermediate step between this first phase and the second phase, the researchers involved in the D'Artagnan project were also asked to devise long questionnaires to be distributed as widely as possible within their countries. These long questionnaires draw, among other sources, on *Switched On* (Kyle, 1992), a survey carried out in the United Kingdom in 1992, which was designed to gather deaf people's views on television subtitling. Although no audiovisual contents were included in this case, the aim is to carry out a large European study of viewers' habits regarding subtitling, which can complement the opinions of the users taking part in the first phase of the project.

Once the viewers' preferences have been identified, the project will move on to the second phase, in which the formal subtitling parameters will be tested again, in this case, with the help of eye-tracking technology. By doing this, the subjective data obtained in the first phase can be compared with empirical evidence indicating the adequacy of the different fonts, sizes, positions, identification methods and justification with regard to legibility. Finally, once these tests have been carried out, the eye-tracker will also be used to test language comprehension of the subtitles of the chosen film.

2.3. Timescale

For reasons of feasibility, especially with regard to the eye-tracking tests, the countries involved in the D'Artagnan project have been divided into three groups: group A (Italy and the United Kingdom), group B (Denmark and Poland) and group C, the control group (Spain). It should be noted that with the exception of the Universitat Autònoma de Barcelona, which is responsible for collating the results of the consortium of universities, it is individual researchers from every country involved who take part in the D'Artagnan project, not their universities as a whole. The timeline for the project, spanning two years in total, is as follows:

GROUP A: Italy and the United Kingdom;
GROUP B: Poland (Denmark will join the group in month 8);
GROUP C: (control group): Spain

	FIRST YEAR				SECOND YEAR		
				12	16	22	24
TASK 1 – Formal subtitling parameters: LAYOUT							
1.1.1 Font		■					
1.1.2 Size		■					
1.1.3 Character identification		■					
1.1.4 Position		■					
1.1.5 Justification		■					
TASK 2 – Formal subtitling parameters: LEGIBILITY							
2.1 Boxes		■					
2.2 Border		■					
2.3 Shadow		■					

TASK 3 – Formal subtitling parameters: INNOVATION								
3.1 Emoticons			█					
3.2 Icons			█					
TASK 4 – Drafting long questionnaires								
4.1 Drafting comprehensive questionnaires to be completed	█	█						
TASK 5 – Compilation of long questionnaires								
5.1 Compilation of questionnaires and data processing		█	█	█	█			
TASK 6 – Verification with eye-tracking								
6.1 Verification of formal subtitling parameters (phases 1 / 2 / 3) with eye-tracking + comprehension			█	█	█			
TASK 7- Testing language comprehension								
7.1 Verbatim							█	
7.2 Standard							█	
7.3 Adapted							█	
TASK 7- Testing comprehension								
8.1- Final Report								█

2.4. Initial results

Given that the project is still at a very early stage, only group A and group C have started the tests (see month 1 in the first year of the timescale). As a matter of fact, we are only now beginning to analyse results from the tests in Spain and the United Kingdom. In Spain, the tests were carried out by Ana Pereira (Universidade de Vigo) in Madrid and by Anjana Martínez Tejerina and Eduard Bartoll (Universitat Autònoma de Barcelona) in Barcelona. In the United Kingdom, the researchers involved in these tests were Pablo Romero-Fresco (Roehampton University) and Steve Emery (University of Bristol).[7] The methodology of the experiments mirrored what was described in Section 2.2., with researchers initially testing the formal subtitling parameters regarding layout, namely font, size, position and identification. Justification still needs to be tested.

2.4.1. Font and size

The fonts tested in Spain were Arial, Verdana and Tiresias, and the sizes were 26, 32 and 40. As explained in Section 2.2., participants were asked not only about their general preferences but also about specific issues such as legibility, distinction of characters within a word, distinction of two lines in long subtitles, etc. Overall, the preferred option appeared to be Arial 32 (9.36 out of 10), which was favoured in virtually all specific questions and in the general question on preference. Verdana 40 (9.24) and Verdana 32 (9.06) were chosen as second and third options respectively. Particularly noticeable was the general rejection of Tiresias, especially by the deaf and hard of hearing groups.

Using, as pointed out in Section 2.2., Spain as a control group, the experiments in the United Kingdom tested the same fonts but narrowed down the font sizes to 28, 32 and 36. As far as fonts were concerned, there seemed to be an extremely close call between Verdana and Arial, the latter being slightly favoured in specific questions but with both fonts obtaining the same ranking as far as overall preference was concerned (7.4). With regard to size, 28 was the unrivalled first choice of all three groups tested (9.5), followed by 32 (5.4) and then 36 (4.1), which was generally deemed too big. Although further analysis is needed, two key points seem to emerge from these initial results. Firstly, participants once again rejected Tiresias as a subtitling font (regardless of the size). Many of the participants even went out of their way to point out that Tiresias was too chunky or that it stood out too much. This is particularly interesting given that Tiresias was specially designed to be used in subtitles (Silver, Gill, Sharville, Slater & Martin, 1998). Secondly, it must be mentioned that several participants from all three groups commented on how difficult it was to distinguish one font size from another. Not surprisingly, this was especially problema-

---

7   The tests in the United Kingdom were carried out in Edinburgh, given that, at the time, both researchers were employed by Heriot-Watt University.

tic for the hard of hearing viewers, whose average age was 79.2 years, which calls into question the results obtained regarding this parameter.

2.4.2. Position

The results obtained in Spain with regard to the parameter position are discussed in detail by Bartoll and Martínez Tejerina (this volume). Based on the information gathered from the guidelines in use in the different European countries involved in the project, the three positions tested were bottom (the most recurrent one), mixed (dialogue at the bottom and extralinguistic information in the top-right corner, as is the case in Spain) and top position (common in theatre and opera). Once again, participants were asked about specific issues, such as legibility or the distinction of sound and dialogue, and then more generally about preference. Overall, the Spanish tests showed a close call between the bottom (8.8) and the mixed (8) positions, whereas the top position was clearly the least favoured (3.2). As pointed out by Bartoll and Martínez Tejerina (this volume), the choice of bottom and mixed as the preferred positions may be explained by habit or convention, as the former is used on Catalan channels and the latter on Spanish channels. As for the top position, the authors point out that it passed all specific questions on legibility and understandability, but clearly failed with regard to overall preference. Once again, this may be due to habit, given that few viewers are used to seeing subtitles "located at the top of the screen in the opera or in art exhibitions" (ibid.). It is for this reason that Bartoll and Martínez Tejerina suggest carrying out experiments with participants who are not used to reading subtitles to find out whether results would still be the same. In any case, the mismatch between the answers given to the specific questions and the participants' overall preference is not anecdotal and merits further discussion in this article.

In the United Kingdom, the same three positions were tested. The results showed a clear preference for the bottom position (9.2), followed by the mixed position (6) and then the top position (5.1). Although these results also corresponded to the conventional placement of SDH in the United Kingdom, they yielded interesting ideas. First of all, it should be noted that the hearing group consisted of viewers who were not accustomed to SDH or indeed to subtitles at all. Interestingly enough, these viewers regarded the mixed position to be as adequate as the bottom position (both in the specific questions and in the overall preference). Furthermore, it is also worth mentioning that the top position, unfamiliar to most of the viewers, was also highly valued. The hard of hearing group chose this position over the mixed position as the second option, and viewers from all groups made specific comments such as "It would take some getting used to it, but I like it" or "I'd like to see more of this".

2.4.3. Identification

Although the analyses of the results obtained regarding this parameter (character identification by colours, tags and displacement) are still being carried out, some initial conclusions may already be drawn. In Spain, colours were clearly chosen as the preferred option (7.3), followed, at a significant distance, by displacement (3.2) and tags (2.8). Yet, it is worth noting that colours ranked last in some of the specific questions, notably when participants were asked about the best method to identify characters. As it happened in the case of position, the answers to specific questions about the suitability of different subtitling options did not correspond to the answers regarding overall preference, which were largely determined by conventions (colours are used for identification on Spanish and Catalan channels). Additionally, the results analysed so far yielded some more interesting ideas about the participants' views on tags and displacement. Thus, the deaf did not appear to favour the use of tags, whereas the hard of hearing group ranked tags highly and was firmly opposed to the use of displacement.

In the United Kingdom, the results regarding character identification have proven particularly difficult to interpret since no clear common pattern emerged across the three groups. The hearing group favoured displacement and labels (both 7.5) over colours (5). The hard of hearing chose tags as their preferred option (9.1), followed by colours (8.3) and, at a significant distance, displacement (5.5). Finally, the members in the deaf group opted for displacement as their first choice (7.5), colours as second (7) and labels as third (5). In spite of their heterogeneity, the results seem to point to some possible patterns. Firstly, the deaf group seemed happy with the idea of displacing subtitles for character identification but, as was the case in Spain, not with the use of tags. This was in sharp contrast with the views of the hard of hearing group, which opted for tags as the preferred choice, giving displacement a very low rating. A case could be made for the use of colours as an identification method, which is currently common practice in Spain, given that neither the deaf nor the hard of hearing oppose it. However, unlike in the tests carried out in Spain, colours were never chosen as the preferred option by any of the groups, which questions this argument and further illustrates the difficulty of finding one 'best' type of SDH for all viewers.

3. Conclusions

In the face of the imminent analogue switch-off, the part of the DTV4ALL project described in this contribution seeks to evaluate access services such as SDH and audio description and to make recommendations to relevant bodies representing stakeholders in the access service value chain so that appropriate measures for promotion can be taken at a European level. The Pear Tree Stories is the part of the DTV4ALL project dealing with audio description, whereas the D'Artagnan project presented in this contribution addresses SDH. A very small study regarding audio subtitling will also be part of the DTV4All project.

D'Artagnan is thus concerned with the optimisation and potential harmonisation of SDH across Europe as far as digital TV is concerned. The project is divided into two parts and involves researchers from five European countries (Denmark, Italy, Poland, Spain and the United Kingdom). The first phase consists of gathering the viewers' preferences with regard to a given set of subtitling parameters and collecting extensive questionnaires dealing with general views on subtitling. In the second phase, these views will be checked against the objective data obtained with eye-tracking technology. Thus, over a period of two years, the D'Artganan project will have all researchers working for one SDH standard, that is, one standard for all viewers.

Although still at a very early stage, some initial complications have been identified. The first problem is related to the heterogeneity of both the viewers and of the results obtained in the different countries. Although participants in the experiment have been divided into three groups (hearing, deaf and hard of hearing) and all the groups have been narrowed down as far as age is concerned, it is still difficult to have comparable groups across countries and, sometimes, to find common patterns in the results. Another problem arises from the sheer number of partners involved in the DTV4All project, from broadcasters to service providers and frontline researchers. This situation is preventing the project from reaching consensus at a fast pace. However, these are minor drawbacks, which may actually be regarded as advantages. First of all, although comparability and coherence are considered important in the tests, the differences found across countries may reveal important national subtitling (or even cultural) practices or habits, all of which are to be taken into account when analysing the results and indeed when considering how to provide SDH for digital TV. As for the number of partners involved in the DTV4All project, although it may account for slow but steady progress in some aspects of the project's work, the involvement of broadcasters and service providers in the project guarantees that the work carried out by the researchers in the consortium of universities will have practical implications for the subtitles shown on digital TV across Europe.

As far as the tests on formal subtitling parameters are concerned, the analysis of the first results, however tentative the conclusions may be, shows interesting patterns. With regard to the subtitling font, whether opting for Arial (Spain) or Arial/Verdana (United Kingdom) as first choices, all viewers seem to reject the use of Tiresias. Although further tests with larger samples of viewers should be carried out, this calls into question the suitability of this font, which was created precisely for subtitling purposes in the United Kingdom. With regard to font size, Spanish participants chose 32, whereas in the United Kingdom 28 was preferred. Much bigger or smaller sizes were ruled out. Also worth noting is that many of the British participants, especially the hard of hearing ones (aged 65+), found it extremely difficult to distinguish the different sizes (28, 32 and 36), which questions the validity of this particular test for these participants. With regard to position, convention proved to be a decisive factor. Thus, Spanish viewers preferred the bottom and mixed positions (shown on Catalan and Spanish channels respectively) while British viewers chose only the bottom position. Habits and convention may also explain why colours were favoured as the first choice for speaker identification in Spain, whereas the results in the United Kingdom present a different and more complex landscape. Yet, some interesting implications are emerging here. For instance, the deaf, not only in the United Kingdom but also in the Spain, seemed to like displacement and colours, but not tags. In contrast, the hard of hearing clearly preferred tags and rejected displacement. This may be a result

of the age factor. The deaf viewers taking part in the tests were aged between 22 and 45 years old and were used to reading colours and chasing
information on a screen, whether on TV or on a computer screen. The
hard of hearing are generally older and less used to doing this. For them,
tags pose fewer problems for speaker identification. Needless to say, both
groups are potential members of the subtitling audience, which illustrates
the difficulty of finding a standardised form of SDH that will please all of
its users.

Finally, a further comment is in order with regard to the importance
of conventions in the tests. In the Spanish tests on position and identification, the participants' views regarding specific issues did not seem to correspond to their views on overall preference. In other words, whereas they
identified a given method as the best position or the best way to identify
speakers, they then chose another one, usually the one applied in their
country, as their preferred position or identification method. It would
appear that they objectively admitted the validity of a given method but
ended up choosing what is conventional in their country. This mismatch
has also been found in recent experiments with eye-tracking technology
(Tuominen, 2008), in which the viewers' preferences did not correspond
to what had been identified as objectively better by the eye-tracker. In
these cases, and given the aforementioned importance awarded to empirical research, should broadcasters and service providers go with the eye-
tracking evidence and, consequently, against the viewers' stated preferences? Would this not be a form of enlightened despotism, where all is
done for the viewers, but nothing by the viewers? Would it be better instead to disregard the empirical evidence and go with the viewers' stated
preferences, given that they are ultimately the consumers? Although it is
still too early to answer any of these questions, it seems advisable to look
for a happy medium between considering that the consumer is always
right and regarding the eye-tracker as the be-all and end-all of the research. The approach adopted in the D'Artagnan project is to regard viewers' preferences and empirical research as complementary. The initial steps
towards the optimisation of SDH in digital TV on this basis have been
outlined in this contribution.

References

Arnáiz Uzquiza, V. (2007). Research on subtitling for the deaf and hard of hearing: TOP SECRET?. *Translation Watch Quarterly, 3*(2), 10–15.

Arnáiz Uzquiza, V. (2008). La objetividad en el subtitulado: Justificación de los parámetros formales mediante *eye tracking*. In Á. Pérez-Ugena & R. Vizcaíno-Laorga (Eds.), *ULISES: Hacia el desarrollo de tecnologías comunicativas para la igualdad de oportunidades* (pp. 73–82). Madrid: Observatorio de las Realidades Sociales y de la Comunicación.

Díaz Cintas, J. (2003). *Teoría y práctica de la subtitulación inglés – español.* Madrid: Ariel.

d'Ydewalle, G., & Gielen, I. (1992). Attention allocation with overlapping sound, image, and text. In K. Rayner (Ed.), *Eye movements and visual cognition* (pp. 415–427). New York: Springer.

Gielen, I., & d'Ydewalle, G. (1992). How do we watch subtitled television programmes? In A. Demetriou, A. Efklides, E. Gonida, & M. Vakali (Eds.), *Psychological research in Greece: Vol. 1, Development, learning, and instruction* (pp. 247–259). Thessaloniki: Aristotelian University Press.

Gottlieb, H. (2005). Texts, translation and subtitling: In theory, and in Denmark. In H. Gottlieb (Ed.), *Screen translation: Eight studies in subtitling, dubbing and voice-over* (pp. 1–40). Copenhagen: University of Copenhagen.

Ivarsson, J. (1992) *Subtitling for the media: A handbook of an art.* Stockholm: TransEdit.

Kirkland, C.E. (1999). Evaluation of captioning features to inform development of digital television captioning capabilities. *American Annals of the Deaf, 144*(3), 250–260.

Kyle, J. (1992). *Switched on: Deaf people's views on television subtitling.* Bristol: Centre for Deaf Studies, University of Bristol.

Neves, J. (2005). *Audiovisual translation: Subtitling for the deaf and hard of hearing.* Unpublished doctoral dissertation, Roehampton University, United Kingdom. Retrieved 17 July 2008, from <http://roehampton.openrepository.com/roehampton/bitstream/10142/12580/1/neves%20audiovisual.pdf>.

Neves, J. (2007). There is research and research: Subtitling for the deaf and hard of hearing (SDH). In C. Jiménez Hurtado (Ed.), *Traducción y accesibilidad. Subtitulación para sordos y audiodescripción para ciegos: Nuevas modalidades de traducción audiovisual* (pp. 27–40). Frankfurt: Peter Lang.

Peli, E., Goldstein, R.B., & Woods, R.L. (2005). Scanpaths of motion sequences: Where people look when watching movies. *Computers in Biology & Medicine, 37*(7), 957–964.

Pereira, A., & Lorenzo, L. (2005). Evaluamos la norma UNE 153010: Subtitulado para personas sordas y personas con discapacidad auditiva. Subtitulado a través del teletexto. *Puentes, 6,* 21–26.

Silver, J., Gill, J., Sharville, C., Slater, J., & Martin, M. (1998). *A new font for digital television subtitles.* Retrieved 4 August 2008, from <http://www.tiresias.org/fonts/screenfont/report_screen.htm>.

Tuominen, T. (2008). Reception or resistance? Some observations on the reception of subtitled films. Paper presented at *Multidisciplinary Approaches,* University of Montpellier 3.

GILLES BOULIANNE, JEAN-FRANÇOIS BEAUMONT,
MARYSE BOISVERT, JULIE BROUSSEAU, PATRICK CARDINAL,
CLAUDE CHAPDELAINE, MICHEL COMEAU, PIERRE OUELLET,
FRÉDÉRIC OSTERRATH, PIERRE DUMOUCHEL

Shadow speaking for real-time closed-captioning of TV broadcasts in French

Growing needs for French closed-captioning of live TV broadcasts in Canada cannot be met only with stenography-based technology because of a chronic shortage of skilled stenographers. Using speech recognition for live closed-captioning, however, brings with it the challenge of solving several specific problems, such as the need for low-latency real-time recognition, remote operation, automated model updates and collaborative work. In this contribution, we describe our solutions to these problems and the implementation of a live captioning system based on the CRIM speech recogniser. We report results from field deployment in several projects. We also propose a novel approach to measuring shadow speaking performance. The oldest approach in operation has been broadcasting real-time closed-captions for more than five years.

1. Introduction

While closed-captioning of Canadian TV programmes is becoming increasingly available in English (about 90% of televised contents), hardly 60% of broadcast news in French is closed-captioned. For live interviews or reports, the percentage is lower still. This restricted accessibility of information to French-speaking deaf and hearing-impaired viewers is in large part due to a lack of available technologies. The Canadian Radio-Television Telecommunications Commission, a federal government agency that oversees Canadian TV, is aware of the situation and has begun to take action by compelling Canadian broadcasters to improve both the quantity and quality of their closed-captioning, particularly for live broadcasts. By the end of 2010, all French and English programmes will have to be closed-captioned.

In this context, a first prototype was produced in a joint project involving the GTVA Network (the largest North American French private television network) and CRIM's speech recognition team to adapt CRIM's transducer-based large vocabulary French speech recogniser. Trial broadcasts started in 2003 and live news captions have been broadcast on a regular basis since February 2004. Since then, our system has been evaluated in trials for the captioning of Canada's House of Commons parliamentary debates, and it is currently producing live captioning of RDS (*Réseau des sports*, a national sports network) NHL Saturday night hockey games.

Shadow speakers, who listen to the original audio, interpret the audio and repeat it to the system, circumventing the problems of difficult acoustics and speaker variability. Even then, reaching acceptable accuracy under low-latency constraints and evolving news topics remains a challenging problem for current speech recognition technology. We will first describe the system architecture and initial recognition setup. Subsequently, we will look at the methods that we have developed to maintain and enhance initial performance for several years through automated vocabulary, language and acoustic model updates. Finally, we will report on results from three ongoing live captioning projects.

2. Architecture

The overall closed-captioning process proceeds along the following steps. Audio is sourced from a newscaster to a shadow speaker, who repeats the spoken content. The respoken audio is then sent over a computer network to a speech recogniser, which produces transcriptions that are filtered, formatted and fed to the broadcaster's closed caption encoder.

The architecture (see Figure 1) has been designed to allow several shadow speakers to collaborate, during a live session, through a lightweight user interface running on each speaker workstation, a shared database, a speech recognition server and encoder servers, which dispatch captions to Line 21 encoders, all communicating through a TCP/IP-based protocol. System components can be physically located anywhere on the network, which facilitates captioning of remote sites.

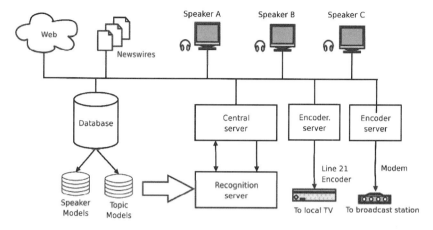

Figure 1. Closed-captioning system architecture

2.1. Server side

The database is the central repository for words and their pronunciations. It tracks the dynamic statuses of words, their associations with topics and their origins. It is also used for administrative tasks such as user profile management and logins.

A captioning 'configuration' is defined as a quadruple CTR = {T, V_T, G_T, A_R}: a topic T, the set of words V_T currently active for this topic (vocabulary), the language model G_T associated with this topic, and an acoustic model A_R for a speaker R. Before a live captioning session, a number of configurations are preloaded in memory, so that switching between topics and speakers happens instantly during the session.

The recognition server handles all speech-related tasks such as recognition, acoustic model adaptation, grapheme-to-phoneme conversion and the storage of recordings. The CRIM recognition engine uses a precompiled, fully context-dependent finite-state transducer (Brousseau et al., 2003) and runs in a single pass at 0.7 times real-time (on average) on a Pentium Xeon 2.8 GHz CPU. There is a minimum delay of one second and a maximum delay of two seconds between the input shadow speech and the text output.

2.2. Client side

The user interface (Figure 2) runs on each shadow speaker workstation and provides user main functionalities: pre-production, production and post-production.

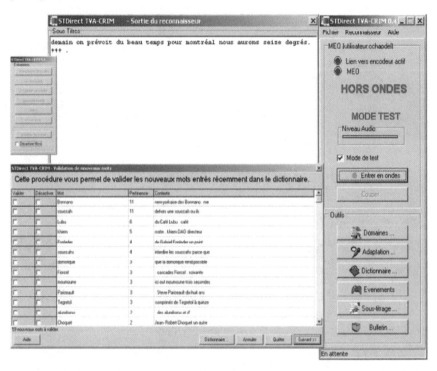

Figure 2. Shadow speaker workstation client software

In the pre-production stage, shadow speakers use the dictionary editor interface to verify the pronunciation of words, to check word association with topics, to add new words or to validate new entries proposed daily by the system. They also select an encoder configuration (which will establish a modem connection if needed).

During live production, shadow speakers listen and repeat through a head-mounted headphone/microphone combination connected to the workstation. They change topics, insert punctuation, indicate speaker turns and insert other symbols while speaking and do so by using a video-game control pad.

After the session has ended, shadow speakers use a correction interface to listen to their recorded voice and correct any recognition errors. These data are stored and are used later for the supervised adaptation of acoustic and language models.

3. System initialisation

In this section we describe the baseline models that served as the starting point of the French broadcast news system. Section 4 will then describe how the baseline system is adapted every night to yield the actual production system used in everyday operations.

3.1. Acoustic models

Baseline acoustic models are speaker-independent, gender-dependent, continuous Hidden Markov Models (HMM are models used in all state-of-the-art speech recogniser), with 5535 cross-word triphone models sharing 1606 state output distributions, each a mixture model of 16 Gaussians with individual diagonal covariances.

Input parameters are 39-dimensional vectors of 13 static MFCC plus energy with first- and second-order derivatives. The models were trained on the *Transtalk* database, which contains 40 hours of clean speech read by 30 French Canadian speakers.

3.2. Language model

The starting point for the language model is a collection of French Canadian newspapers, news reports collected from the Web and broadcaster news archives. This collection provided us with a total of 175 million words of text. Here, we describe the procedure used to estimate language models for the news domain. Other domains, such as parliamentary debates and hockey games, follow the same procedure but use fewer sub-topics.

News texts are automatically classified into eight pre-defined topics: *culture, economy, world, national, regional, sports, weather, traffic* using a Naive Bayes classifier (Schapire & Singer, 2000) trained on topic-labelled newspapers articles. For each topic, larger text sources are also ordered chronologically to be partitioned into older and newer data sets.

A different mixed-case vocabulary is selected for each topic using counts weighted by source size (Matsui, Segi, Kobayashi, Imai & Ando, 2001). For each vocabulary, pronunciations are derived using a rule-based phonetiser augmented with a set of exceptions added by hand. The phoneme inventory contains 37 French phonemes and 6 English phonemes.

Using topic-specific vocabularies, a 3-gram language model is estimated for each time/topic partition. Another 3-gram generic language model is also estimated by merging all topics together. The most recent 1% of the texts is withheld from training, and topic- and time-dependent and generic language models are interpolated together to optimise perplexity of these data, to yield 8 topic-specific language models. Finally, language models are pruned to a reasonable size using entropy-based pruning (Stolcke, 1998).

For weather and traffic, no adequate written source could be found to train a language model. We resorted to synthetic texts produced from a grammar generalised from a few examples and from manual transcriptions. Using even such a small amount of in-domain data resulted in better language models than using a more general topic model such as *regional*.

4. System update

The topics, words, vocabularies, and pronunciations from the baseline system are entered into the database to form the initial captioning system. From that point onwards, the database content will evolve in time as a result of automatic updates and manual corrections, and all recognition models will be derived from the content of the database.

4.1. Unsupervised vocabulary adaptation

In the news, words are introduced every day. Names such as *Katrina* or *tsunami* appear suddenly while others fade out of frequent usage. Yet, out-of-vocabulary (OOV) words are an important component of the word error rate. Substituting a place or a person's name has a worse effect on under-standing than using the wrong number or gender agreement (another fre-quent source of errors in French). Thus, it is important that new words are automatically added to each topic vocabulary every day. This adaptation is unsupervised, in the sense that word-topic associations are not given *a priori*, but must be estimated by the adaptation procedure itself.

The system uses a configurable web crawler, which extracts texts from a number of websites, newswire feeds and the broadcaster's internal ar-chives. These texts are stored in an XML database together with meta-data collected by the crawler. The topic classifier (see Section 3.2) assigns to each text a probability for each topic.

Each day, newly collected texts are compared against the current topic-specific vocabularies (captions corrected in post-production are also con-sidered a source of text). Potential new words are passed through a series of garbage filters and are automatically accepted, automatically rejected or accepted temporarily but proposed to the user for acceptance.

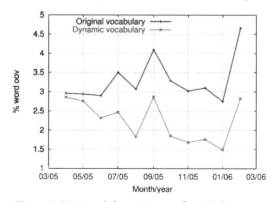

Figure 3. Static and dynamic out-of-vocabulary rates

The crawler retrieves about one million words of text every night. On average 6000 of these words are unknown to the system, but only 200 words or so will survive the garbage filters and be added to the database and proposed to the user for verification.

Associations between words and topics have limited lifetimes, so words become inactive in a topic after 60 days. Words from the initial baseline vocabularies never become inactive. In this way vocabularies never grow too large or too small.

Figure 3 illustrates the evolution, over almost a year, of the out-of-vocabulary rate for a 20K word topic-independent vocabulary, relative to the reference texts (corrected captions). The full line shows the static vocabulary OOV rate obtained for the unchanging initial vocabulary. The dashed line shows the dynamic vocabulary OOV rate obtained when the vocabulary is updated every day. The vocabulary update is effective, allowing the dynamic vocabulary to produce only around half the static vocabulary OOV rate towards the end of the period.

4.2. Unsupervised language model adaptation

Language models must be adapted in two ways. First, new words must be provided with an adequate language model probability even if they have not been seen in training. Second, all probabilities in the language model, including higher-order n-grams, should be adapted to reflect changes in word usage. Both of these adaptations can use only a small amount of text collected in the last few days, or no data at all in the case of new words added directly by the user. In both cases, adaptation is unsupervised, in the sense that adaptation text has to be classified into topics automatically by the web crawler.

We interpolate the existing language model unigrams with a unigram model estimated from the adaptation data (before interpolation, in each unigram model, words in the vocabulary that were not observed in training are assigned the same probability as the least frequently observed word in the model). Then, higher-order n-gram probabilities in the background model are adjusted using minimum discriminant estimation (MDE), which finds an adapted language model that is as close as possible (in the Kullback-Leibler sense) to the background model and has the adaptation unigram probabilities as its marginal distribution (Niesler & Willett, 2002). This procedure has been found to provide good recognition of words added with very small amounts of context (such a the list of hockey players in a team that was not part of the training set) while not degrading the accuracy for already well-trained words.

4.3. Acoustic model incremental adaptation

Acoustic models are subject to gradual performance degradation over long time periods, In addition, changes in the acoustic environment (noise, wall reverberation), voice or microphone positioning also affect the recognition performance. To counter these effects, we use both short-term and long-term adaptation of the speaker-dependent models.

Short-term adaptation (also called *session adaptation*) is done at the beginning of each captioning session. A short news extract is played and repeated by the shadow speaker so that an MLLR transform can be estimated (Leggetter & Woodland, 1995). This procedure does not substantially affect average accuracy, but it reduces variations in error rate across captioning sessions.

Long-term adaptation is performed every night. Audio and text from the day's production of each shadow speaker are aligned using its current model. If enough aligned data have accumulated for a speaker since its model was last updated (typically 40 minutes are required), its model undergoes an MLLR transformation (Leggetter & Woodland, 1995) followed by an MAP adaptation (Gauvain & Lee, 1994). A small part of the data (five minutes) is held out. If its likelihood is improved, the adapted model becomes the current model. If there is no update, the data are kept available for subsequent training. Using an MAP adaptation scheme guarantees that, over long periods, the adapted model will asymptotically converge to the maximum likelihood model. At the time of enrolment, new shadow speakers start with a copy of the gender-dependent model.

4.4. Real-time correction

CRIM has developed a correction module (Cardinal, Boulianne, Comeau & Boisvert, 2007) that allows a user to intercept the real-time caption stream and correct it before broadcasting. The correction software allows editing of the closed-captions by intercepting them while they are being sent to the encoder. Both assisted and manual corrections can be applied to the word stream. Assisted correction reduces the number of operations by presenting a list of alternate words, so that a correction can be carried out with a simple mouse click. Manual correction requires editing the word to be changed and is more expensive in terms of delay. Consequently, the number of these

operations should be reduced to a strict minimum. The user interface
shown in Figure 4 has been designed with this consideration in mind.

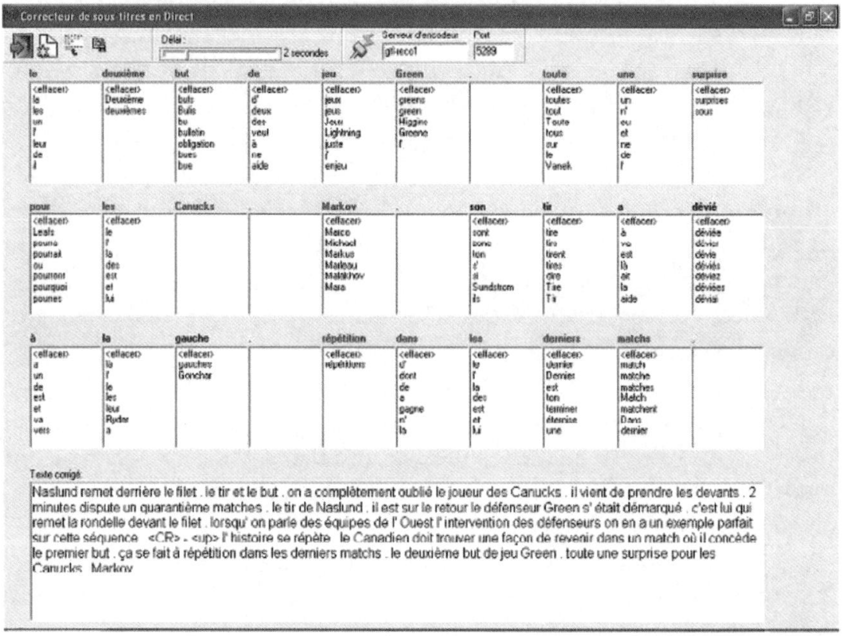

Figure 4. Corrector software interface

A test with a 30-minute hockey game description was set up with two user
delays: 2 and 15 seconds (Table 1). It shows that the word error rate (WER)
is reduced from 6.8% to 6.1% and from 6.2% to 2.5% in a context of
2-second and 15-second user delay respectively.

	Delay	
	2 seconds	15 seconds
Test duration	30 minutes	8 minutes
# of words	4631	1303
# of editions	21	28
WER before	6.8%	6.2%
WER after	6.1%	2.5%
GAIN (relative %)	8.1%	58.7%

Table 1. Error Rate after user correction

5. Results

In this section we summarise results obtained over a period of a few years, while producing closed-captions in live trials in the course of three research projects.

The first project goal was closed-captioning live parts of the three daily news shows broadcast by GTVA, the largest North American French private network. This is the most complex task, requiring the eight topics mentioned in Section 3.2. Captioning has been done on-site, with GTVA-trained personnel, since February 2004.

The second project is the captioning of Canada's House of Commons (HoC) parliamentary debates. This is a more restricted domain, but captions must be verbatim. In addition, shadow speakers mostly work on French coming from simultaneous translation, as parliament members use French only one third of the time. Simultaneous translation is more difficult to repeat due to hesitations and abrupt changes in speaking rate. Several trials have taken place since February 2002.

The third project, with the national sports network (RDS), was started in October 2005, and provides closed-captions for NHL Saturday night hockey games with Montreal's Canadiens. Two topics are required, one for the description of the game in action, and the other for more general interviews and reports between periods. Game action descriptions *must* be summarised by the shadow speakers because captioning becomes unreadable at rates greater than 200 words per minute.

5.1. Shadow speaking results

We observed that a person with no previous experience attains a good performance in less than three weeks of practice with the system. Figure 5 was obtained when we introduced the new task of hockey games to our speakers. It shows a typical rate of progress for a new task or new shadow speakers.

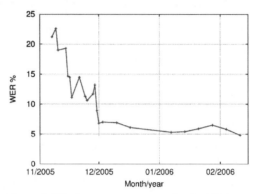

Figure 5. Word error rate progress for the RDS project

Shadow speakers can work for relatively long periods without a break, depending on the task difficulty. In general, they introduce a delay of one second or less and relay each other every 15 to 20 minutes.

Respoken speech is more difficult to recognise than read speech. We suspect phenomena like the Lombard effect, interference in speech planning and wider speaking rate variations to be among the factors explaining this phenomenon. A five per cent word error rate when reading typically jumps to 20% at first when respeaking.

In some applications, summarisation is essential to making captions readable, but the additional cognitive load can reduce accuracy. Similarly, spontaneous speech in live reports or discussions may require a 'simultaneous translation' to a language closer to the written form in order to be readable in captions.

5.2. Recognition accuracy

Table 1 summarises the characteristics of current language models and vocabularies. In Table 2, we report recognition error rates following the usual convention of counting insertion, substitution and deletion errors relative to a reference text that corresponds to the words *actually spoken by the shadow speaker*, obtained by manual correction of the speech recogniser output. Errors as a result of homophony are counted, but capitalisation errors are not. We did not explore the use of on-the-fly editing (Ando, Imai, Kobayashi, Isono & Nakabayashi, 2000), although some other applications could tolerate a longer delay in exchange for error-free captions.

In all these projects, closed-captions were presented to panels of deaf and hard of hearing viewers and they received good comments. As a rough comparison, the actual live captioning of nine US news programmes was observed to have an average word error rate of 11.9% using the same metric (Martone, Taskiran & Delp, 2004).

Topic	V_t	OOV	G arcs	Ppx
news_culture	38 K	1.3%	889 K	114
news_economy	28 K	1.0%	870 K	95
news_world	28 K	1.4%	887 K	86
news_national	30 K	1.2%	884 K	106
news_regional	30 K	1.3%	884 K	106
news_sports	25 K	1.2%	893 K	125
news_traffic	20 K	1.9%	484 K	83
news_weather	20 K	1.4%	448 K	72
news_inter	23 K	1.8%	2.3 M	70
hockey_game	23 K	1.6%	2.3 M	54
hoc_debates	21 K	1.0%	2.4 M	55

Table 2. Vocabulary size, out-of-vocabulary rate, number of language

Project	Measurement period	Hours	Words	WER
GTVA	11/2005–12/2005	26	83 K	11.0%
HoC	09/2005–11/2005	20	163 K	8.8%
RDS	12/2005–03/2006	33	195 K	7.2%

Table 3. Results obtained during live trial periods

6. End-to-end performance metric

In a real situation, shadow speakers will correct input errors such as repetitions. They will wrap up dialogue with high word rate to facilitate the reading, will substitute words that are not recognised by the recogniser or difficult to understand for a specific clientele such as children, etc. Shadow speakers will also make errors by mispronunciation, by skipping words, by incorrectly relocating words, etc. Some of the changes introduced by the shadow speakers should be counted as errors, but others should not when they preserve the original meaning.

When we evaluate performance with the word error rate (WER) metric, we use the shadow speaker text as a reference. Thus, we calculate the performance of only the speech recogniser. We estimate how accurately a recogniser is able to convert shadow speaker speech into text. The whole performance of the process of respeaking by a shadow speaker as well as converting respoken speech into text by a speech recogniser as shown in Figure 6 is not taken into account when evaluating WER.

If we use the original speech transcript as a reference, WER will take into account both shadow speaker and speech recogniser errors. But it will also count as errors any summarisation or rephrasing done by the shadow speaker since it cannot distinguish between incorrect substitutions and correct ones which preserve the original meaning. Unfortunately, even with verbatim text, WER cannot tell us which errors come from the shadow speaker and which come from the speech recogniser. In addition, hesitations and restarts in the original speech, which were correctly removed by the shadow speaker, will still be counted as errors.

In order to evaluate both shadow speaker and recogniser performances, we are proposing the end-to-end (ETE) performance metric. ETE is a metric for comparing an original text with text uttered by a shadow speaker and converted by a speech recogniser (caption), ignoring differences that preserve meaning.

Shadow Speaker   Speech Recognizer
Performance   Performance

Figure 6. Left is original speech, middle is shadow speaker speech, right is closed-caption

To evaluate the ETE metric, we first automatically align a verbatim transcript of the original speech with the shadow speaker text. This is achieved with an algorithm based on the Levenstein distance or by using the Wagner-Fisher algorithm. Figure 7 shows an example of an alignment. The shadow speaker text is obtained by manually correcting the speech recogniser output.

Figure 7. Example of automatic alignment between verbatim text (left column) and corrected text from shadow speaker speech (right column)

Graphical comparison software is used to highlight misaligned text. In the example of Figure 7, the first misalignment consists of *C'est pour ça qu'il s'y oppose* vs. *C'est pourquoi il s'y oppose*. Both utterances have the same meaning. For this example, the shadow speaker has decided to use different words. The second misalignment shows *Opposition* vs. *Monsieur le Président*.

Opposition was deleted. In this situation, *Opposition* was deleted since it was displayed on the television and the shadow speakers had the directive of not repeating displayed text. The third misalignment consists of *La vérité, Monsieur le Président, …* vs. *Monsieur le Président. La vérité …* It is explained by phrase inversion produced by the shadow speaker and should not be considered as an error. The last misalignment consists of *de rendre* vs. *pour entre.* This misalignment is probably a speech recogniser error.

By aligning verbatim text with caption text, one could mediate and explain (at least guess) where the error has come from (from the shadow speaker or the speech recogniser). To confirm the source of errors a mediator is required. The mediator has the task of processing and identifying the type of errors as well as its gravity on the quality of performance. For this reason, we suggest that mediation should be realised by a deaf or hard of hearing person. When this mediation process has been completed, we can count the number of errors introduced by the shadow speaker as well those introduced by the speech recogniser.

7. Conclusion

Our speech recognition-based captioning system has been deployed successfully in the course of several projects. It has demonstrated its self-maintaining capability over long periods of time. Because shadow speakers can be trained in a short time, the system is already a viable solution for rapidly increasing the amount of closed-captioned programming. We are currently investigating its use to produce offline captions in quasi real time.

8. Acknowledgments

This work was funded in part by GTVA, CANARIE Inc. and the Canada Heritage Fund for New Media Research Networks, and in partnership with the *Regroupement Québécois pour le sous-titrage*, an association which promotes deaf and hard of hearing rights to closed-captioning.

References

Ando, A., Imai, T., Kobayashi, A., Isono, H., & Nakabayashi, K. (2000). Real-time transcription system for simultaneous subtitling of Japanese broadcast news programs. *IEEE Trans. Broadcasting*, 46(3), 189–196.

Brousseau, J., Beaumont, J.-F., Boulianne, G., Cardinal, P., Chapdelaine, C., Comeau, M., et al. (2003). Automated closed-captioning of live TV broadcast news in French. *Proceedings of the 8th European Conference on Speech Communication and Technology (Eurospeech 2003/Interspeech 2003)*, 1245–1248.

Cardinal, P., Boulianne, G., Comeau, M., & Boisvert, M. (2007). Real-time correction of closed-captions. *Proceedings of 45th Annual Meeting of the Association for Computational Linguistics*, 2007, 113–116.

Gauvain, J.-L., & Lee, C. H. (1994). Maximum *a posteriori* estimation for multivariate Gaussian mixture observations of Markov chains. *IEEE Trans. SAP*, *2*, 291–298.

Leggetter, C., & Woodland, P. (1995). Maximum likelihood linear regression for speaker adaptation of continuous density hidden Markov models. *Computer Speech and Language*, *9*, 171–185.

Martone, A., Taskiran, C., & Delp, E. (2004). Automated closed-captioning using text alignment. *Proc. SPIE Int. Conf. on Storage and Retrieval Methods and Applications for Multimedia*, 108–116.

Matsui, A., Segi, H., Kobayashi, A., Imai, T., & Ando, A. (2001). *Speech recognition of broadcast sports news*. Tech. Rep. No. 472, NHK Laboratories.

Niesler, T., & Willett, D. (2002). Unsupervised language model adaptation for lecture speech transcription. *Proceedings of the International Conference on Acoustics, Speech, and Signal Processing (ICASSP)*, 1413–1416.

Schapire, R. E., & Singer, Y. (2000). Boostexter: A boosting-based system for text categorization. *Machine Learning*, *39*(2/3), 135–168.

Stolcke, A. (1998). Entropy-based pruning of backoff language models. *Proceedings DARPA Broadcast News Transcription and Understanding Workshop*, 270–274.

Álvaro Pérez-Ugena, Ricardo Vizcaíno-Laorga,
Deborah Rolph

Subtitles for the deaf and hard of hearing within a virtual avatar environment: ULISES

Subtitling for the deaf and hard of hearing (SDH) is a great complement when used within virtual avatar environments. However, much research needs to be done in order to ascertain the optimal formal features required to ensure the best possible reception among users. Avatar subtitles do not require the same format as subtitles used in other media such as digital TV or DVD. The ULISES project (Utilización Lógica e Integrada del Sistema Europeo de Signos/Señas, *The logical and integrated use of the European System of Sign Language) is an accessible initiative to help the deaf and hard of hearing through the use of virtual avatars and two other tools to enhance understanding: subtitles and contextual pictures. This contribution describes the ULISES project and indicates some features which may prove useful for SDH when used in conjunction with avatars.*

1. Introduction

The ULISES project (*Utilización Lógica e Integrada del Sistema Europeo de Signos/Señas,* The logical and integrated use of the European System of Sign Language) is an accessible project which marks the first step in the development of an avatar oriented towards meeting the needs of the deaf-signing community. Help that members of this community often do not receive because of their minority status. The original project proposed the development of a prototype that would allow, by means of a virtual interpreter (a so-called 'signing avatar') (see Figure 1), information to be made available at airports in sign language. Two other tools were added to enhance comprehension: subtitles and contextual pictures. In fact, subtitles have proved to be a great complement when used within virtual avatar environments, although much research needs to be done to ensure the best possible reception among users because avatar subtitles do not require the same format as subtitles used in other media such as digital TV or DVD.

Figure 1. The avatar designed for the ULISES project

After presenting sign language as a complement to communication, this contribution describes both the genesis and results of the ULISES project. It also indicates some features which may prove useful for SDH when used in conjunction with avatars. The results of the project are shown by means of a survey carried out among 47 airport terminal users, between the cities of Madrid and Barcelona.

2. Sign language as a complement to communication

The evident difficulties propounded by the lack of a 'European' Sign Language (international or general) meant that the initial proposal was to address the challenge of establishing a design oriented towards the Spanish language, but with the intention of making the design as widely comprehensible as possible. Therefore, the original idea behind the ULISES project was to equip the signing avatar with a complementary visual component that would help in the comprehension of the information that the virtual interpreter was transmitting, thus converting ULISES into a potentially integrative element which would serve as a complement to other systems such as subtitles and vice versa. In fact, investigations carried out into

TESSA (the interpreter present at post offices in the United Kingdom) have concluded that people with visual disabilities prefer to have information provided in both texts form and sign language form (Cox et al., 2002).

Figure 2. TESSA, the UK Post Office Sign Language interpreter

However, the inclusion of both forms in the same platform raises several issues, in particular, the question of the validity of previous research conducted into the use of typography, its positioning and length of time on-screen in subtitles for mixed-media environments. In the United Kingdom, one attempt to unite both forms was SIMON, a project carried out by the Independent Television Commission (ITC), which consisted of a televirtual character which was able to translate written text (subtitles) into sign language (Pérez-Ugena, 2008).

 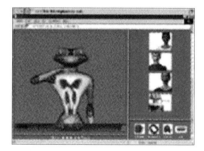

Figure 3. SIMON from the ITC project

Subtitling alone, without the support of additional visual information, does not appear to provide a satisfactory solution, even for those members of the deaf community who are able to read well, as the usual reading methods are different to those of a non-disabled person. Herrera (2006), quoting Andrews and Mason (1991), describes some of the causes of the failure to read for people with auditory disabilities:

1. "The lack of knowledge of the medium and scarce previous experience of the principle themes of the texts" that presumes that deaf people will begin the formal learning process of reading with a reduced linguistic and conceptual repertoire (and which in itself causes a poor level of reading).
2. "Poverty in oral linguistic ability [...] in that limited lexical range is presented, poorer understanding of polysemantic words, a lack of knowledge of idiomatic expressions and difficulties experienced with figurative language, syntactic forms and inferences".
3. The different structure of sign language with respect to spoken language.

In short, the patent differences in lexical, syntactic, semantic and pragmatic abilities between people with and without auditory capacity explain the difficulties in reading experienced by the deaf community. Therefore, the inclusion of elements of visual support in subtitles (and not necessarily just sign language, but contextual visual support such as the support proposed by the ULISES project) will enhance the comprehension ability of people with auditory disabilities. Further studies should be carried out to quantify this improvement in comprehension and to decide what form such visual support for subtitles should adopt, both in their graphic configuration as in their position, size and location on the screen. Such studies should consider these aspects of both subtitles and their visual support elements since it is anticipated that the perception of subtitles will be affected by such visual components.

3. The ULISES project: Development and results

The idea behind the ULISES project was initially raised during the conference of the CEPPAC network, held on 21 April 2006 at the Faculty of Translation and Interpretation of the Universitat Autònoma de Barcelona. The project was presented to the Spanish Ministry of Work and Social Services as part of the public invitation to tender projects competitively, by the Universidad Rey Juan Carlos in conjunction with the Universitat Autònoma de Barcelona, the Universidad Complutense de Madrid, the Universidad Politécnica de Madrid and the Fundación Barcelona Media-Universitat Pompeu Fabra and obtained financing in the amount of 78,000 Euros out of a possible maximum amount of 90,000 Euros.

3.1. Development of the project

It was proposed that the ULISES project would involve seven significant components:

1. The elaboration of a repertoire of needs that people with auditory disabilities might face in an airport environment;
2. The recording, by means of sign language interpreters, of both elementary linguistic units and models of phrases to serve as a reference for the animators;
3. Developing, through the work carried out with the interpreters, the possible structural sign language models capable of generating variants on questions and answers would be generated. This model was to serve as a base from which to transform the recordings of real interpreters into virtual characters;
4. Elementary units would then be fused;
5. The ULISES project model would generate questions and answers in real time, which would require the design of a transition engine and the administration of a database, which would provide individual access to the different pre-existing videos;
6. The need to check the appropriateness of the prototype being generated. In order to prevent and solve previously committed errors, similar projects would be reviewed;
7. Designing a dissemination plan in order to make the project known and widely available.

Given the limited environmental application of the project, the design of a linguistically based model was substituted for a logical model drawn from the repertoire of needs (question and answer map). To achieve this end the following models, categories and units were designed, which the database (administered by the Universidad Politécnica de Madrid) would be able to recognise. For example, *Welcome to Madrid airport* was a model of a phrase that would generate the following mode:

Model: Welcome to Madrid airport

Combination of categories: D_009 (Airport) L_01(to) F (City) G_002 (Welcome)

In this case, the category that would be left open is F (City), which could give rise to the name of any city. Fourteen logical categories were tentatively established, whose objectives were the ability to combine structures and the implementation and growth of the system. The aim was not only to manage the combination of the many structures but also the development and growth of the system.

These logical categories were

1. Type of sentence
2. Type of structure
3. Language
4. Name
5. Action
6. Location/City/Country
7. Adjective/Estate

8. Alphabet/Firm
9. Numeral (palm of the hand outside)
10. Numeral (palm of the hand inside)
11. Ordinal
12. Hours
13. Minutes
14. Prepositional sense

Section of the table with the categories used in ULISES

A (Type of sentence)		B (Type of structure)		C (Language)		D (Name)		[...] F (Location/City)	
00	Prerecorded	001	See table	00	International	001	Ticket	001	Sevilla
01	Generated	002	with models	01	Spanish	[...]	[...]	002	Aquí
		003		02	English	007	Flight	003	Madrid
		004		03	Catalan	[...]	[...]	004	Barcelona
		005		04	[...]	015	Boarding gate	005	La Coruña
		[...]		[...]	[...]	[...]	[...]	[...]	[...]
		999		99	[...]	999	[...]	999	[...]

Section of table with models used in ULISES

Prerecorded		Generated	
001	Welcome to ULISES	001	Welcome to [Madrid] airport
002	Click on the screen to have information regarding flights	002	Write the flight no. [destination]
003	Choose one option to get information	003	Click on the letters to write the [flight no./destination/airline]
004	Choose a sign language and a language	004	Destination/airline UNKNOWN
[...]	[...]	[...]	[...]
999	[...]	999	[...]

As is visible in the two tables, each category was given a letter (A, B, C, etc.). The category 'Type of sentence' was divided into two subcategories: prerecorded and generated. Prerecorded sentences were those which had already been recorded while generated sentences were those related to a model of a phrase with a determined structure where, by combining its elements, ULISES would be able to generate different sentences.

The interface that would serve to request and receive information at the airport was designed in parallel with the 3D animation. The first important issues requiring evaluation that were raised by the study, centred on what type of equipment would be appropriate (tactile screen, keyboard, virtual keyboard, etc.) and the administration of the information (web or closed circuit). Subsequent to these decisions, the project proceeded to work on the visual design of the interface, which itself passed through various stages. Once the first draft was ready, the next fundamental step centred on the design of the elements and their functions on each of the screens. 'Elements' (characters) and 'Types of elements' (functions that could be assigned to a character) were established. The list of information provided by the Universidad Rey Juan Carlos to the Universidad Politécnica de Madrid (which was in charge of the execution of the interface) allowed work to proceed without any ambiguities and as fast as possible.

The Fundación Barcelona Media-Universitat Pompeu Fabra was in charge of the design and 3D animation as well as the administration of the transition engine. To this end, a pre-existing system, NINOS, was modified and can currently be found working in the form of MeteoSam, in the production of high-quality emissions for television in Catalonia, on digital channels and in MMS technology for mobile telephones.

After carrying out appropriate tests, the option of expanding the features of the character animation engine with the intention of obtaining more natural animations was explored. The most important change centred on the flexibility of the timing of the interpolation between the different animations.

The initial proposal was to capture movements using real people (signers) and systems for the capture of movement. However, it became evident that the available systems did not meet the requirements of the project. Therefore, a 'manual' system was developed using the videotaped recordings, which served to configure the different formative parameters of the signs: hand configurations (the shape adopted by the hand and the fingers), the place of articulation (the concrete space in which the sign is made), the movement (the action made by the hand, which can imply a trajectory) and the orientation (of the palm of the hand and the fingers).

Finally, in order to avoid the problem of delimiting and identifying each of the sign's parameters and to facilitate the treatment of the videos, the signed phrases were annotated using the ELAN program (EUDICO Linguistic Annotator). This allowed both the sign language annotations to be synchronised with the video archives and the segmentation and classification of the different signs. The annotation was simplified to as much as possible: the translation of the phrases into oral language, and the approximate translation of all of the signs and their locations in neutral space where they form part of a sign alphabet or numerical sequence were specified (González-Bolea et al., 2008).

Those involved in the technical development and the visual design of the first prototypes (whose background scenery and character were developed using 3DStudio Max by Autodesk) left aside some important aspects related to sign language, such as the lack of contrast with hands, or the creation of a two-dimensional physical conception of the avatar's characters and their environments (hair, inadequate scenery), which was progressively corrected in the successive versions of the characters.

3.2. Results

In order to verify the usefulness of the system, a survey was carried out among 47 airport terminal users, between the cities of Madrid and Barcelona, for the duration of the system's development. The use of these two cities would assure a high degree of validity given the linguistic differences (with respect to sign language) that exist between these two zones.

The profile of the subjects polled included a similar number of men and women, 49% and 51% respectively. 81% of the subjects were single and 45% had enjoyed a form of higher education.

The level of education appeared to condition the results in terms of level of comprehension. The subsection of subjects with no higher education or those who had not continued in education following school preferred or requested subtitles with eye-catching colours and simple wording while those with higher education (degrees and/or postgraduate studies) were indifferent to the colours of the subtitles and understood the wording with ease. There were even subjects who preferred to maintain a certain amount of incomprehension to broaden the vocabulary of other deaf users.

The majority of the subjects (71%) polled considered the information provided on the principal screen to be sufficient while 20% thought that it should be simplified, as they did not consider some of the secondary information (lost property, transport, weather and other services) to be of genuine use, or that in spite of being useful, the information was felt to be harder to absorb when it was concentrated on the same screen at the same time.

On the other hand, the subjects polled agreed about the necessity of including facial expressions as an essential element of the avatar to ensure correct understanding. And although not initially forecast for inclusion, subtitles were included in the videos to make some of the animations more intelligible. The NINOS system already allows the introduction of subtitles into the videos by means of superimposing them on the images.

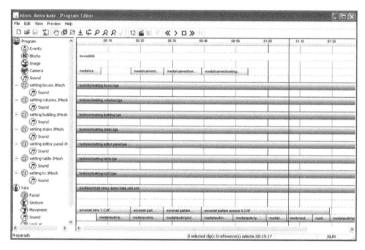

Figure 4. NINOS screen

Due to the quantity of subtitling necessary, the subtitles were generated using an automated software program. However, due to the limitations of the project, the inclusion of contextual information to assist in the comprehension of the conveyed messages was not carried out. The possibility of adding such images at a later date will be possible through the use of a similar automated system as that used for the subtitles. Such contextual images are available to the project through the contribution of the bank of images compiled by the Hervás and Panduro Centre, Cooperative Society of Madrid.

And lastly, 84% of the subjects polled considered the implementation of the project to be useful for the deaf community and 55% considered it to be a way of reducing the communication barriers and of increasing personal independence and security, in addition to reducing concern about travelling.

4. Conclusions

The project, in adding to the contributions made by previous developments, presents the challenge of integrating sign language into a system which would generate the signs automatically. Technically this is possible, even though it may require adjustments in both the mode of generating transitions and impact by means of reducing redundant information both visual (contextual images) and textual (subtitles).

In addition to being a system which provides assistance, ULISES is, above all, an acknowledgement, a way of making the deaf community visible by means of the contribution of a system. Although, at first glance, the system may be considered of use exclusively for a small community, it could be of use to anyone, especially with regard to emergency warnings and basic information. The development of a system with semi-universal comprehension is the goal of the system that is trying to use avatars as a way of humanising channels of information.

References

Andrews, J. F., & Mason J. M. (1991). Strategy usage among deaf and hearing readers. *Exceptional Children, 57*(6), 536–545.

Cox, S. J., Lincoln, M., Tryggvason, J., Nakisa, M., Wells, M., Tutt, M., et al. (2002, July). TESSA: *A system to aid communication with deaf people.* SSETS 2002, Fifth International ACM SIGCAPH Conference on Assistive Technologies. Edinburgh. Scotland, 205–212. Retrieved 15 March 2008, from <http://www.visicast.cmp.uea.ac.uk/Papers/Cox-Assets-2000.pdf>.

González-Bolea, E., Juliá, A., Fort, S., & Blat, J. (2008). Generación automática de lengua de signos con avatares. In Á. Pérez-Ugena & R. Vizcaíno-Laorga (Eds.), *ULISES: Hacia el desarrollo de tecnologías comunicativas para la igualdad de oportunidades. Retos y perspectivas para discapacitados sensoriales* (pp. 35–49). Madrid: Observatorio de las Realidades Sociales y la Comunicación.

Herrera, V. (2006). Educación especial y sordera. *Estudios Pedagógicos, XXXI, 2*, 121–135.

Pérez-Ugena, Á., & Vizcaíno-Laorga, R. (2008). *Primeros pasos de ULISES (Utilización Lógica e Integrada del Sistema Europeo de Signos/Señas).* Paper presented at the conference Amadis 2008. Granada.

ANA PEREIRA, VERÓNICA ARNÁIZ UZQUIZA

A comprehensive bibliography on subtitling for the deaf and hard of hearing from a multidisciplinary approach[1]

Asociación Española de Normalización y Certificación (AENOR). (2003). *Norma UNE 153010: Subtitulado para personas sordas y personas con discapacidad auditiva. Subtitulado a través del teletexto.* Madrid: Asociación Española de Normalización y Certificación.

Araújo, V. (2004). Closed subtitling in Brazil. In P. Orero (Ed.), *Topics in audiovisual translation* (pp. 99–212). Amsterdam: John Benjamins.

Arnáiz Uzquiza, V. (2007a). *El subtitulado para sordos en España.* Unpublished master's thesis, Universitat Autònoma de Barcelona, Spain.

Arnáiz Uzquiza, V. (2007b). Research on subtitling for the Deaf and Hard of Hearing: Top secret?. *Translation Watch Quarterly, 3*(2), 10–25.

Arnáiz Uzquiza, V. (2008). La objetividad en el subtitulado: justificación de los parámetros formales mediante *eye tracking*. In Á. Pérez-Ugena & R. Vizcaíno-Laorga (Eds.), *ULISES: Hacia el desarrollo de tecnologías comunicativas para la igualdad de oportunidades: Retos y perspectivas para sordos signantes* (pp. 73–84). Madrid: Observatorio de las Realidades Sociales y de la Comunicación.

Arumí, M., Matamala, A., Orero, P., & Romero-Fresco, P. (2009). L'ensenyament de la subtitulació mitjançant reconeixement de parla. *V Congrés Internacional Docència Universitària i Innovació: El canvi de la cultura docent universitària.* Girona: Universitat de Girona. CD-ROM.

Arumí, M., & Romero-Fresco, P. (2008). A practical proposal for the training of respeakers. *Journal of Specialised Translation, 10.* Available at <http://www.jostrans.org/issue10/art_arumi.php>.

Austin, B. (1980) The deaf audience for television. *Journal of Communication, 30*(2), 25–30.

Baaring, I. (2006). Respeaking-based online subtitling in Denmark. *Intralinea, Special Issue: Respeaking 2006.* Available at <http://www.intralinea.it/specials/respeaking/eng_more.php?id=446_0_41_0_M>.

---

1   This paper is part of the research project *La subtitulación para sordos y la audiodescripción: Primeras aproximaciones científicas y su aplicación* (Subtitling for the Deaf and Hard of Hearing and Audiodescription: First scientific approaches and their application) (reference HUM2006-03653FILO) funded by the Spanish ministry of education.

Badia, T., & Matamala, A. (2007). La docencia en accesibilidad en los medios. *Trans. Revista de Traductología, 11,* 61–71. Available at <http://www.trans.uma.es/pdf/ Trans_11/%20T.61-71BadiayMatamala.pdf>.

Baker, D. (2001). Television captioning frequently asked questions-FAQs. *Hearing Loss, the Journal of Self Help for Hard of Hearing People, 6,* 18–19.

Baker, R. G., Lambourne, A., & Rowston, G. (1984). *Handbook for television subtitlers.* Winchester: University of Southampton and Independent Broadcasting Authority.

Baker, R. G. (1982). *Monitoring eye-movements while watching subtitled television programmes: A feasibility study.* London: Independent Broadcasting Authority.

Baker, R. G., Lambourne, A., Downtown, A. C., & King, A. W. (1984). *Oracle subtitling for the deaf and hard of hearing.* Southampton: Department of Electronics and Information Engineering.

Ball, J. E. (1988). Closed-captioned television improves resident well-being. *Provider, 14*(12), 41–42.

Ballester, A., Lorenzo, L., Matamala, A., Orero, P., & Pereira, A. (2006). La formación del audiodescriptor y el subtitulador para sordos: Un reto europeo para la Universidad española'. In *Adaptar la igualdad, normalizar la diversidad. II Congreso Nacional sobre Universidad y Discapacidad* (pp. 410–421). Madrid: Vicerrectorado de Estudiantes, UCM.

Bartoll, E. (2006). Subtitling for the Hard of Hearing on Catalan TV. *VI International Conference and Exhibition 'Languages and the Media'.* Available at <http://www. languages-media.com/lang_media_2006/protected/Bartoll_Eduard.pdf>.

Blatt, J. (1981). Captioned television and hearing-impaired viewers: The report of a national survey. *American Annals of the Deaf, 126*(9), 1017–1023.

Braverman, B. (1981). Television captioning strategies: A systematic research and development approach. *American Annals of the Deaf, 126*(9), 1031–1036.

British Broadcasting Corporation (BBC). (1996). *BBC subtitling style guide.* London: British Broadcasting Corporation.

British Broadcasting Corporation (BBC). (1998). *BBC subtitling guide.* London: British Broadcasting Corporation.

Burnham, D., Leigh, G., Noble, W., Jones, C., Tyler, M., Grebennikov, L., et al. (2008). Parameters in television captioning for deaf and hard of hearing adults: Effects of caption rate versus text reduction on comprehension. *Journal of Deaf Studies and Deaf Education, 3*(1), 391–404.

Canadian Association of Broadcasters (CAB). (2008). *Closed captioning standards and protocol for Canadian English language broadcasters.* Ottawa: Joint Societal Issues Committee on Closed Captioning Standards. Available at <http://www.cab-acr.ca/english/ social/captioning/captioning.pdf>.

Carney, E. (1987). Caption decoders: Expanding options for hearing impaired children and adults. *American Annals of the Deaf, 132*(2), 73–77.

Carrera, J. (2007). *La subtitulación para sordos: El caso de las variedades del español.* Unpublished master's thesis, Universidad de Valladolid, Spain.

Carrera, J., & Lorenzo, L. (2008). Variedades de español en subtitulación para sordos: Análisis de casos y propuesta de marcadores. In C. Jiménez & A. Rodríguez (Eds.),

Accesibilidad a los medios audiovisuales para personas con discapacidad AMADIS '07 (pp. 79–89). Madrid: Real Patronato sobre Discapacidad.

Chapdelaine, C., Gouaillier, V., Beaulieu, M., & Gagnon, L. (2007). Improving video captioning for deaf and hearing-impaired people based on eye movement and attention overload. Retrieved 23 July 2009, from <http://www.crim.ca/Publications/2007/documents/plein_texte/VIS_ChaCals_SPIE6492.pdf>.

Danan, M. (2004). Captioning and subtitling: Undervalued language learning strategies. *Meta*, *49*(1), 67–78.

Described and Captioned Media Program (DCMP). 2008. *Captioning key: Guidelines and preferred Techniques.* Spartanburg: National Association of the Deaf. Available at <http://www.dcmp.org/captioningkey/captioning-key.pdf>.

De Graef, P., Van Rensbergen, J., & d'Ydewalle, G. (1985). *User's manual for the Leuven Eye Movement Registration System* (Psychological Reports No. 52). Leuven: University Press of Leuven.

De Jong, F. (2004). *Access Services for Digital Television. EBU Technical Review.* Grand-Saconnex: EBU Project Group. Available at <http://www.ebu.ch/en/technical/trev/trev_300-de_jong.pdf>.

De Korte, T. (2006) Live inter-lingual subtitling in the Netherlands. *Intralinea, Special Issue: Respeaking 2006.* Available at <http://www.intralinea.it/specials/respeaking/eng_more.php?id=454_0_41_0_M>.

de Linde, Z. (1995). Read my lips: Subtitling principles, practices and problems. *Perspectives: Studies in Translatology*, *3*(1), 9–20.

de Linde, Z. (1996). Le sous-titrage intralinguistique pour les sourds et les mal entendants. In Y. Gambier (Ed.), *Les transferts linguistiques dans les medias audiovisual* (pp. 165–183). Paris: Presses Universitaires du Septentrion.

de Linde, Z. (1997). *Linguistic and visual complexity of television subtitles.* Unpublished doctoral dissertation, University of Bristol.

de Linde, Z. (1999). Processing subtitles and film images: Hearing vs. deaf viewers. *The Translator*, *5*(1), 45–60.

de Linde, Z., & Kay, N. (1999). *The semiotics of subtitling.* Manchester: St. Jerome.

Díaz Cintas, J. (2006). *Competencias profesionales del subtitulador y el audiodescriptor.* Report written in September 2006 at the request of the Centro Español de Subtitulado y Audiodescripción (Spanish Centre for Subtitling and Audio Description, CESyA). Retrieved 6 May 2008, from <http://www.cesya.es/estaticas/jornada/documentos/presentacion_CESyA.pdf>.

Díaz Cintas, J. (2007). Por una preparación de calidad en accesibilidad audiovisual. *Trans. Revista de Traductología*, *11,* 45–60.

d'Ydewalle, G., & Van Rensbergen, J. (1987). Reading a message when the same message is available auditorily in another language: The case of subtitling. In J.K. O'Regan & A. Lévy-Schoen (Eds.), *Eye movements: From physiology to cognition* (pp. 313–321). Amsterdam: Elsevier Science.

d'Ydewalle, G., & Van Rensbergen, J. (1989). Developmental studies of text-picture interactions in the perception of animated cartoons with text? In H. Mandl & J.R. Levin (Eds.), *Knowledge acquisition from text and pictures* (pp. 233–248). Amsterdam: Elsevier Science.

d'Ydewalle, G., Warlop, L., & Van Rensbergen, J. (1989). Television and attention: Differences between young and older adults in the division of attention over different sources of TV information. *Medienpsychologie: Zeitschrift für Individual- und Massenkommunikation, 1,* 42–57.

d'Ydewalle, G., Praet, C., Verfaillie, K., & Van Rensbergen, J. (1991). Watching subtitled television: Automatic reading behavior. *Communication Research, 18,* 650–666.

d'Ydewalle, G., & Gielen, I. (1992). Attention allocation with overlapping sound, image, and text. In K. Rayner (Ed.), *Eye movements and visual cognition* (pp. 415–527). New York: Springer.

Earley, S. (1978). Developments in communication technology for the hearing impaired. *American Annals of the Deaf, 123*(6), 655–662.

Eugeni, C. (2006) Introduzione al rispeakeraggio televisivo. *Intralinea, Special Issue: Respeaking 2006.* Available at <http://www.intralinea.it/specials/respeaking/eng_more. php?id=444_0_41_0_M>.

Eugeni, C. (2007) Il rispeakeraggio televisivo per sordi: Per una sottotitolazione mirata del TG. *Intralinea, 9.* Available at <http://www.intralinea.it/volumes/eng_more.php?id= 513_0_2_0_M60%>.

Eugeni, C. (2008). A sociolinguistic approach to real-time subtitling: Respeaking vs. shadowing and simultaneous interpreting. In C. J. Kellett Bidoli & E. Ochse (Eds.), *English in international deaf communication* (pp. 357–382). Bern: Peter Lang.

Eugeni, C. (2008). Respeaking political debate for the deaf: The Italian case. In A. Baldry & E. Montagna (Eds.), *Interdisciplinary perspectives on multimodality: Theory and practice* (pp. 191–205). Campobasso: Palladino Editore.

Eugeni, C. (2009). Respeaking the BBC news: A strategic analysis of respeaking on the BBC. *The Sign Language Translator and Interpreter, 3*(1), 29–68.

European Broadcasting Union (EBU). 2004. *EBU Recommendation R-110-2004: Subtitling for digital television broadcasting.* European Broadcasting Union Committee – PMC and BMC. 11 March. Available at <http://www.ebu.ch/CMSimages/fr/tec_text _r110-2004_tcm7-10501.pdf>.

Federal Communications Commission (FCC). (2004). *Consumer facts: Closed captioning,* Washington: Federal Communications Commission, Consumer and Governmental Affairs Bureau. Available at <http://www.fcc.gov/cgb/consumerfacts/closedcaption. html>.

Fitzgerald, M. (1981). Closed-captioned television viewing preference. *American Annals of the Deaf, 126*(5), 536–539.

Franco, E., & Araújo, V. (2003). Reading television. *The Translator, 9*(2), 249–267.

Gaell, R. (Ed.) (1999). *Subtitling consumer report.* London: Royal National Institute for Deaf People.

Gielen, I., & d'Ydewalle, G. (1992). How do we watch subtitled television programmes? In A. Demetriou, A. Efklides, E. Gonida, & M. Vakali (Eds.), *Psychological research in Greece: Vol. 1, Development, learning, and instruction* (pp. 247–259). Thessaloniki: Aristotelian University Press.

Gregory, S., & Sancho-Aldridge, J. (1997). *Dial 888: Subtitling for Deaf children.* London: Independent Television Commission.

Independent Television Commission (ITC). (1999). *ITC guidance on standards for subtitling*. London: Independent Television Commission. Available at: <http://www.ofcom.org.uk/tv/ifi/guidance/tv_access_serv/archive/subtitling_stnds/itc_stnds_subtitling_word.doc>.

Independent Television Commission (ITC). (2001). *ITC code on subtitling, sign language and audio description*. London: Independent Television Commission. Available at <http://www.ofcom.org.uk/static/archive/itc/uploads/ITC_Code_on_Subtitling_Sign_Language_and_Audio_Description.doc>.

Ivarsson, J. (1992). *Subtitling for the media*. Stockholm: TransEdit.

Ivarsson, J., & Carroll., M. (1998). *Subtitling*. Simrishamn: TransEdit.

Izard, N. (2001). La subtitulación para sordos del teletexto en Televisión Española. In L. Lorenzo & A. Pereira (Eds.), *Traducción subordinada inglés-español/galego II: El subtitulado* (pp. 169–194). Vigo: Servicio de Publicacións de la Universidade de Vigo.

Jensema, C. J. (1981). Background and initial audience characteristics of the closed caption television system. *American Annals of the Deaf, 126*(1), 32–36.

Jensema, C. J. (1997a). Instant reading incentive: Understanding TV caption. *Perspectives Education and Deafness, 16*(1), 6–7. Available at <http://clerccenter2.gallaudet.edu/products/perspectives/sep-oct97/instant.html>.

Jensema, C. J. (1997b). A demographic profile of the closed-caption television audience. *American Annals of the Deaf, 132*(6), 389–392.

Jensema, C. J. (1997c). *Presentation rate and readability of closed caption television: Final report*. Washington: Office of Educational Technology. Available at <http://eric.ed.gov/ERICDocs/data/ericdocs2sql/content_storage_01/0000019b/80/15/75/be.pdf>.

Jensema, C. J. (1998). Viewer reaction to different television captioning speeds. *American Annals of the Deaf, 143*(4), 318–324.

Jensema, C. J. (2000). A study of the eye movement strategies used in viewing captioned television. Retrieved 20 May 2008, from <http://www.dcmp.org/caai/nadh7.pdf>.

Jensema, C. J. (2003). *Final report: The relation between eye movement and reading captions and print by school-age deaf children*. Washington: Department of Education, Technology, Educational Media and Materials for Individuals with Disabilities. Available at: <http://www.dcmp.org/caai/nadh134.pdf>.

Jensema, C., McCann, R., & Ramsey, S. (1996). Closed-captioned television presentation speed and vocabulary. *American Annals of the Deaf, 141*(4), 284–292.

Jensema, C., & Burch, R. (1999). *Caption speed and viewer comprehension of television programs final report (SuDoc ED 1.310/2:434446)*. Washington: U.S. Department of Education, Educational Resources Information Center. Available at: <http://eric.ed.gov/ERICDocs/data/ericdocs2sql/content_storage_01/0000019b/80/15/e3/70.pdf>.

Jensema, C., Sharwaky, S., Danturthi, R. S., Burch, R., & Hsu, D. (2000). Eye-movement patterns of captioned-television viewers. *American Annals of the Deaf, 145*(3), 275–285.

Jensema, C., Danturthi, R. S., & Burch, R (2000) Time spent viewing captions on television programs. *American Annals of the Deaf, 145*(5), 464–468.

Jordan, A. J. et al. (2003). *The state of closed-captioning services in the United States: An assessment of quality, availability, and use*. Philadelphia: The Annenberg Public Policy Center of the University of Pennsylvania.

Justo Sanmartín, N. (forthcoming). El subtitulado para sordos y personas con discapacidad auditiva en Inglaterra. In Elena Di Giovanni (Ed.), *Entre texto y receptor: Accesibilidad, doblaje y traducción. Between text and receiver: accessibility, dubbing and translation.* Frankfurt: Peter Lang.

King, C., & LaSasso, C. (1992). Research project to determine preferences of deaf and hard of hearing viewers about current and future captioning. *SHHH Journal, 13*(5), 14–16.

King, C., LaSasso, C., & Short, D. D. (1994). Digital captioning: Effects of color coding and placement in synchronized text-audio presentations. In H. Maurer (Ed.), *Educational Multimedia and Hypermedia* (pp. 329–334). Charlottesville, Vancouver: Assoc for the Advancement of Computing in Educ., June 25–29.

King, C. & LaSasso, C. (1994). Caption format preferences. *NAD Broadcaster, 16*(11), 5–6.

Kirkland, C. E. (1999). Evaluation of captioning features to inform development of digital television captioning capabilities. *American Annals of the Deaf, 144*(3), 250–260.

Kyle, J. (1992). *Switched on: Deaf people's views on television subtitling.* Bristol: Centre for Deaf Studies, University of Bristol.

Lambourne, A., Hewitt, J., Lyon, C., & Warren, S. (2004). Speech-based real-time subtitling services. *International Journal of Speech Technology, 7*(4), 269–279.

Lambourne, A. (2006) Subtitle respeaking: A new skill for a new age. *Intralinea, Special Issue: Respeaking 2006.* Available at <http://www.intralinea.it/specials/respeaking/eng_more.php?id=447_0_41_0_M>.

Lorenzo, L., & Pereira, A. (forthcoming). Deaf children and their access to audio-visual texts: school failure and the helplessness of the subtitler. In E. Di Giovanni (Ed.), *Entre texto y receptor: Accesibilidad, doblaje y traducción. Between text and receiver: accessibility, dubbing and translation.* Frankfurt: Peter Lang.

Marsh, A. (2006). Respeaking for the BBC. *Intralinea, Special Issue: Respeaking 2006.* Available at <http://www.intralinea.it/specials/respeaking/eng_more.php?id=484_0_41_0_M>.

Martínez Ortiz, M. (2007). *Subtitulado para sordos: análisis, procedimiento y problemática del subtitulado de Harry Potter y la Cámara Secreta.* Unpublished undergraduate thesis, Universidad de Valladolid, Soria.

Mellors, W., Hodgkinson, R., & Miller, C. (2006). Access symbols for use with video content and ITC devices. Sophia-Antiopolis: 20th International Symposium on Human Factors in Telecommunication, 20–23 March 2006. <http://www.hft.org/HFT06/paper06/09_Mellors.pdf>.

Méndez Brage, B. (2003). *El subtitulado para sordos.* Unpublished undergraduate thesis, Universidade de Vigo, Spain.

Miller, C. (2007). Access symbols for use with video content and information and communication technology services. In J. Díaz Cintas, P. Orero & A. Remael (Eds.), *Media for all: Subtitling for the deaf, audio description, and sign language* (pp. 53–69). Amsterdam: Rodopi.

Möck, J. (2002). Workshop: Subtitling for the deaf and hard of hearing. *VI International Conference and Exhibition 'Languages and the Media'.* Berlin.

Moreira Brenlla, E. (2008). *Análisis de la representación del sonido en el SPS de películas infantiles.* Unpublished pre-doctoral dissertation, Universidade de Vigo, Spain.

Moreira Brenlla, E. (forthcoming). Subtítulos para sordos en la televisión alemana. In E. Di Giovanni (Ed.), *Entre texto y receptor: Accesibilidad, doblaje y traducción. Between text and receiver: accessibility, dubbing and translation.* Frankfurt: Peter Lang.

Muzii, L. (2006) Respeaking e localizzazione. *Intralinea, Special Issue: Respeaking 2006.* Available at: <http://www.intralinea.it/specials/respeaking/eng_more.php?id=446_0_41_0_M>.

National Center for Accessible Media (NCAM). n/d. *Projects: ATV Closed Captioning.* Boston: National Center for Accessible Media. Available at: <http://ncam.wgbh.org/projects/atv/atvccsumm.html>.

Neves, J. (2005). *Audiovisual translation: Subtitling for the deaf and hard of hearing.* Unpublished PhD Thesis. Roehampton University, London. Available at: <http://roehampton.openrepository.com/roehampton/bitstream/10142/12580/1/neves%20audiovisual.pdf>.

Neves, J. (2007a). A world of change in a changing world. In J. Díaz Cintas, P. Orero & A. Remael (Eds.), *Media for all: Subtitling for the deaf, audio description, and sign language* (pp. 89–98). Amsterdam: Rodopi.

Neves, J. (2007b). There is research and research: Subtitling for the deaf and hard of hearing (SDH). In C. Jiménez Hurtado (Ed.), *Traducción y accesibilidad. Subtitulación para sordos y audiodescripción para ciegos: Nuevas modalidades de traducción audiovisual* (pp. 27–40). Frankfurt: Peter Lang.

Neves, J. (2008). 10 fallacies about subtitling for the d/Deaf and the hard of hearing. *The Journal of Specialised Translation, 10,* 128–143.

Neves, J., & Lorenzo, L. (2007). La subtitulación para Sordos: Panorama global y prenormativo en el marco ibérico. *Trans. Revista de Traductología, 11,* 95–113. Retrieved 1 May 2008, from <http://www.trans.uma.es/pdf/Trans_11/T.95-113Lourdes.Lorenzo.pdf>.

National Institute on Deafness and Other Communication Disorders (NIDCD). (2002). *Captions For deaf and hard of hearing viewers.* Bethesda: National Institute on Deafness and Other Communication Disorders. Available at <http://www.nidcd.nih.gov/health/hearing/caption.asp>.

O'Connell, E. (2003). *Minority language dubbing for children.* Bern: Peter Lang.

Ofcom. (2005). *Subtitling: An issue of speed?.* London: Office of Communications. Available at <http://www.ofcom.org.uk/research/tv/reports/subt/subt.pdf>.

Orero, P., Pereira, A., & Utray, F. (2007). Visión histórica de la accesibilidad en los medios en España. *Trans. Revista de Traductología, 11,* 31–43. Available at http://www.trans.uma.es/pdf/Trans_11/T.31-43OreroPereiraUtray.pdf>.

Pazó Lorenzo, I. (2006). *Propuesta de subtitulación para sordos de* La edad de hielo: *Búsqueda de la convergencia entre lenguas orales y signadas.* Unpublished undergraduate thesis, Universidade de Vigo, Spain.

Pazó Lorenzo, I. (forthcoming). La adaptación del subtitulado para personas sordas. In E. Di Giovanni (Ed.), *Entre texto y receptor: Accesibilidad, doblaje y traducción.* Frankfurt: Peter Lang.

Pardina i Mundó, J. (1999) El futuro de la subtitulación para personas sordas o con pérdidas auditivas. *Fiapas, 68,* 38–41. Madrid: Confederación Española de Familias de personas sordas. Available at <http://www.terra.es/personal6/932108627/Articulos/arti3-C.htm>.

Pardina i Mundó, J. (2000). *Estudio sobre el servicio audiovisual de subtitulación para personas sordas o con pérdidas auditivas en el mercado televisivo español*. Barcelona: Dirección Audiovisual de la CMT. Available at <http://www.cmt.es/es/publicaciones/anexos/subtitula.pdf>.

Pereira, A. (2005). El subtitulado para sordos: estado de la cuestión en España. *Quaderns: Revista de traducció, 12*, 161–172. Available at <http://ddd.uab.es/pub/quaderns/11385790n12p161.pdf>.

Pereira, A., & Lorenzo, L. (2005). Evaluamos la norma UNE 153010: Subtitulado para personas sordas y personas con discapacidad auditiva. Subtitulado a través del teletexto. *Puentes, 6*, 21–26. Available at <http://www.ugr.es/~greti/puentes/puentes6/03%20Ana%20M%20Pereira.pdf>.

Pereira, A., & Lorenzo, L. (2006). La investigación y formación en accesibilidad dentro del ámbito de la traducción audiovisual. In C. Gonzalo, C. & P. Hernúñez (Coord.), CORCILLVM. *Estudios de traducción, lingüística y filología dedicados a Valentín García Yebra* (pp. 649–658). Madrid: Arco Libros.

Pereira, A., & Lorenzo, L. (2007). Teaching proposals for the unit 'subtitling for the deaf and hard of hearing' within the subject audiovisual translation (English – Spanish*). Translation Watch Quarterly, 3*(2), 26–37.

Pérez de Oliveira, A. (forthcoming). El subtitulado para sordos en las principales cadenas de televisión en España. In E. Di Giovanni (Ed.), *Entre texto y receptor: Accesibilidad, doblaje y traducción. Between text and receiver: accessibility, dubbing and translation*. Frankfurt: Peter Lang.

Prada González, M. (2004). Buscando a Nemo: *Propuesta de subtitulado para sordos a partir del análisis crítico de cuatro casos reales*. Unpublished undergraduate thesis, Universidade de Vigo, Spain.

Remael, A. (2007). Sampling subtitling for the deaf and hard of hearing in Europe. In J. Díaz Cintas, P. Orero & A. Remael (Eds.), *Media for all: Subtitling for the deaf, audio description, and sign language* (pp. 23–52). Amsterdam: Rodopi.

Remael, A., & van der Veer, B. (2006). Real-time subtitling in Flanders: Needs and teaching. *Intralinea, Special Issue: Respeaking 2006*. Available at <http://www.intralinea.it/specials/respeaking/eng_more.php?id=446_0_41_0_M>.

Rico, A. (2002). Subtitling for deaf people and language contact in Catalonia. *IV International Conference and Exhibition 'Languages and the Media'*, Berlin.

RNIB. 2000. *Tiresias Screenfont: A typeface for television subtitling*. London: Royal National Institute for the Blind. Available at <http://www.tiresias.org/fonts/screenfont/about_screen.htm>.

Robson, G. (2004). *The closed captioning handbook*. Oxford: Elsevier.

Robson, A. (n/d). *Early Ceefax subtitling: Adrian Robson remembers*. Teletext: Then and Now. Available at <http://teletext.mb21.co.uk/timeline/early-ceefax-subtitling.shtml>.

Romero-Fresco, P. (2009) La subtitulación rehablada: palabras que no se lleva el viento. In Á. Pérez-Ugena & R. Vizcaíno-Laorga (Eds.), *ULISES: Hacia el desarrollo de tecnologías comunicativas para la igualdad de oportunidades* (pp. 49–71). Madrid: Observatorio de las Realidades Sociales y de la Comunicación.

Romero-Fresco, P. (2009). More haste less speed: Edited vs. verbatim respoken subtitles, *VIAL (Vigo International Journal of Applied Linguistics), 6*, 109–133.

Sancho-Aldridge, J., & IFF Research Ltd. (1996). *Good news for deaf people: Subtitling of national news programmes*. London: Independent Television Commission.

Schmidt, M. (1992). The older hearing-impaired adult in the classroom: Real-time closed captioning as a technological alternative to the oral lecture. *Educational Gerontology, 18*(3), 273–276.

Shulman, J. (1979). Multilevel captioning: A system for preparing reading materials for the hearing impaired. *American Annals of the Deaf, 124*(5), 559–567.

Silver, J., Gill, J., Sharville, C., Slater, J., & Martin, M. (1998). A new font for digital television subtitles. Available at <http://www.tiresias.org/fonts/screenfont/report_screen.htm>.

Silver, J., Gill, J.M., & Wolffsohn, J.S. (1995) Text display preferences on self-service terminals by visually disabled people. *Optometry Today, 35*(2), 24–27.

Stehle, M. (2002) Workshop: Subtitling for the deaf and hard of hearing. *IV International Conference and Exhibition 'Languages and the Media'*, Berlin.

Stewart, D. (1984). Captioned television for the deaf. *Journal of Special Education, 8*(1), 61–69.

Stoddart, P., 1983, 'Working with the sound of silence', *Broadcast U.K.,* October 14, 22.

Stone, C. (2007). Deaf access for Deaf people: The translation of the television news from English into British Sign Language. In J. Díaz Cintas, P. Orero & A. Remael (Eds.), *Media for all: Subtitling for the deaf, audio description, and sign language* (pp. 71–88). Amsterdam: Rodopi.

Tercedor Sánchez, I., Lara Burgos, P., Herrador Molina, D., Márquez Linares, I., & Márquez Alhambra, L. (2007). Parámetros de análisis en la subtitulación accessible. In C. Jiménez Hurtado (Ed.), *Traducción y accesibilidad. Subtitulación para sordos y audiodescripción para ciegos: Nuevas modalidades de TAV* (pp. 41–51). Frankfurt: Peter Lang.

Utray, F., Orero, P., & Pereira, A. (2009). The present and future of audio description and subtitling for the deaf and hard of hearing in Spain. *Meta, 54*(2), 248–263.

van der Veer, B. (2008). De tolk als respeaker: Een kwestie van training. *Linguistica Antverpiensia New Series, 6*, 315–328.

Varela, S. (forthcoming). Subtitulado para sordos. Camino hacia una normative: Análisis del éxito comunicativo de *Chicken Run* y *Pinocho 3000*. In E. Di Giovanni (Ed.), *Entre texto y receptor: Accesibilidad, doblaje y traducción*. Frankfurt: Peter Lang.

VOICE (1999). *VOICE: Giving a voice to the deaf by developing awareness on voice-to-text recognition capabilities*. Ispra: European Commission Joint Research Centre. Available at <http://voice.jrc.it/home/pamphlet/pamphlet_en.doc>.

Walleij, S. (1987). Teletext subtitling for the Deaf. *EBU Review, Programmes, Administration, Law, 38*(6), 26–27.

Ward, P., Wang, Y., Peter, P., & Loeterman, M. (2007). Near verbatim captioning versus edited captioning for students who are deaf or hard of hearing. *American Annals of the Deaf, 152*(1), 20–28.

WGBH. (2001). *The Caption Centre online: FAQs – Frequently asked questions about captioning*. Boston: Media Access Group at WGBH. Available at <http://main.wgbh.org/wgbh/pages/mag/services/captioning/faq/>.

Notes on contributors

VERÓNICA ARNÁIZ UZQUIZA has a BA in Translation and Interpreting and an MA in Specialised Translation, both from the Universidad de Valladolid in Spain. In addition, she also has an MA in Audiovisual Translation from the Universitat Autònoma de Barcelona. She is currently employed as a lecturer at the Universidad de Valladolid in the official postgraduate master in Professional and Institutional Translation. Her fields of interest are audiovisual translation, subtitling for the deaf and hard of hearing and accessibility. She is a member of the research group Transmedia Catalonia.

INMACULADA BÁEZ MONTERO, a graduate in Spanish Philology from the Universidad de Salamanca (1983), has a PhD from the Universidad de Santiago de Compostela (1995). She is currently a senior lecturer in the Spanish Language department at the Universidade de Vigo. From the academic year 2004–2005, she has coordinated the PhD programme *Language and the Information Society: Linguistics and its applications* (with MEC Quality Award 2004/00215), which consists of, among other modules, a sign language oriented module. She is also responsible for the Sign Language and Spanish as a Foreign Language courses at the Universidade de Vigo. She has published several works on grammar, research methodology, sociolinguistics and the history of sign languages. She has also been in charge of research aimed at developing sign language in people with developmental difficulties with therapeutic outcomes. She has co-supervised Ana Fernández Soneira's thesis and several Diplomas of Advanced Studies on bilingualism and subtitling for the deaf. She has been the chief researcher in different state-financed research projects carried out by the Sign Languages Research Unit at the Universidade de Vigo since the unit was founded in 1992.

EDUARD BARTOLL is an audiovisual translator, who translates mainly from English and German, but also from French, Portuguese and Italian, into Catalan and Spanish. He has subtitled more than 500 films and he translates plays too. He works at the Universitat Pompeu Fabra, in Barcelona, as a lecturer in translation (German into Catalan), and in the Master in Audiovisual Translation, at the Universitat Autònoma de Barcelona, also in its online version. His PhD on subtitling will soon be published in Catalan. In addition, he is a member of the research group Transmedia Catalonia.

JEAN-FRANÇOIS BEAUMONT was a research assistant at the Centre de recherche informatique de Montréal (CRIM). He has a degree in electrical engineering from the École de technologie supérieure (ÉTS) and an MA in Computer Engineering from McGill University.

MARYSE BOISVERT is a research assistant at the Centre de recherche informatique de Montréal (CRIM). She is trained in the field of statistical learning, specialising in natural language processing. She joined the Speech Recognition team in 2004. She is involved in the development of domain-specific language models.

GILLES BOULIANNE is a senior advisor at the Centre de recherche informatique de Montréal (CRIM). He received BS degrees in systems engineering from UQAC, Chicoutimi, and mechanical engineering from INSA, Toulouse (1984), and an MS degree in Telecommunications from INRS-Télécommunications, Montreal (1988). From 1986 to 1990 he developed linguistic research tools and an articulatory speech synthesiser in the Linguistics department at the Université du Québec à Montréal. Subsequently, he worked on very large vocabulary speech recognition as a research assistant at INRS-Telecommunications and at Spoken Word Technologies until 1998, when he joined CRIM. There, his explorations of finite-state transducers for speech recognition resulted in the implementation of CRIM's FST-based speech recognition engine. He is in charge of the speech recognition efforts in several projects with industrial partners such as Nortel Networks, Locus Dialogue, Ryshco Media, and the House of Commons, as well as large collaborative projects such as MADIS, RAP, C3Grid, and E-Inclusion (see www.crim.ca), each involving several academic and industrial partners. In the course of these projects, he also had the opportunity of co-supervising several students, two of which completed their MS degrees and became full-time CRIM research assistants. He is currently director of the CRIM speech recognition group.

JULIE BROUSSEAU is production director of the Centre de recherche informatique de Montréal's close-captioning bureau (CRIM). She has over fifteen years of experience in the field of speech recognition. She launched her career at Dragon Systems as the manager of an R&D project related to adapting the DragonDictate commercial system to Canadian French. At CRIM since 1993, Julie Brousseau was originally responsible for experiments that led to the prototyping of an automatic translation assistance system. She is involved in the application of new approaches focusing on the continuous improvement of French language speech recognition.

CARMEN CABEZA-PEREIRO has a degree and a PhD in Spanish Philology, both from the Universidad de Santiago de Compostela in Spain. She lectures General Linguistics at the Universidade de Vigo in Spain. During the last fifteen years, she has focused her research on Spanish Sign Language grammar and on the sociolinguistics and other relevant features of deaf communities, their lifestyles and their ways of communicating. She is also interested in methodological issues related to signed language research. She has been the first director of the Centre of Languages at the Universidade de Vigo, where she has promoted Spanish Sign Language as a second language to be learned as a part of the complementary curriculum. She is currently vice-rector of Cultural Affairs and Students.

PATRICK CARDINAL is an advisor at the Centre de recherche informatique de Montréal (CRIM). He joined the CRIM team in 2000. He is currently pursuing his doctorate in computer science at the École de technologie supérieure (ÉTS). He is involved in transducer research techniques and parallel programming.

CLAUDE CHAPDELAINE is a senior research advisor at the Centre de recherche informatique de Montréal (CRIM). She has an MASc. in the field of human-machine interaction. A CRIM team member since 1997, her interests are mostly in the design and evaluation of human performance using software in the fields of automatic speech recognition, vision and imaging. She was responsible for an eye-tracking analysis of deaf and hearing impaired people to improve the production of captions. Presently, she is involved in the production of video description for the blind and visually impaired using video detection techniques.

MICHEL COMEAU was a research agent at the Centre de recherche informatique de Montréal (CRIM). He received his doctorate in chemistry. Over the last two years, he has worked extensively in the field of internet applications. He joined the Speech Recognition team in 2000 while working on speech modelling methods and interfaces.

CLARA CIVERA has a degree in English from the Universitat de València, and an MA in Audiovisual Translation from the Universitat Autònoma de Barcelona in Spain. She has worked as a freelance translator of subtitles. Her research interest lies in the optimisation of subtitle reception. She works at the Universitat Miguel Hernández, where she teaches English.

PIERRE DUMOUCHEL, BEng. (Université McGill), MSc, PhD (INRS-Télécommunications), is currently Scientific Vice-President at the Centre de recherche informatique de Montréal (CRIM) and full professor at the École de technologie supérieure (ÉTS) of the Université du Québec. He was the vice-president CRIM Research and Development from 1999 to 2004. Before that, he was the Principal Researcher of the CRIM's Automatic Speech Recognition team and a scientific columnist at Radio-Canada, the French Canadian National Radio. He has more than 23 years of expertise in Speech Recognition Research, six years in managing a research team and three years in managing the Research and Development unit of CRIM. His research has resulted in many technology transfers to such companies as Nortel, Locus Dialog, Canadian National Defence, Le Groupe TVA, as well as many SME, as such as Ryshco Media. His research interests are speech recognition, speaker recognition and emotion detection from speech. He favoured applications of speech recognition for the hard of hearing and audiovisual film indexation. He received the 2004 IWAY Award, for outstanding achievements in Adaptive Technology for his work in the real-time close-captioning production tool for the Groupe TVA and the House of Commons.

ANA Mᴬ FERNÁNDEZ SONEIRA is assistant lecturer in the Department of Spanish Language at the Universidade de Vigo, where she obtained her PhD with a dissertation on the expression of quantification in Spanish Sign Language (SSL). She is also member of the Sign Languages Research Unit at the Universidade de Vigo and has researched widely on SSL-related linguistic subjects. She has authored many articles on such topics and has just finished a volume: *La cantidad a manos llenas. La expresión de la cuantificación en la lengua de signos española*, Madrid, Fundación CNSE. She also teaches Sign Language courses, in collaboration with deaf people, at the Universidade de Vigo Language Centre. More recently she has begun to work in the field of Spanish teaching to the deaf and to prepare teaching resources for this purpose.

PETER OLAF LOOMS is senior consultant, Strategy & Development Projects Unit, DR Media (1 July 2001 – present). At DR, the main emphasis of his work is on media and service convergence, standards and interoperability, and the development of solutions at European and international level. Recent work includes participation in the EICTA/EBU/European Commission / Handicap body consultative forum on e-inclusiveness and access services on Digital Television; participation in EBU initiatives on access services.

LOURDES LORENZO has a degree in English Philology from the Universidad de Santiago de Compostela (Spain) (1992) and obtained a European Doctorate in Translation Studies (Universidade de Vigo) in 1999. She has been teaching Translation (English into Spanish and Galician) since 1995 at the Universidade de Vigo and from 2002 onwards she has also been teaching Screen Translation (dubbing, subtitling and subtitling for people with hearing impairment) to postgraduate students at the Universitat Autònoma de Barcelona (Online Master in Audiovisual Translation), Universidad de Valladolid and Universitat Jaume I (Castelló). Her main areas of research are the translation of metaphor and intertextuality, the translation of children's literature, and screen translation, especially subtitling for the deaf. She has published more than 50 books and articles related to these fields, both as editor and as author.

ANJANA MARTÍNEZ TEJERINA obtained her degree in Translation and Interpretation from the University of Alicante in 2003. A year later, she obtained the Sworn Translator Title and was awarded with a Leonardo grant to work as an Assistant Teacher in London for two years. She obtained an MA in Audiovisual Translation at the Universitat Autònoma de Barcelona in 2007 and holds a PhD in Translation by the Universidad de Alicante, with a thesis on the dubbing of wordplay in the Marx Brothers films. She is currently working for a subtitling company and is also a member of the research group Transmedia Catalonia.

ANNA MATAMALA is a full-time lecturer at the Universitat Autònoma de Barcelona, where she coordinates the MA in Audiovisual Translation (<www.fti.uab.es/audiovisual>) and teaches audiovisual translation. She has been working as an audiovisual translator for more than ten years for the Catalan television (TVC) and holds a PhD in Applied Linguistics from the Universitat Pompeu Fabra. Her main interests are audiovisual translation, media accessibility and applied linguistics. Anna Matamala has taken part in many regional, national and international funded research projects on audiovisual translation and media accessibility, and has published in international refereed journals such as *The Translator*, *Catalan Journal of Linguistics* and *Perspectives*. She is a member of the research group Transmedia Catalonia.

JOSÉ ANTONIO MOREIRO is the author of three books about the Bio-Bibliography of Agustín Millares Carlo, nine books about Bibliography and History of IS, and about Document Content Analysis. In addition, he has contributed to different IS journals, fifteen of which published articles about Document Content Analysis. He has collaborated in several projects of the UNESCO, CNP (Brazil), FAPESP (Sao Paulo, Brazil), FEDER (European Union) and CICYT (Spain). He has developed consulting and research activities in several organisations and enterprises. He has taught as visiting professor or lecturer at thirty universities in France, Portugal, Brazil, Colombia, Uruguay, Peru and Spain. He has been part of the organisation of fifty conferences in different academic and cultural scopes. In addition, he has supervised twenty PhD dissertations in the scope of the Library and Information Science.

PILAR ORERO holds an MA in Translation from the Universitat Autònoma de Barcelona (Spain) and a PhD in Translation from UMIST (United Kingdom). She is a lecturer at the Universitat Autònoma de Barcelona, where she also coordinates the Online Master in Audiovisual Translation (<http://www.fti.uab.es/onptav/>). She is the co-editor of *The Translator's Dialogue* (1997) and the editor of *Topics in Audiovisual Translation* (2004), both published by John Benjamins. She is co-writer of a book on voice-over, which is in the process of being published. In the field of media accessibility she is co-editor of *Media for All: Subtitling for the Deaf, Auidio Description and Sign Language*, published in Amsterdam by Rodopi. She is the guest editor of the special issue of TRANS 11 on *Media Accessibility in Spain*. She is the leader of two university networks (CEPACC and RIID-LLSS) which group 24 Spanish universities devoted to media accessibility research and quality training. She is a member of the Editorial Board of *The Journal of Specialised Translation* (<http://www.jostrans.org>) and *Monographs in Translation and Interpreting* (<http://www.ua.es/en/dpto/trad.int/publicaciones/index.html>). Her research interests are nonsense literature, audiovisual translation and media accessibility. She has numerous research projects on media accessibility funded by the Spanish and Catalan Governments and is the leader of the research group Transmedia Catalonia.

PIERRE OUELLET is a senior research agent at the Centre de recherche informatique de Montréal (CRIM). He completed the courses required for his MSc, however, he interrupted his studies to pursue a career in speech and speaker recognition. He started at CRIM in 1998 and is involved in projects relating to finite-state transducer based representations, the implementation of efficient algorithms, and applicable modifications to parameters and acoustic models.

FRÉDÉRIC OSTERRATH is a research agent at the Centre de recherche informatique de Montréal (CRIM). After receiving his bachelor's degree in electrical engineering from the (ÉTS) in 2001, he joined the CRIM team in 2002. He is involved in developing prototypes and applications mostly relating to closed captioning using speech recognition and networked speech applications.

ANA PEREIRA graduated in 1989 from the Universidad Complutense de Madrid (Spain) with a Licenciatura en Filología Inglesa. In 1992, she obtained a postgraduate diploma in Translation, followed by a doctorate in Applied Linguistics (1998) both at the Universidad Complutense de Madrid. Since 1993, she has been teaching Translation from English into Spanish at the Universidade de Vigo (Spain). She also teaches subtitling for people with hearing impairment to postgraduate students at the MA in Audiovisual Translation and

Online MA in Audiovisual Translation (Universitat Autònoma de Barcelona), and at the PhD programme Language and the Information Society: Linguistics and its Applications (MEC Quality Award 2004/00215). Dr. Pereira is the leader of the project SUBSORDIG. Her main areas of research are the comparative study of English and Spanish genres and registers within Systemic Functional Linguistics, the translation of children's literature, and screen translation, especially subtitling for the deaf. She has written books and numerous articles related to these fields.

ÁLVARO PÉREZ-UGENA is tenured Assistant Professor in Communication. Member of Experts Committee for development of Standard AENOR for Audio Description. Member of MHP Technology forum and Digital TV for Accessibility. Author of *La evolución de la TV y los pasos hacia la Accesibilidad* (Development and way to the Accessible TV) and *TV digital e integración* (Digital TV and integration). Organiser of International Seminars in Aranjuez, Spain, 2005 and Altea, Spain, 2004, and arbitrator of the European Arbitral Tribunal Association. Some articles: *Perspectiva global de la integración de las personas discapacitadas* (A global view of the integration for disabilities, Estudios sobre la Constitución Europea, 2004), *ULISES. Utilización Lógica e Integrada del Sistema Europeo de Signos / Señas. Un proyecto de intérpretes virtuales para personas sordas en lugares de alto tránsito* (ULISES, Integrated and Logical Use of the European Signal System. A project for deaf people using virtual avatars in places with large amounts of users; Pérez-Ugena & Vizcaíno-Laorga, 2006) and *Nuevos retos de la accesibilidad en los medios* (New challenges for media accessibility; Pérez-Ugena, Linares & Vizcaíno-Laorga, 2007). Research Projects: Accessible Digital Television for Disabilities (Profit 2004–2005). Interactive Digital Television (URJC 2004). Leader with Ricardo Vizcaíno-Laorga of ULISES Project. Member of SUBSORDIG Project. Member of GICOMSOC (Communication, Society and Culture Research Group), Universidad Rey Juan Carlos (Spain).

PABLO ROMERO-FRESCO has a degree in Translation and Interpreting from the Universidade de Vigo and a PhD in Audiovisual Translation from Heriot-Watt University. He is now a Senior Lecturer in Audiovisual Translation at Roehampton University, where he teaches dubbing, subtitling and respeaking. He has also taught respeaking as part of the MA programmes on Audiovisual Translation at the Università di Bologna (Forlì) and Universitat Autònoma de Barcelona, both on-campus and online. He is a member of the research group Transmedia Catalonia, for which he co-ordinates the EU-funded research project D'Artagnan (DTV4ALL), which focuses on the optimisation of subtitling for the deaf and hard of hearing on digital TV.

BELÉN RUIZ holds a PhD in Physics by the ETSI Telecommunications of the Universidad Politécnica de Madrid. She is currently a professor in the Information Technology Department of the Universidad Carlos III de Madrid and Technical Director of the Spanish Centre for Subtitling and Audio Description (CESYA) under the Royal Council for Disability. She is the Deputy Director of the Institute for Technological Development and Innovation Promotion Pedro Juan de Lastanosa and is responsible for the laboratory on disability. She is Deputy Vice-Chancellor for Scientific Technological Park. She is a member of the Centre for Technological Innovation in Disability and the Elderly and she has led a course on technological support for people with disabilities on the Universidad Carlos III. She has led several national and international projects on voice recognition, human-computer interaction, mobile systems analysis and audiovisual accessibility. She is the author and co-author of several national and international publications in this field of research. She has recently published in the area of audiovisual accessibility in national and international conferences (IBERDISCAP) and she has taken part in summer courses such as the Information Technology and Communications in the Personal Autonomy (Poio 2006) with a dissertation about audiovisual disability, or in the Master in Communication without Barriers (Valencia, 2005–2006).

DEBORAH ROLPH has an MA in Translation from the Universitat Autònoma de Barcelona in Spain and is currently working on a PhD in audiovisual translation at the Universitat Autònoma de Barcelona, where she lectures English. She is the co-author of *Accessibility: Raising awareness of audio description in the UK* (in P. Orero, A. Remael & J. Díaz Cintas (Eds.), *Media for All: Subtitling for the Deaf, Audio Description and Sign Language* (Amsterdam: Rodopi, 2007). In a previous incarnation she worked as a psychologist, managing a community-based psychiatric crisis team and she has kept her interest in how the mind works.

FRANCISCO UTRAY is an Associate Lecturer in Audiovisual Communication at the Universidad Carlos III de Madrid. He is currently developing a research project on Accessibility of Disabled People to Digital Television in the Spanish Centre for Subtitling and Audio Description (CESyA). He has participated in the work groups Forum for TDT aimed at implementing Accessible Digital TV in Spain.

RICARDO VIZCAÍNO-LAORGA has a Communications Degree (Universidad Complutense de Madrid), Education Degree (UNED) and a PhD in Communication (UCM). He is a member of GICOMSOC (Communication, Society and Culture Research Group) at the Universidad Rey Juan Carlos in Spain. Social Communication for Energy Master's Degree (UCM) and Educational Projects and Culture for Peace studies (Pontificia Universidad Católica de Perú). Research Personnel in Training (Universidad Complutense de Madrid, 1999–2002), Assistant Professor (Universidad Católica San Antonio de Murcia, 2002–2004; Universidad Rey Juan Carlos, 2004–2008). Research stage in New York (USA) and Wrocław (Poland). His fields of research include the following: disabilities and communication, internet (users), graphic design and immigration and communication. He is a member of SUBSORDIG and leader with Álvaro Pérez-Ugena of the ULISES project.